MANU FEILDEL is the French—Australian co-owner and executive chef of the acclaimed L'étoile restaurant in Sydney's Paddington. He is well known and loved for his role as a co-host on Channel 7's *My Kitchen Rules*, and from Channel 10's *Ready, Steady, Cook* as well as the Lifestyle Channel's *Boys Weekend*.

MANU'S FRENCH BISTRO

MANU FEILDEL

PHOTOGRAPHY BY **CHRIS CHEN**

LANTERN
an imprint of
PENGUIN BOOKS

'COOKING FRENCH WITH LOVE & PASSION'

CONTENTS

INTRODUCTION	1
ENTREES	7
MAINS	79
DESSERTS	157
BASICS	201
GLOSSARY	208
MERCI	211
INDEX	212

INTRODUCTION

The restaurant business is in my blood, and I grew up cooking and eating the classic bistro fare that French cuisine is renowned for all over the world, such as vichyssoise, goat's cheese salad, coq au vin and duck confit. My father was a chef who ran his own bistro in Saint-Nazaire, France. The restaurant served simple food, such as salads, pates and terrines, and was always filled with workers from the town's shipping industry. After a brief stint as a circus performer in my early teens (seriously!), I realised that circus life wasn't for me. So, every night after school, from the age of 15, I worked at my dad's restaurant, serving customers and cleaning up after they had gone home.

Eventually I moved behind the scenes and into the kitchen, where I specialised in preparing the entrees, a job that I loved. These were all cold dishes, prepared in advance and stored in the fridge, then plated up at the last moment. As the kitchen was only small, the menu was quite limited. Even so, with just Dad and me in the kitchen, we still managed to serve an average of 200 customers every day for lunch. Dad also ran the hotel attached to the restaurant, so I soon took over behind the restaurant burners at night and didn't get to bed until after midnight. It was a busy life, but it gave me a taste for cooking.

From the moment I set foot in a restaurant kitchen, I knew this was what I wanted to do. Filled with enthusiasm for my new profession, I returned to my home town of Nantes, where I began my two-year apprenticeship at a restaurant called Rôtisserie du Palais. It was the hardest job I have ever had! The head chef was a bit scary, and I had to juggle my work as the only apprentice in a very busy kitchen with studying the theory of classic cuisine at the French equivalent of TAFE. The experience in my father's bistro stood me in good stead, as I specialised in cold entrees when I started. The life of a chef isn't glamorous, and one of my tasks was to clean all the fish for the restaurant (and I was only allowed one apron each week!) – it was horrendous. However, many of my friends had also decided to become chefs and their apprenticeships were equally challenging, so I figured it wasn't so bad. The second year I worked there, the head chef and I decided to work our way through the French master chef Escoffier's complete works. Not only was this an excellent grounding in the basic techniques and dishes of my homeland's cuisine, but it was also an amazing experience that I still treasure, as it laid the foundations for what I do today.

With my apprenticeship behind me, the adventurer in me led me to London, where I landed without knowing a single word of English. I lucked into a job in the kitchen of the institution that was the Café Royal. Not only was it said to be Oscar Wilde's favourite watering hole, but Winston Churchill famously waited there to find out his political fate. (Sadly, it became a victim of the GFC in 2008, when it closed its doors for the last time after 143 years.) Compared to small bistro kitchens in France, it was a revelation to be part of a kitchen brigade of over 30 chefs. Somehow, I again started off making cold entrees – which may be why there are so many recipes for these in this book!

After working in various London restaurants over the next five years, I joined the acclaimed seafood restaurant Livebait, initially in Waterloo and then in Covent Garden. Each day we would order the finest fish from our suppliers, then devise a menu of five entrees and five mains to make the most of what was available, and bake our own bread in the tiny kitchen. I thrived on the challenge of creating a fresh menu every day, eventually becoming head chef. I relished the freedom and creativity involved in running such a small but perfectly formed place, and was thrilled when Livebait was nominated for best seafood restaurant in the UK in 1998.

Once again, the urge to travel struck, so in 1999 I set off for Australia, to try my luck here and follow my dream of one day owning my own restaurant. The rest, as they say, is history. After spending some time in Melbourne, I came to Sydney to visit a friend. Taking my CV with me on my first trip to Bondi Beach, I got a call back from Hugo's in Bondi. I was asked to run Hugo's Lounge in Kings Cross when it originally opened, and that's how I ended up meeting Pete Evans, my mate and co-host on *My Kitchen Rules*.

After stints in restaurant kitchens around town, including six years at Bilson's (which was awarded three chef's hats by the *Sydney Morning Herald Good Food Guide* for three years running while I was head chef), I finally had the opportunity to open my very own French bistro, L'étoile, in Sydney's Paddington. This is where I get to serve the kind of bistro food that I love from my formative years in France, and it is what inspired the idea for the collection of recipes I share here. This book is a tribute to my favourite classic bistro dishes, such as Twice-baked Cheese Souffles (see page 23), Confit Pork Belly with Apple Puree (see page 130) and Raspberry Souffles (see page 161), as well as those that I have taken inspiration from and then played with over the years, giving them my own little twist, such as Chilled Tomato Consomme with Prawn Salad (see page 18), Tuna Rossini (see page 84) and Chocolate Creme Brulee (see page 164). I love taking everything I have learnt as a chef over the years and injecting it with my own personality and tastes. I hope that you will love to cook and eat these dishes as much as I do.

SPRING

MENU

ENTREES

Asperges blanches 'en barigoule'
White asparagus barigoule 30

Ceviche de 'kingfish', vinaigrette à la coriander et au pignons
Kingfish ceviche with coriander & pine-nut dressing 66

Pâté de tête au sauce gribiche
Smoked ham hock terrine with gribiche sauce 73

Tartare de chevreuil
Venison tartare 24

Soupe de petits-pois froide et sa salade de crabe, d'huile d'olive noir
Chilled pea soup with crab salad & black olive oil 14

MAINS

'Black flathead', salade tiède de haricots blanc vinaigrette
Black flathead with warm white bean salad 100

Filet de Saint-Pierre, chou-fleur et noisette
Pan-fried John Dory with cauliflower & hazelnuts 88

Supreme de volaille, petits navets glacés et parfumé á l'estragon
Pan-roasted chicken breasts with baby turnips 111

Romsteck d'agneau aux flageolets
Lamb rump with spiced flageolet beans 153

Steak à l'échalote
Sirloin steak with eschalot sauce 135

DESSERTS

Tarte au citron en verrine
Verrine of lemon 'tart' 180

Mousse au chocolat blanc et tuile de chocolat amer
White chocolate mousse with dark chocolate tuiles 186

Omelette Norvègienne
Bombe Alaska 171

Baba au rhum
Rum baba 189

CAULIFLOWER SOUP WITH ROQUEFORT

WHITE ASPARAGUS BARIGOULE

RILLETTES DE LAPIN
RABBIT RILLETTES

ENTRÉES

CROQUETTES D'ESCARGOTS AU BEURRE D'AIL

TUNA & CRAB 'CANNELLONI' WITH AVOCADO CREAM

KINGFISH CEVICHE WITH CORIANDER & PINE-NUT DRESSING

JOHN DORY CHOWDER

VENISON TARTARE

PARISIAN-STYLE GNOCCHI
GNOCCHI À LA PARISIENNE

'CHOWDER' DE SAINT-PIERRE
JOHN DORY CHOWDER

I've always loved a chowder, a creamy seafood soup whose origins lie in the New England region of the United States. Here I've added my own touch by making a sauce rather than a soup and adding a perfectly cooked piece of John Dory, one of my favourite types of fish. The fish is the hero here.

SERVES 4

80 ml olive oil
200 g clams, soaked in cold water for 20 minutes
3 eschalots, 1 thinly sliced, 2 finely chopped
3 sprigs thyme
1 bay leaf
8 flat-leaf parsley stalks, leaves picked and chopped, stalks reserved
100 ml white wine
1 carrot, finely chopped
1 stick celery, finely chopped
2 cloves garlic, finely chopped
1 litre Fish Stock (see page 205)
1 desiree potato, finely chopped
180 ml pouring cream
sea salt and freshly ground black pepper
4 × 150 g John Dory fillets, skin-on, pin-boned
40 g unsalted butter
lemon juice, to taste
chervil sprigs (optional), to serve

1. Heat 1 tablespoon of the olive oil in a heavy-based saucepan over medium heat. Add the clams, thinly sliced eschalot, thyme, bay leaf, parsley stalks and white wine. Cover and cook for 6–8 minutes or until the clams open. Remove the opened clams from the pan and set aside. Strain the cooking juices and reserve, discarding the solids.

2. Heat 2 tablespoons of the olive oil in a heavy-based saucepan over medium heat. Add the carrot, celery, garlic and remaining eschalot and cook for 3–4 minutes or until golden. Add the reserved cooking juices and fish stock and bring to the boil, then reduce the heat to low and simmer for 5–6 minutes or until the vegetables are almost tender. Add the potato to the pan and simmer for 5 minutes. Add the cream and continue to simmer for 10–15 minutes or until the sauce has reduced by half and the vegetables are tender. Season to taste with salt and pepper. Return the clams to the pan and keep warm.

3. Heat the remaining olive oil in a large heavy-based frying pan over medium heat. Season the fish with salt and pepper, then cook, skin-side down, for 4–5 minutes or until golden. Turn the fish over, then cook for another minute. Add the butter to the pan and continue to cook for 1–2 minutes or until the fish is cooked through.

4. To serve, add the chopped parsley to the sauce, then divide among wide shallow bowls and top with a John Dory fillet, skin-side up. Add a squeeze of lemon juice and scatter with chervil sprigs, if desired.

VELOUTÉ DE CHOU-FLEUR ET ROQUEFORT
CAULIFLOWER SOUP WITH ROQUEFORT

The tangy saltiness of crumbled Roquefort cheese plus the smooth silkiness of this creamy cauliflower soup equals a culinary match made in heaven. If you can find a good-quality loaf of walnut sourdough, serve it alongside. The richness and crunch of walnuts is a classic accompaniment to blue cheese.

SERVES 4

40 g unsalted butter
1 small head cauliflower (about 1 kg), core removed, cut into small florets
1 litre White Chicken Stock (see page 204)
100 g creme fraiche
100 g Roquefort cheese, crumbled
sea salt and freshly ground black pepper
extra virgin olive oil, finely chopped chives and walnut bread (optional), to serve

1. Melt the butter in a heavy-based saucepan over medium heat. When the butter starts to foam, add the cauliflower and stir for 3–4 minutes – you do not want it to take on any colour. Add the stock and bring to the boil, then reduce the heat to low and simmer for 20 minutes or until the cauliflower is very tender.

2. Puree the soup in a blender until smooth. Whisk in the creme fraiche, then sprinkle over the Roquefort cheese and season to taste with salt and pepper. Drizzle with olive oil and sprinkle with chives. Serve with walnut bread, if desired.

SOUPE À L'AIL
GARLIC SOUP

This traditional soup is perfect for lovers of garlic. The onion, eschalot and garlic are gently sauteed in olive oil, bringing out their natural sweetness. The resulting soup has such a deep flavour it almost tastes like a rich chicken broth. I love it.

SERVES 6

50 ml olive oil
1 small onion, finely chopped
2 eschalots, finely chopped
4 heads garlic, cloves separated and peeled
1 kg potatoes, diced
2 litres White Chicken Stock (see page 204)
250 g creme fraiche
sea salt and freshly ground black pepper

1. Heat the olive oil in a large heavy-based saucepan over medium heat. Add the onion, eschalot and garlic and cook for 10 minutes or until translucent. Add the potato, then stir for 1–2 minutes. Pour in the stock and bring to the boil. Reduce the heat to low and simmer for 20 minutes or until the potato is tender.

2. Puree the soup with a stick blender or blender until smooth, then press through a fine-mesh sieve into a clean pan.

3. Add the creme fraiche and stir to combine, then season to taste with salt and pepper. Divide the soup among bowls and serve.

VELOUTÉ DE TOPINAMBOUR
JERUSALEM ARTICHOKE SOUP

Funnily enough, Jerusalem artichokes are not from Jerusalem, nor are they part of the artichoke family – in fact, they belong to the sunflower family. One theory as to how they got their name is that it came from the Italian word for sunflower, *girasole*. Whatever their origin, their distinctive sweet, nutty, earthy flavour is really showcased in this simple yet delicious soup.

SERVES 4

1 kg Jerusalem artichokes
½ lemon
50 g unsalted butter
1 onion, finely chopped
3 cloves garlic, crushed
1 litre White Chicken Stock (see page 204)
sea salt and freshly ground black pepper
100 g creme fraiche

1. Peel the artichokes and place them in a large bowl of water with a squeeze of lemon juice added as you go, so they don't discolour. Cut the artichokes into 1 cm thick slices and return to the lemon water.

2. Melt the butter in a large heavy-based saucepan over medium heat. When the butter starts to foam, add the artichoke, onion and garlic and cook for 5 minutes or until softened but not coloured. Pour in the stock and bring to the boil, then reduce the heat to low and simmer for 20 minutes or until the vegetables are soft.

3. Puree the soup in a blender until smooth. Season to taste with salt and pepper, then whisk in the creme fraiche. Divide the soup among bowls and serve.

ENTREES

SOUPE DE PETIT-POIS FROIDE ET SA SALADE DE CRABE, D'HUILE D'OLIVE NOIR
CHILLED PEA SOUP WITH CRAB SALAD & BLACK OLIVE OIL

Pea soup may be very English, but here I serve it chilled, which also makes it French. I added the black olive oil and a lemony crab salad to give it my own personal touch. This soup is great served cold as a refreshing spring or summer starter.

SERVES 4

50 ml olive oil
1 small onion, thinly sliced
2 cloves garlic, crushed
2 sprigs marjoram
650 g fresh or frozen peas
500 ml pouring cream
175 g baby spinach leaves, stalks removed
sea salt and freshly ground black pepper
micro herbs or chervil sprigs (optional), to serve

CRAB SALAD WITH PRESERVED LEMON VINAIGRETTE

30 ml champagne vinegar
100 ml extra virgin olive oil
1 preserved lemon quarter, rinsed, flesh removed and rind finely chopped
1 eschalot, finely chopped
sea salt and freshly ground black pepper
180 g cooked crab meat, picked over to remove any shell

BLACK OLIVE OIL (OPTIONAL)

250 g pitted kalamata olives
200 ml olive oil

1. To make the black olive oil (if using), preheat the oven to 60°C. Place the olives on a baking tray and bake for 8 hours or overnight, if time permits, until the olives are firm and dry. Blend the olives and olive oil in a blender until a smooth puree forms. Press the mixture through a fine-mesh sieve into a bowl, discarding the solids. Cover with plastic film and refrigerate until needed. (Makes about 200 ml.)

2. Heat the olive oil in a large saucepan over medium heat. Add the onion and cook, stirring, for 5–6 minutes or until it has softened but not coloured. Add the garlic and marjoram, then cook for 2 minutes, stirring. Add the peas and cook, covered and stirring occasionally, for 5 minutes or until they begin to soften. Add the cream and bring to the boil, then reduce the heat to low and cook, covered, for 3–4 minutes or until the peas are tender. Remove the pan from the heat and stir in the spinach. Cover and leave to stand for 1–2 minutes or until the spinach has wilted.

3. Puree the soup in a blender until smooth. Press the soup through a fine-mesh sieve into a large bowl, then season to taste with salt and pepper and set aside to cool. Cover and chill in the fridge.

4. To make the crab salad, place the vinegar and olive oil in a bowl and whisk to combine well. Add the preserved lemon and eschalot and season to taste with salt and pepper. Add the crab meat and toss gently to combine.

5. Divide the chilled soup among shallow bowls, then place a generous mound of the crab salad in the centre and scatter with micro herbs or chervil sprigs, if desired. Drizzle the black olive oil around the soup (if using), then serve immediately.

SOUPE VICHYSSOISE ET CHANTILLY À L'HUÎTRES
VICHYSSOISE WITH OYSTER CHANTILLY

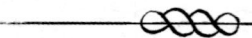

This bistro menu staple has timeless appeal, and here it is set off to perfection by the oyster Chantilly. You can serve it hot, warm or chilled – I leave it up to you.

SERVES 4

50 g unsalted butter
300 g desiree potatoes, halved and thinly sliced
2 leeks (about 500 g), white part only, well washed, halved lengthways and thinly sliced
1 litre water
1 sprig thyme
1 bay leaf
100 g creme fraiche
sea salt and freshly ground black pepper

OYSTER CHANTILLY
2 oysters, shucked
60 ml pouring cream
sea salt and freshly ground black pepper

1. To make the oyster Chantilly, place the oysters in a food processor and process until a smooth puree forms. Press the oyster puree through a fine-mesh sieve into a bowl; discard any solids. Using hand-held electric beaters, whisk the cream until soft peaks form. Add the oyster puree to the cream, then whisk to combine. Season with salt and pepper, then cover with plastic film and refrigerate until needed. (Makes about 125 ml.)

2. Melt the butter in a large heavy-based saucepan over low heat. When the butter starts to foam, add the potato and cook, stirring, for 5 minutes – you don't want it to take on any colour. Add the leek and cook, stirring, for 3 minutes or until just softened. Add the water, then increase the heat to high and bring to the boil. Add the thyme and bay leaf. Simmer for 20 minutes or until the potato is tender when pierced with a knife. Discard the thyme and bay leaf.

3. Puree the soup in a blender until smooth, then transfer to a large bowl and whisk in the creme fraiche. Season to taste with salt and pepper, then divide among bowls and serve, topped with a small spoonful of oyster Chantilly. If serving cold, cover with plastic film and refrigerate until required.

GASPACHO AUX AMANDES ET SA SALADE DE CRABE
ALMOND GAZPACHO WITH CRAB & ALMOND SALAD

When you think of gazpacho, you usually think of the traditional Spanish chilled tomato-based soup. This less well-known, but equally delicious, almond-based version is the perfect antidote to a hot summer's day, and the crab and almond salad makes it extra special. You can buy cold-pressed French almond oil from specialty food stores. Cooked and picked crab meat is available from good fishmongers (or you can cook the crabs and pick the meat yourself). You'll need to start this recipe the day before you wish to serve it, and it can easily be doubled to serve eight.

SERVES 4

- 320 g flaked almonds
- 310 ml milk
- 125 g sourdough bread, crusts removed, torn into chunks
- 1 teaspoon almond oil
- 100 ml extra virgin olive oil
- 325 ml water
- sherry vinegar (see page 209), to taste
- sea salt and freshly ground black pepper

CRAB & ALMOND SALAD

- 240 g cooked crab meat, picked over to remove any shell
- 2 tablespoons finely chopped chives
- 40 g flaked almonds, roasted (see page 209)
- finely grated zest and juice of 1/2 lemon
- sea salt and freshly ground black pepper
- extra virgin olive oil, for drizzling

1. Combine the flaked almonds, milk, sourdough, almond oil, olive oil and 200 ml of the water in a large bowl. Cover and refrigerate overnight.

2. The next day, transfer the mixture to a blender with the remaining 125 ml water and process until smooth (alternatively, use a stick blender). Press the soup twice through a fine-mesh sieve into a large bowl; the soup should be smooth and silky. Taste and season with sherry vinegar, salt and pepper as required. Cover with plastic film and chill in the fridge until ready to serve.

3. Just before serving, make the crab salad. Combine the crab meat, chives, almonds, lemon zest and juice in a small bowl. Season to taste with salt and pepper, then drizzle with a little olive oil and toss gently to combine.

4. Divide the gazpacho among bowls, then top with the crab salad and drizzle with more olive oil. Serve.

CONSOMMÉ DE TOMATES ET SALADE DE CREVETTES
CHILLED TOMATO CONSOMME WITH PRAWN SALAD

You will need to start this the day before you serve it because the rich, concentrated tomato flavour and almost translucent appearance of the soup is only achieved by straining the ingredients overnight. The result tastes like a liquid tomato salad in a bowl and, to me, is the essence of summer. The prawn salad brings a touch of saltiness that contrasts perfectly with the slightly sweet flavour of tomato. This is best served cold, in keeping with the long tradition of chilled French soups.

SERVES 4–6

2 kg ripe tomatoes, coarsely chopped
juice of 1 orange
juice of 1 lemon
large handful basil leaves
Tabasco sauce, to taste
sea salt and freshly ground black pepper

PRAWN SALAD

1 large ripe tomato, peeled (see page 209) and seeded
1 small Lebanese cucumber, finely diced
sea salt and freshly ground black pepper
12 cooked king prawns, peeled and cleaned
French tarragon sprigs (see page 208) and finely chopped chives, to serve

1. Working in batches if necessary, place the tomato, orange juice, lemon juice and basil in a food processor or blender and process until a smooth thick puree forms. Season to taste with Tabasco sauce, salt and pepper.

2. Line a large fine-mesh sieve with muslin, then place over a large bowl. Transfer the puree to the muslin-lined sieve, then refrigerate overnight to drain. Clear juices will slowly drip through the muslin and collect in the bowl.

3. To make the salad, cut the tomato flesh into fine dice. Combine the tomato and cucumber and season to taste with salt and pepper.

4. Place two or three prawns in the centre of each serving bowl, then top with a spoonful of the tomato and cucumber mixture and a sprig of tarragon. Spoon the tomato consomme around the prawn salad, scatter with chives and serve immediately.

TARTIFLETTE
PONT-L'EVÊQUE CHEESE GRATIN

This traditional alpine dish, from the Haute-Savoie region of France, is comfort food at its best. It is traditionally made with the region's most famous cheese, Reblochon, a whole-milk cheese aged in mountain cellars and caves. Here in Australia I like to use Pont-l'Evêque for its creamy, slightly tangy taste. Serve this gratin with a glass of red wine on a wintry night and then sit back and enjoy.

SERVES 6

1.2 kg desiree potatoes, cut into 2 cm cubes
sea salt
olive oil, for cooking
1 onion, thinly sliced
200 g speck (see page 209) or bacon, cut into 3 cm × 1 cm strips (lardons, see page 208)
unsalted butter, for greasing
2 tablespoons creme fraiche
1 × 240 g square Pont-l'Evêque cheese, thinly sliced

1. Place the potato in a large saucepan, cover with water and season with salt, then bring to the boil. Remove the pan from the heat and leave to cool to room temperature for 1 hour; the potato should be firm but fully cooked. Drain and set aside.

2. Meanwhile, heat a large heavy-based frying pan over medium–high heat and drizzle in a little olive oil. Add the onion and fry for 3–4 minutes, then add the speck or bacon and cook for a further 3 minutes or until golden brown.

3. Preheat the oven to 220°C.

4. Butter the base of a 1 litre capacity gratin dish (mine is 25 cm × 20 cm), then add the potato, followed by the onion and bacon mixture. Spoon over the creme fraiche and top with the sliced cheese.

5. Bake for 20–25 minutes or until the cheese has melted and is golden brown. Serve immediately.

GÂTEAUX TIÈDE AUX MARRONS ET À L'HUILE D'OLIVE ET SON 'CHUTNEY' DE TOMATES
WARM CHESTNUT & OLIVE CAKE WITH TOMATO CHUTNEY

Over the last few years I've noticed an increase in demand for vegetarian dishes at L'étoile. It is a constant challenge to come up with new ideas, but I think you'll like this sophisticated and slightly unusual starter, best served in autumn, when fresh chestnuts are in season. Store the leftover tomato chutney in an airtight container in the fridge for up to 5 days, and serve it as a condiment with cold or hot meats.

SERVES 8

175 g fresh chestnuts
100 ml olive oil, plus extra for greasing
4 eggs, lightly beaten
100 ml white wine
450 g plain flour, sifted
1 teaspoon baking powder
125 g gruyere cheese, finely diced
200 g pitted black olives, sliced
200 g pitted green olives, sliced
80 g prosciutto or spicy salami (optional), thinly sliced
sea salt and freshly ground black pepper

TOMATO CHUTNEY

30 ml olive oil
1 small onion, thinly sliced
3 cloves garlic, crushed
½ teaspoon French Dijon mustard (see page 208)
1 tablespoon soft brown sugar
2 tablespoons champagne vinegar
4 over-ripe tomatoes, sliced
1 tablespoon chopped flat-leaf parsley
sea salt and freshly ground black pepper

1 Preheat the oven to 220°C.

2 Cut a cross in the base of each chestnut with a small sharp knife; this prevents the chestnuts from exploding in the oven. Place the chestnuts on a baking tray with the crosses facing upwards. Roast for 20–30 minutes or until they burst open and are golden brown. Remove from the oven and set aside until cool enough to handle. While still warm, peel off the shells, then chop. Set aside.

3 Grease a 1.5 litre capacity loaf tin or brioche mould with olive oil.

4 Place the egg and wine in a large bowl and stir with a wooden spoon until just mixed. Add the flour and baking powder, stirring continuously until the mixture is just combined; do not over-mix as the batter will become too dense. Fold in the 100 ml olive oil, gruyere, olives, chestnuts and prosciutto or salami (if using), then season with salt and pepper.

5 Spoon the batter into the prepared tin; there should be a 1 cm gap at the top. Wrap the tin in foil and bake for 45 minutes. Remove the foil and bake for a further 12–15 minutes or until the top is golden and a skewer inserted into the middle comes out clean. Leave to cool in the tin for 5 minutes, then turn out on a wire rack to cool a little.

6 Meanwhile, to make the tomato chutney, heat the olive oil in a heavy-based saucepan over medium heat. Add the onion and cook for 4–5 minutes or until light golden, then add the garlic and cook for another 2 minutes. Add the mustard, sugar and vinegar and stir until well combined, then add the tomato. Reduce the heat to low and cook for 30 minutes or until the tomato has softened. Stir in the parsley and season to taste with salt and pepper. (Makes about 250 ml.)

7 Serve slices of the chestnut cake warm with the tomato chutney. (Leftover chestnut cake can be stored in an airtight container in a cool, dark place for up to 3 days.)

ENTREES

SOUFFLÉS AU GRUYÈRE
TWICE-BAKED CHEESE SOUFFLES

These bistro staples sell like hotcakes at my restaurant. Just make sure you use the best-quality gruyere cheese you can find. The souffles are baked twice, which makes this dish particularly good for entertaining. You can complete the first stage of cooking in advance (up to a day ahead), then finish the second stage of cooking just before serving, when the souffles will puff up again beautifully.

SERVES 4

50 g unsalted butter, plus extra for greasing
30 g plain flour, plus extra for dusting
1 small onion, finely chopped
1 teaspoon finely chopped thyme
150 ml milk
45 g grated gruyere cheese
2 eggs, separated
small pinch cream of tartar
80 ml pouring cream
25 g grated parmesan
green salad (optional), to serve

1. Preheat the oven to 150°C.

2. Grease four 250 ml capacity ramekins or souffle dishes with butter and dust with flour, shaking out the excess.

3. Melt 20 g of the butter in a small frying pan over medium heat, then add the onion and thyme and cook, stirring, for 4–5 minutes or until the onion has softened but not coloured. Set aside to cool.

4. Heat the milk in a small saucepan over medium heat until it is almost simmering.

5. Meanwhile, melt the remaining 30 g butter in a heavy-based saucepan over medium heat, then add the flour and stir for 2–3 minutes or until combined and smooth. Cook, stirring, for another 3 minutes, then gradually add the hot milk, stirring continuously to prevent lumps forming. Bring to a simmer, then cook for 2 minutes. Stir in the gruyere.

6. Place the onion mixture in a food processor and blend until a smooth puree forms, then add the gruyere sauce and blend until just combined. Leave to cool slightly, then add the egg yolks and pulse until just combined. Transfer to a large bowl.

7. Using hand-held electric beaters, whisk the egg whites and cream of tartar until soft peaks form. Gently fold this mixture through the cheese mixture.

8. Divide the cheese mixture among the prepared ramekins until three-quarters full. Place the ramekins in a roasting pan and add enough boiling water to the pan to come halfway up the sides of the ramekins. Bake for 20 minutes or until set. Carefully remove the ramekins from the pan and place in the fridge to cool for 1 hour or until needed.

9. Preheat the oven to 180°C.

10. Remove the ramekins from the fridge and leave at room temperature for 10 minutes. Remove the souffles from the ramekins and place on a baking tray. Evenly pour a little cream over each souffle and top with parmesan. Bake for 10–15 minutes or until the parmesan has melted and is golden. Serve with a green salad, if desired.

TARTARE DE CHEVREUIL
VENISON TARTARE

I can hear you saying, 'What? Raw venison?', but I urge you to try it – you'll be pleasantly surprised at how good it is. I think this combination of raw venison with ground juniper berries works beautifully, producing a dish with a light, gamey flavour and a beautiful aroma. Start preparing the venison just before you intend to serve this to prevent it from oxidising.

SERVES 4

1 × 800 g venison fillet
4 egg yolks
40 g cornichons (see page 208), finely chopped
30 g baby salted capers, rinsed very well and finely chopped
4 eschalots or spring onions, finely chopped
3 tablespoons finely chopped curly parsley
crusty bread, to serve

TO TASTE:
French Dijon mustard (see page 208)
tomato sauce
Worcestershire sauce
Tabasco sauce
ground juniper berries
sea salt and freshly ground black pepper

1. Use a large sharp knife to cut the venison into very fine dice. (Don't be tempted to use a food processor as it will make a paste rather than a dice.)

2. To serve, divide the meat into four even portions, then shape each portion into a mound on a serving plate. Make a shallow indent in the centre of each mound and carefully slide in an egg yolk, taking care not to break the yolk. Top with some of the cornichons, capers, eschalot or spring onion and parsley. (Alternatively, mix the venison with the cornichons, capers, eschalot or spring onion and parsley, then divide into four even portions and add an egg yolk to each one.)

3. Serve with mustard, tomato sauce, Worcestershire sauce, Tabasco, ground juniper and salt and pepper to the side. Your guests can season their tartare to taste with their chosen condiments.

CARPACCIO NOIX DE SAINT-JACQUES
CARPACCIO OF SCALLOP

This elegant, special-occasion dish is very simple to make. The scallops are 'cooked' in the dressing, and just melt in your mouth. The saltiness of the salmon roe provides a lovely counterpoint to the sweetness of the scallops. As an extra indulgence, I sometimes add a few shavings of bottarga (salted dried mullet roe), which is available from specialty food stores and delicatessens.

SERVES 4

600 g raw scallops, roe removed
60 g Avruga herring roe (optional)
60 g salmon or ocean trout roe
60 g bottarga
handful micro herbs (optional)
60 ml lime juice
60 ml extra virgin olive oil
sea salt and freshly ground black pepper

1. Thinly slice the scallops into fine rounds, then place an overlapping layer on 4 plates. Scatter the Avruga, if using, and salmon roe over the scallop carpaccio, then shave a little of the bottarga over each plate. Sprinkle with micro herbs (if using).

2. Combine the lime juice and olive oil, then season to taste with salt and pepper. Spoon the dressing over the carpaccio. Serve.

TARTES D'AUBERGINE ET D'ECHALOTE, CRÈME DE CÊPES
EGGPLANT TARTS WITH CEP CREAM

The versatile eggplant is one of my favourite ingredients. Originating in India some 4000 years ago, its name in Italian, *melanzana*, derives from the Latin word meaning 'apple of madness' – I'm not sure why! You will need to make the cep cream in advance to allow enough time for it to chill.

MAKES 4

olive oil, for cooking
2 large eggplants, thinly sliced lengthways
2 sheets ready-rolled butter puff pastry, thawed
6 eschalots, thinly sliced
20 g unsalted butter
40 g caster sugar
125 ml red wine
1 tablespoon thyme leaves, plus 2 teaspoons finely chopped thyme, extra
freshly ground black pepper
micro herbs (optional) and shaved parmesan, to serve

CEP CREAM
40 g dried cep (porcini) mushrooms (see page 209)
1 tablespoon olive oil
1 tablespoon thyme leaves
freshly ground black pepper
100 ml dry white wine
100 ml White Chicken Stock (see page 204) or Vegetable Stock (see page 205)
200 ml pouring cream

1. To make the cep cream, cook the ceps in a saucepan of boiling water for 2 minutes. Drain, then rinse with cold water and pat dry. Heat the olive oil in a heavy-based saucepan over medium heat, then add the ceps and thyme and cook for 5 minutes. Season to taste with pepper. Add the wine and chicken stock and bring to the boil, then simmer for 6–8 minutes or until reduced by half. Add the cream and simmer for a further 5–6 minutes or until reduced by half. Leave to cool slightly, then transfer to a food processor and process until a smooth puree forms. Place in a bowl, cover with plastic film and refrigerate until cold.

2. Preheat the oven to 180°C.

3. Heat a splash of olive oil in a large heavy-based frying pan and, working in batches, cook the eggplant for 3–4 minutes on each side or until golden, adding more oil to the pan as needed. Drain on paper towel.

4. Place one sheet of the pastry on a heavy-based baking tray lined with baking paper. Place another heavy-based baking tray on top, then bake for 5 minutes; this par-cooking helps to prevent the pastry from shrinking. Using a 10 cm pastry cutter, cut out two 10 cm rounds, discarding the pastry off-cuts. Repeat with the remaining pastry sheet, then place the four pastry rounds on one lined baking tray and bake for a further 8–10 minutes or until golden and crisp. Set aside to cool on the tray.

5. Meanwhile, heat 1 tablespoon olive oil in a heavy-based saucepan over medium heat. Add the eschalot and cook for 5 minutes or until just translucent. Add the butter, caster sugar, wine and thyme leaves and bring to the boil, then cook for 3–4 minutes or until the sauce has reduced to a deep-red syrup. Set aside.

6. Place three slices of eggplant slightly overlapping on a chopping board. Use the 10 cm pastry cutter to cut a round from the eggplant. Repeat with the remaining eggplant; you should have 4 eggplant rounds.

7. Top each pastry round with an eggplant round and one-quarter of the eschalot mixture, then scatter with extra chopped thyme. Return the tarts to the oven for 3–4 minutes or until warmed through.

8. Place some cep cream on each plate, then top with a tart. Place a spoonful of the cep cream on top, then scatter with micro herbs (if using) and add some shaved parmesan.

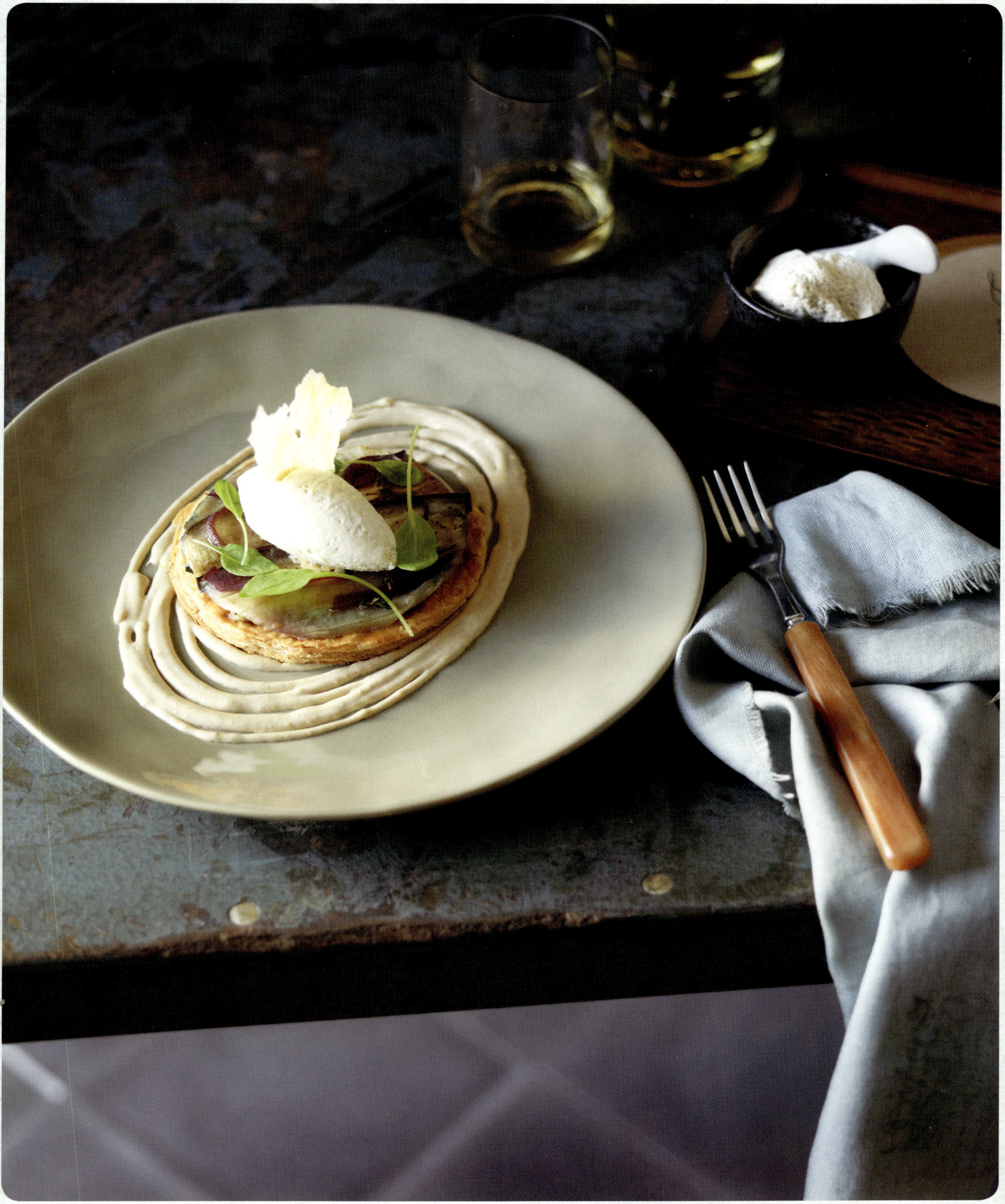

ASPERGES BLANCHES 'EN BARIGOULE'
WHITE ASPARAGUS BARIGOULE

I've always loved the juicy thick stalks and sweet flavour of white asparagus. As a kid, I often ate them at my grandma's house during spring, which is when they are in season. *Barigoule* is a simple but classic Provencal dish typically made with globe artichokes, but it tastes just as good (if not better) with white asparagus instead. Make sure you peel the asparagus as they have quite a tough skin. I like to serve this with aioli.

SERVES 4

100 ml olive oil
3 eschalots, finely chopped
1 small carrot, finely diced
1 small leek, white part only, well washed and finely chopped
2 cloves garlic, thinly sliced
zest of 1 lemon, thinly sliced, white pith removed
2 bunches thick white asparagus, trimmed and peeled
150 ml white wine
350 ml White Chicken Stock (see page 204)
sea salt and freshly ground black pepper
thyme leaves and Aioli (see page 202), to serve

1. Heat the olive oil in a large saucepan over medium heat. Add the eschalot, carrot, leek, garlic and lemon zest and cook for 5 minutes or until starting to colour. Increase the heat to high, then add the asparagus, wine and stock and bring to the boil. Reduce the heat to medium and cook for 5–6 minutes or until the asparagus is just tender.

2. Transfer the asparagus mixture to a platter or individual plates, then season to taste with salt and pepper, scatter with thyme leaves and serve warm or at room temperature with aioli.

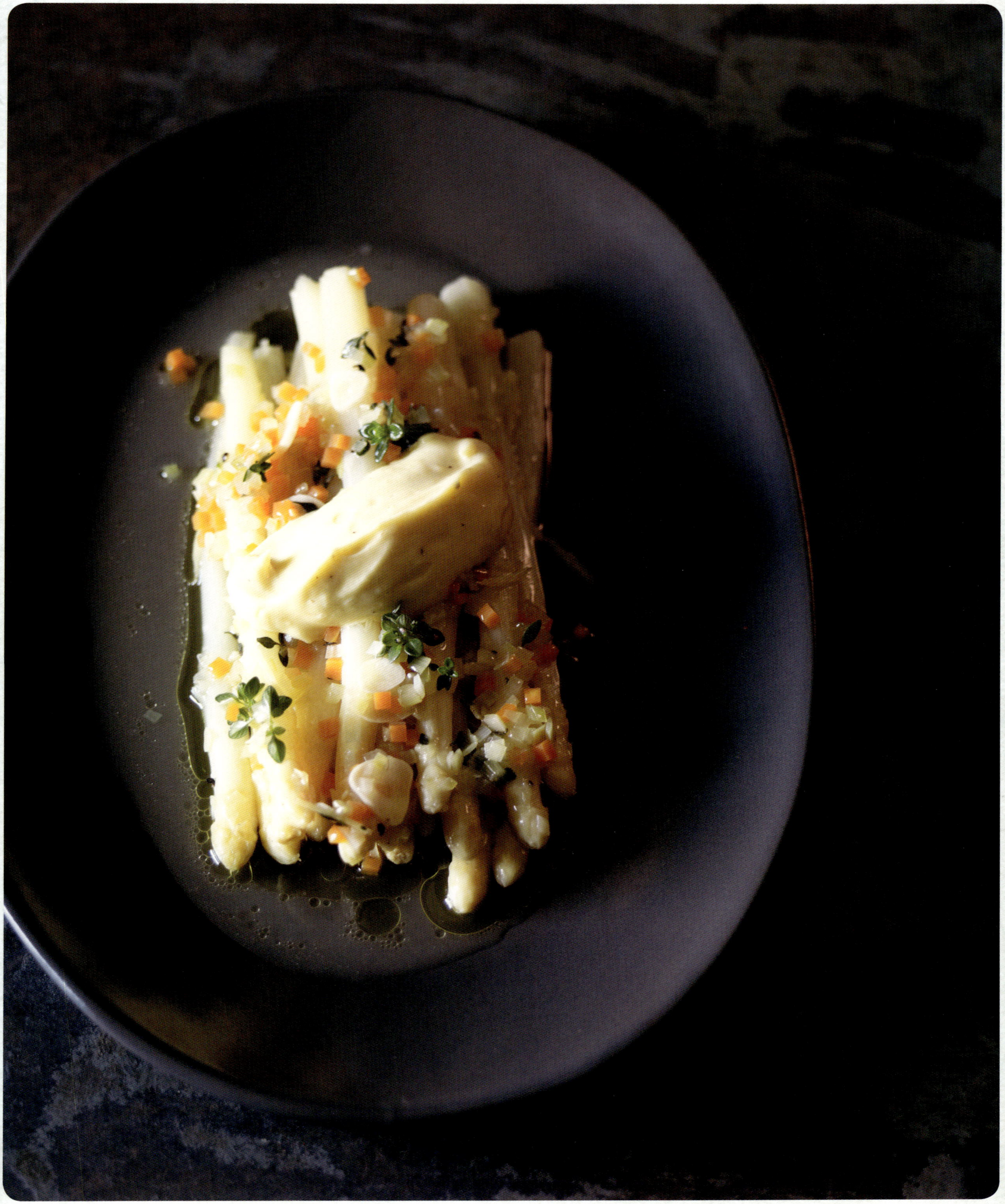

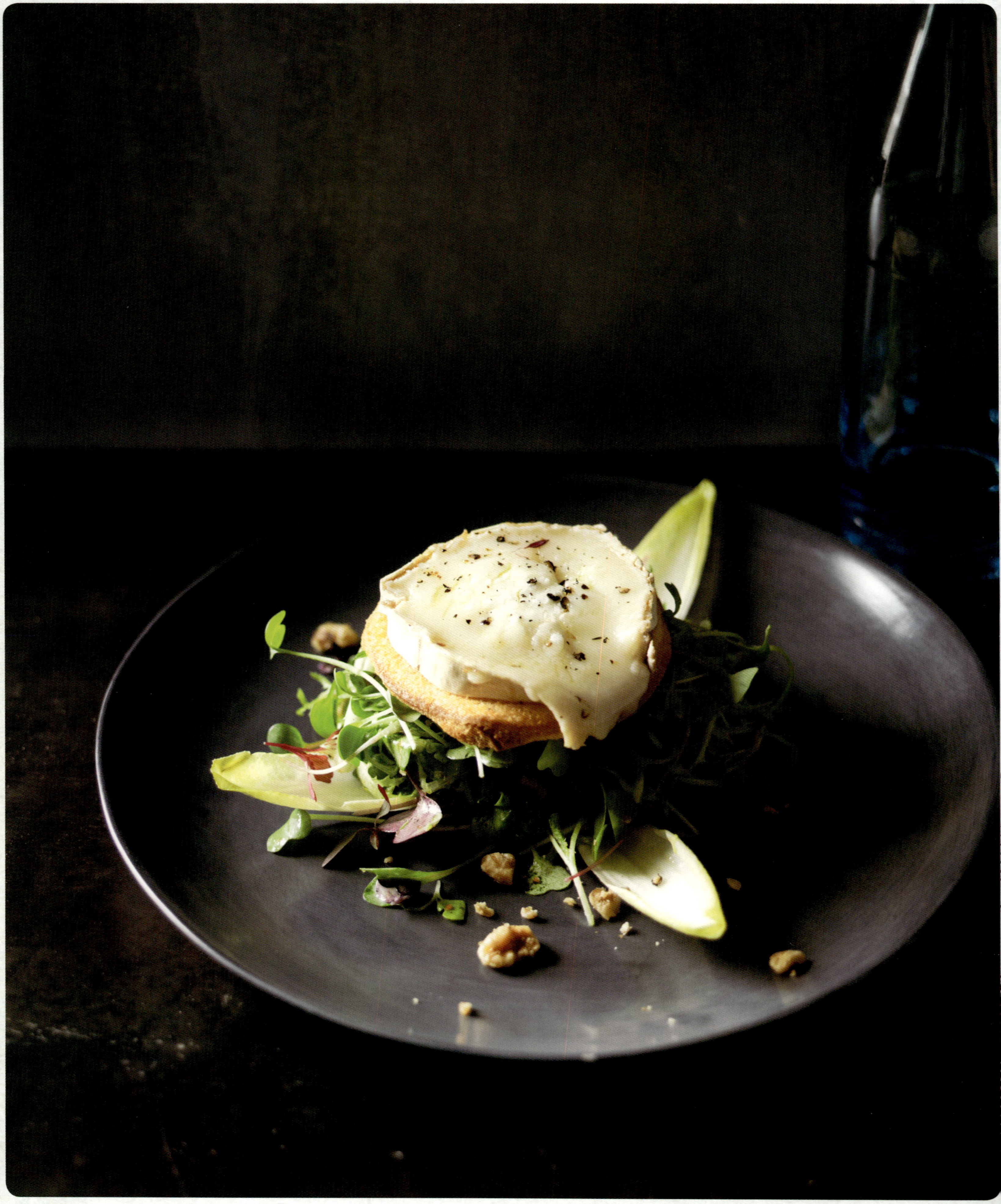

SALADE DE CHÈVRE CHAUD
GOAT'S CHEESE SALAD

This bistro classic reminds me of my childhood as my mum used to make it all the time when she entertained. The bitterness of the leaves, the richness of the goat's cheese and the crunch of the pear combine to make this a really fresh and flavoursome salad, perfect to serve in autumn before a rich main course.

SERVES 4

20 g unsalted butter
75 g walnuts, coarsely chopped
4 slices white sourdough bread, cut into 10 cm rounds with a pastry cutter
olive oil, for brushing
200 g white mould goat's cheese, cut into 1 cm thick rounds
1 pear, halved, cored and thinly sliced
1 head frisee, base trimmed, leaves washed and dried
1 head witlof, base trimmed, leaves washed and dried
large handful micro herbs (optional)
4 chives, cut into 3 cm lengths
freshly ground black pepper

WALNUT DRESSING

1 tablespoon French Dijon mustard (see page 208)
2 tablespoons sherry vinegar (see page 209)
1 tablespoon lemon juice
sea salt and freshly ground black pepper
100 ml olive oil
100 ml walnut oil

1. To make the walnut dressing, place the mustard, vinegar, lemon juice, and salt and pepper to taste in a bowl and whisk to combine well. Whisking continuously, gradually add the oils in a thin steady stream until emulsified.

2. Melt the butter in a small frying pan over medium heat. When the butter starts to foam, add the walnuts and shake the pan for 4–5 minutes or until they are toasted and glossy. Drain on paper towel.

3. Preheat the oven to 200°C.

4. Brush each side of the bread with olive oil, then place on a baking tray and bake for 2 minutes on each side or until golden brown. Place a round of cheese on each crouton and continue to bake for a further 3–4 minutes or until the cheese starts to melt.

5. Meanwhile, place the pear, frisee, witlof, micro herbs (if using), chives and walnuts in a bowl and toss gently to combine. Pour enough walnut dressing over the salad to just coat the leaves, then use your hands to gently combine.

6. Divide the salad among four plates and top with a goat's cheese crouton. Season with black pepper and serve immediately.

BALLOTTINE D'AUBERGINES SAUCE BOIS BOUDRAN
EGGPLANT ROLLS WITH BOIS BOUDRAN DRESSING

Ballottine is a French term generally used to describe a dish of boned meat or poultry that has been stuffed, rolled and cooked. This technique works equally well using tender slices of fried eggplant, which I cut into even slices using a bread knife. This is a delicious vegetarian dish with a flavour I think of as almost like eggplant caviar. Great served as a summer starter.

SERVES 4

200 ml olive oil
2 large eggplants, cut lengthways into 1 cm thick slices
½ teaspoon ground cumin
8 sprigs thyme, leaves picked
1 teaspoon lemon juice
freshly ground black pepper
10 eschalots, unpeeled and halved lengthways
1 bay leaf
2 cloves garlic
2 teaspoons brown sugar
6 roma tomatoes, peeled (see page 209) and seeded
1 tablespoon Bois Boudran Dressing (see page 203)
sea salt
micro herbs (optional), to serve

1. Heat 50 ml of the olive oil in a frying pan over medium heat. Working in batches, fry the eggplant for 2–3 minutes on each side or until golden, adding more oil to the pan as needed. Place on a baking tray lined with paper towel to drain. Set aside.

2. Place 2 eggplant slices, the cumin, half the thyme leaves, the lemon juice, black pepper to taste and 1 tablespoon of the olive oil in a food processor and process until a smooth paste forms. Set aside.

3. Preheat the oven to 180°C.

4. Heat 80 ml olive oil in a frying pan over medium heat. Place the eschalots, skin-side up, in the pan and cook for 5–6 minutes or until golden. Transfer to a baking tray, then add the bay leaf, garlic, brown sugar and remaining thyme leaves. Roast for 10 minutes or until the eschalots are soft but still hold their shape. Set aside. When cool enough to handle, peel and discard the skins.

5. Carefully cut the tomatoes into 5 mm dice, then transfer to a bowl with the dressing, season with salt and pepper and mix until well combined. Set aside.

6. Place 2 slices of the eggplant on a chopping board with the long side facing you, one slightly overlapping the other. Spread 1 teaspoon of the eggplant paste down the centre, then top with 5 eschalot halves and fold up the eggplant to enclose and form a tight log. Repeat with the remaining eggplant slices, paste and eschalots (you should have enough to make four rolls), then transfer to a 1.5 litre capacity baking dish. Roast the eggplant rolls for 5–7 minutes or until heated through.

7. Place an eggplant roll on one side of each plate, then add a line of the tomato mixture alongside. Top with micro herbs (if using), drizzle with the remaining olive oil and serve.

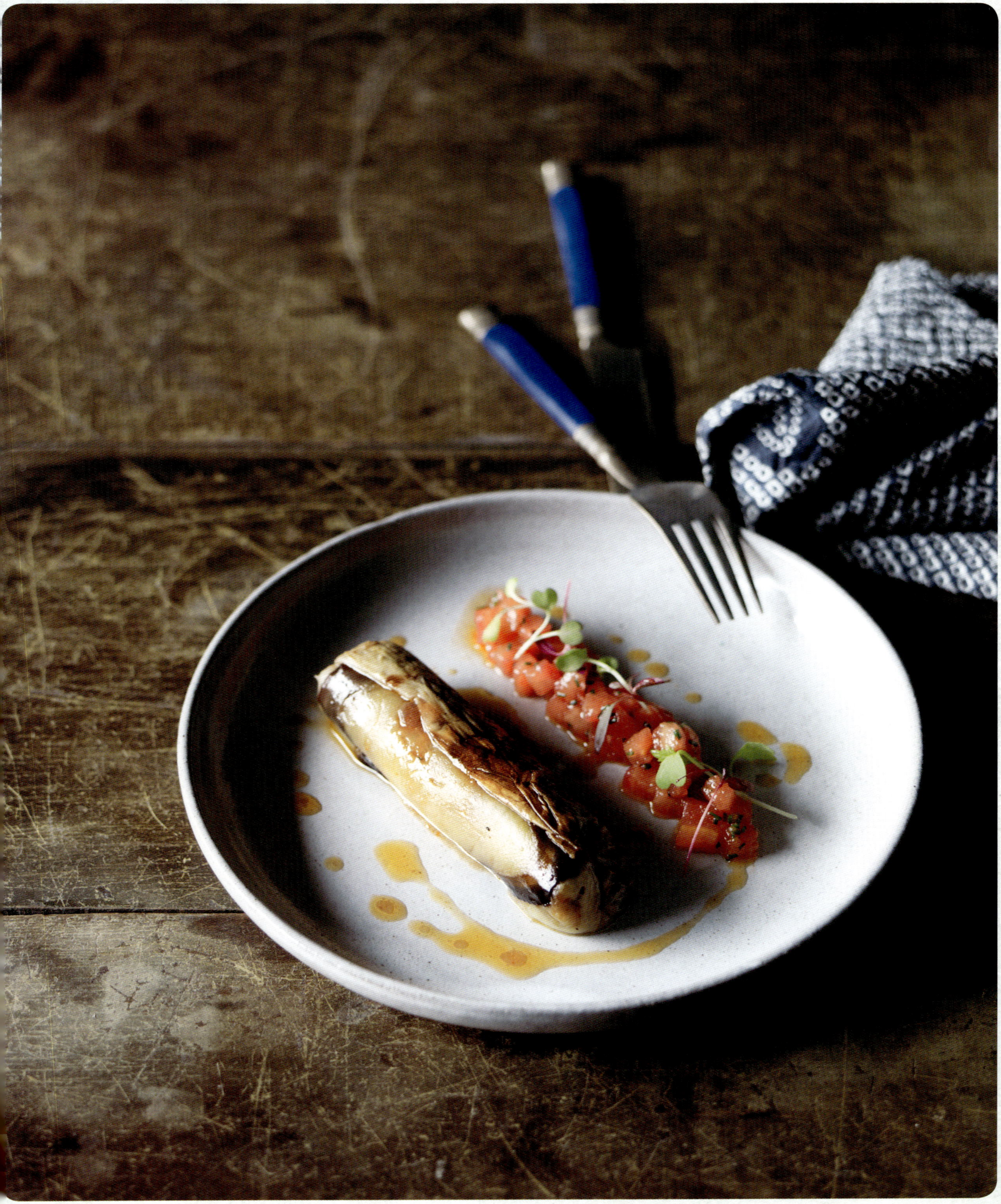

TARTELETTES À L'OIGNON ET AU BACON
ONION & BACON TARTLETS

These little tarts are great to serve as a starter on a cold winter's night, or as a meal in themselves for a light lunch or dinner, with a fresh green salad alongside. They are based on the simple onion tarts that can be found throughout the Alsace region of France, but here I've added a little speck (spiced, salt-cured and smoked pork), just because it is so delicious. If you can't find speck, use the best-quality bacon you can get. For best results, take the time to caramelise the onion properly.

SERVES 4

1 quantity Shortcrust Pastry (see page 207)
2 teaspoons unsalted butter
30 g speck (see page 209) or bacon, cut into thin strips
1 onion, thinly sliced
2 eggs
150 ml milk
150 ml pouring cream
¼ teaspoon freshly grated nutmeg
sea salt and freshly ground black pepper
thyme sprigs (optional), to serve

1. Roll out the pastry on a lightly floured work surface until about 3 mm thick and use to line four 12 cm tart tins with removable bases. Use a small sharp knife to trim off the excess. Prick the pastry shells all over with a fork. Refrigerate for 1 hour.

2. Preheat the oven to 180°C.

3. Line each pastry shell with a piece of baking paper, then fill with pastry weights, dried beans or rice. Place the tart tins on a baking tray and bake for 15 minutes or until the pastry is light golden. Remove the baking tray from the oven, then remove the weights and paper and return the pastry shells to the oven to bake for another 5 minutes or until the pastry is golden and dry. Place on a wire rack to cool completely.

4. Meanwhile, heat the butter in a heavy-based frying pan over low heat. Add the speck or bacon and cook for 5 minutes. Add the onion and cook for another 5 minutes, stirring continuously. Cover and cook over low heat for 30 minutes, stirring every 5 minutes.

5. Whisk the eggs until foamy. Whisk in the milk, cream and nutmeg and season to taste with salt and pepper.

6. Divide the onion mixture evenly among the tart shells and pour over the egg mixture. Bake for 30–35 minutes or until golden and just set. Serve immediately with thyme sprigs, if using.

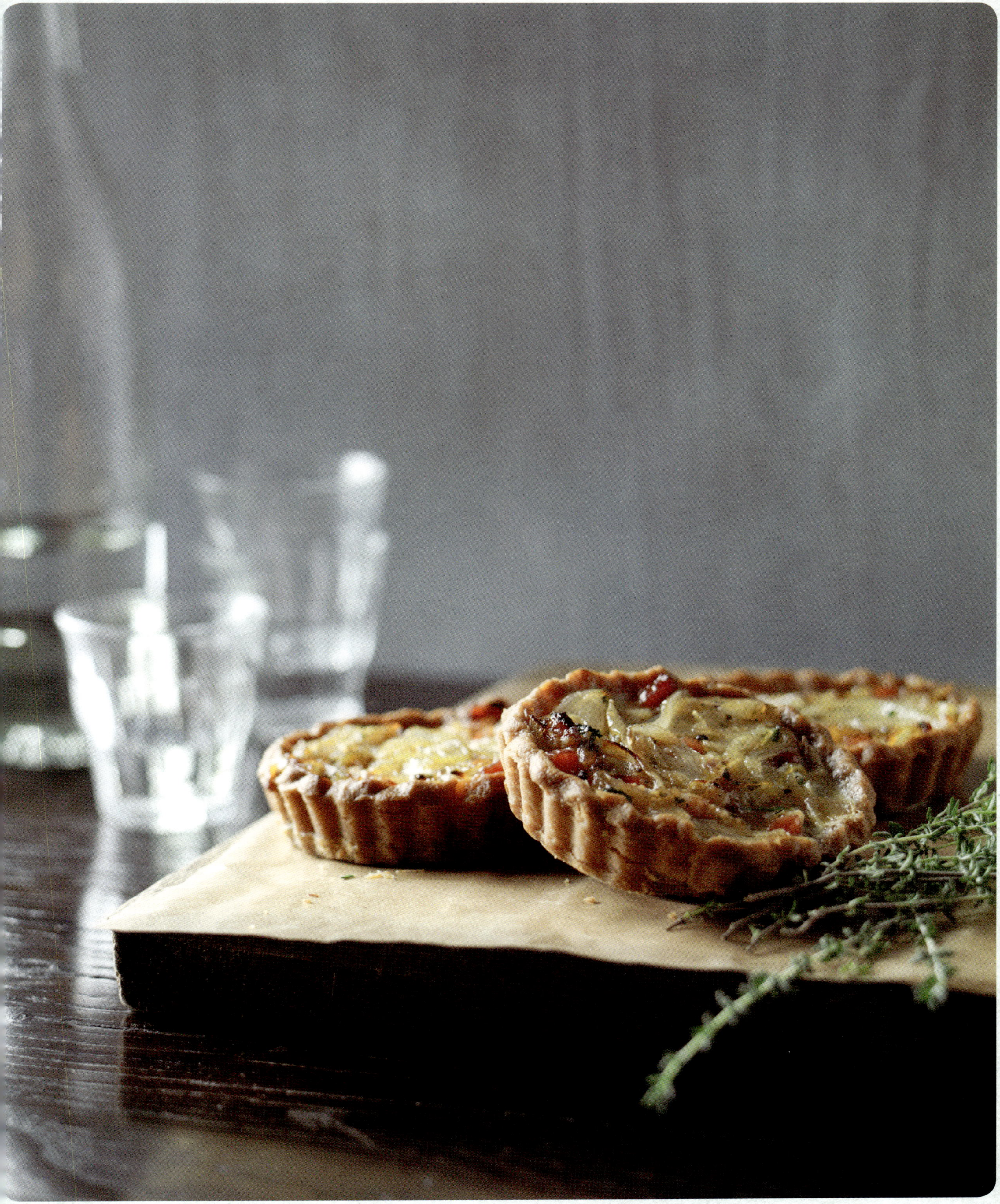

SALADE DE FROMAGE DE CHÈVRE FRAIS ET DE PETITES BETTERAVES
SALAD OF GOAT'S CURD & BABY BEETROOT

This autumn salad is made even more special by using a selection of different-coloured beetroot. If you can't find golden and target beetroot, then regular baby beetroot will still taste fantastic. The creamy, salty flavour of goat's cheese combines with the sweetness of beetroot to create a wonderful marriage of flavours and textures.

SERVES 4

1.5 litres water
450 g white sugar
300 ml champagne vinegar
12 sprigs thyme
6 golden beetroots, well washed and tops trimmed leaving 1 cm stalk intact
6 baby red beetroots, well washed and tops trimmed leaving 1 cm stalk intact
6 target beetroots, well washed and tops trimmed leaving 1 cm stalk intact
large handful micro herbs (such as mache, coriander and red basil)
ice cubes
olive oil, for drizzling
sea salt and freshly ground black pepper

HERBED GOAT'S CURD
200 g soft goat's curd
175 g cream cheese
finely grated zest of 1 lemon
sea salt
2 teaspoons finely chopped chives
freshly ground black pepper

1. To make the herbed goat's curd, place the goat's curd, cream cheese, lemon zest and ½ teaspoon salt in a food processor and blitz until smooth – it should be spreadable but still hold its shape. Transfer to a bowl, add the chives and ½ teaspoon pepper and stir until well combined. Spoon into a log shape on a sheet of plastic film, then roll to enclose. Refrigerate for 1 hour.

2. Take three heavy-based saucepans and add 500 ml water, 150 g sugar, 100 ml vinegar and 4 thyme sprigs to each one. (Each variety of beetroot needs to be cooked in its own pan so it retains its colour and flavour.) Add the different beetroots to one pan each and bring to the boil, then reduce the heat to low and simmer for 30–35 minutes or until a small sharp knife can be inserted into the beetroots without any resistance. Remove the beetroots, reserving the liquid from one pan, then peel them while still warm (wear disposable food-grade gloves if desired). Cut the larger beetroots in half, and leave the smaller ones whole.

3. Bring the reserved cooking liquid to the boil. Reduce the heat and simmer for 10–12 minutes or until reduced to a nice syrup; this will be your dressing.

4. Place the micro herbs in a bowl of iced water to make them crisp. Just before you're ready to serve, drain them and pat dry on paper towel.

5. To serve, unwrap the herbed goat's curd and place on a platter with the beetroot and herbs. Drizzle with olive oil and dressing, then season to taste with salt and pepper.

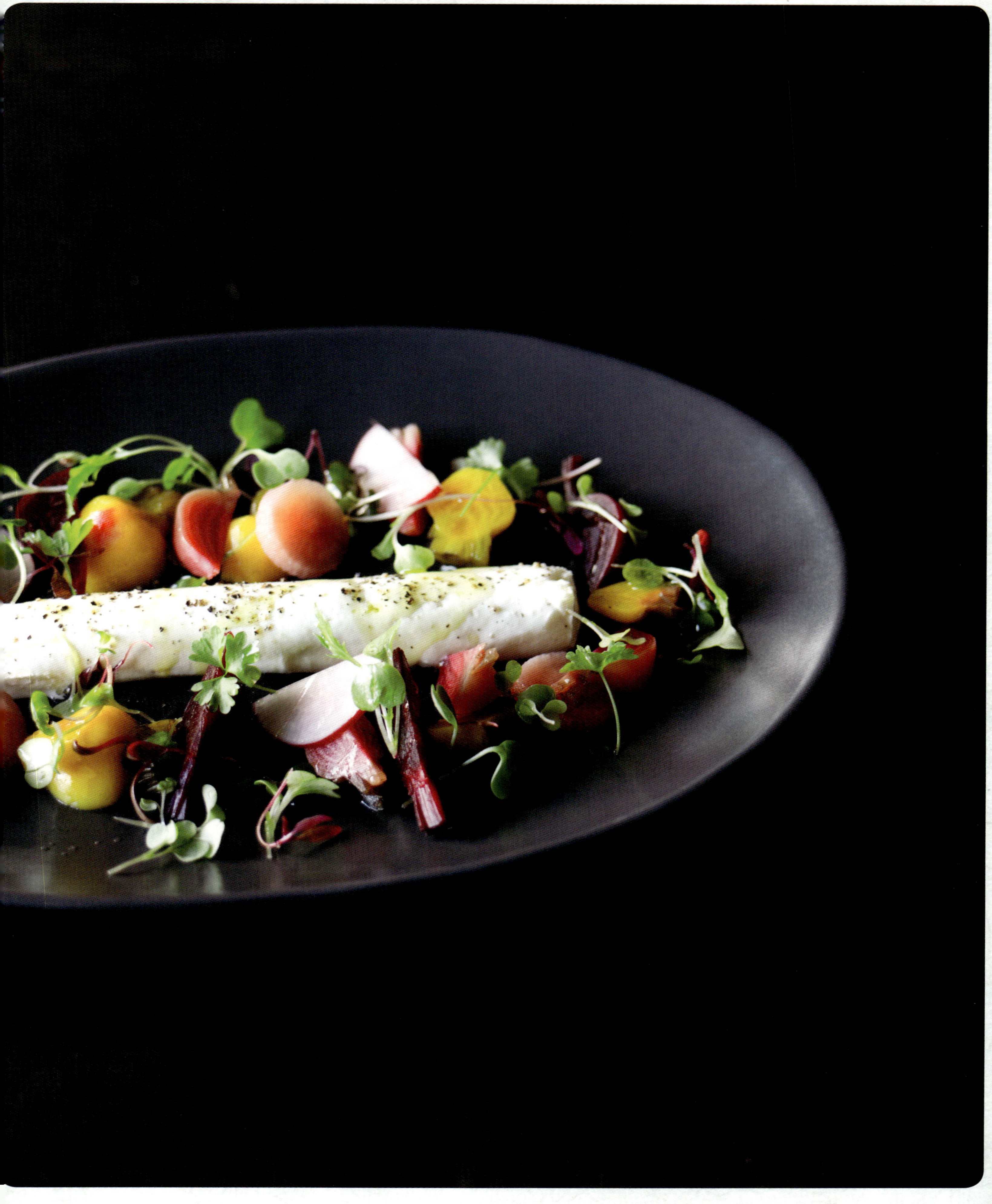

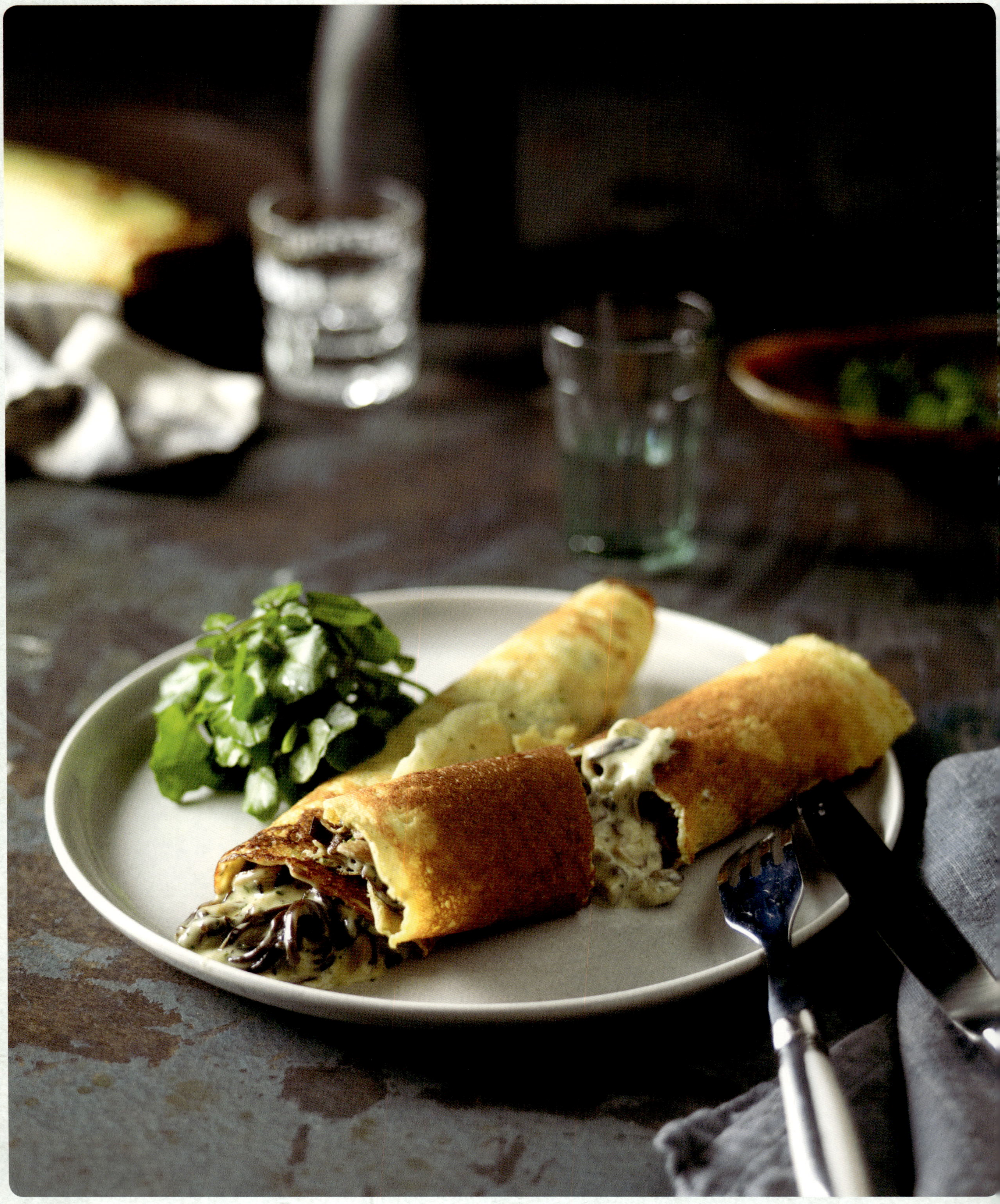

CRÊPES À LA FARINE DE POIS CHICHE FOURRÉES AUX CHAMPIGNONS SAUVAGES
CHICKPEA CREPES FILLED WITH WILD MUSHROOMS

I have given this old-fashioned recipe a modern twist by using chickpea flour in the crepes. This makes it great for people with an intolerance to wheat or gluten, and gives the crepes a distinctive nutty flavour. Use fresh wild mushrooms in autumn, when they are in season – otherwise, you can find dried wild mushrooms from specialty food stores.

SERVES 4

4 eggs
550 ml milk
200 g chickpea flour (available from health food stores and specialty food stores)
30 g unsalted butter, melted, plus extra for cooking
1 tablespoon finely chopped chives
4 handfuls watercress
lemon juice, to taste
extra virgin olive oil, for drizzling

WILD MUSHROOM FILLING

50 g dried morel mushrooms (see page 209)
80 g dried cep (porcini) mushrooms (see page 209)
100 ml olive oil
2 eschalots, finely chopped
2 cloves garlic, crushed
1 tablespoon finely chopped thyme
sea salt and freshly ground black pepper
250 g button mushrooms, trimmed and cut into quarters
125 g cream cheese
375 ml pouring cream
2 tablespoons finely chopped curly parsley

1. Place the eggs and milk in a large bowl and whisk to combine. Whisk in the chickpea flour, melted butter and chives and season to taste with salt and pepper. Cover, then refrigerate for 1 hour.

2. To make the mushroom filling, cook the morels and ceps in a saucepan of boiling water for 5 minutes. Drain, then rinse with cold water to remove any grit or stones that may be in the morels and pat dry. Coarsely chop the mushrooms and set aside.

3. Heat the olive oil in a frying pan over medium heat. Add the eschalot and cook for 4–5 minutes or until softened, then add the garlic and thyme and cook for a further 5 minutes. Season to taste with salt and pepper, then transfer to a bowl and set aside. Add the remaining olive oil to the pan and saute the button mushrooms for 5–6 minutes or until golden. Add the morels, ceps and eschalot mixture and cook for 5 minutes. Add the cream cheese and cream to the pan and simmer over medium heat for 8–10 minutes or until reduced to a sauce consistency. Stir in the parsley and set aside.

4. Heat a 22 cm non-stick frying pan over medium heat. Add a little butter, then ladle in 60 ml of the batter at a time, swirling to make sure the base of the pan is covered with a layer of batter. Cook on one side until you see the edges turn golden brown or bubbles form on the surface, then turn the crepe over with a spatula. Cook for a further 2–3 minutes or until the crepe is golden and crisp, then transfer to a plate and keep warm. Repeat with the remaining batter. (Makes about 10 crepes.)

5. Place the watercress in a bowl, then add lemon juice to taste and a drizzle of olive oil and toss to coat.

6. Gently reheat the mushroom mixture, then divide among the crepes and roll up tightly. Serve immediately, with watercress on the side.

CASSOLETTES D'ESCARGOT À L'AIL
GARLIC SNAIL PIES

Here I started with the timeless French combination of garlic and snails and turned it into a pie filling — and my, what a pie!

SERVES 4

2 bulbs fennel, trimmed, quartered and cores removed
90 ml olive oil
60 g unsalted butter, chopped
2 carrots, cut into julienne (see page 208)
sea salt and freshly ground black pepper
2 eschalots, finely chopped
3 teaspoons fennel seeds
8 cloves garlic, finely chopped
200 ml dry white wine
200 ml White Chicken Stock (see page 204)
150 ml pouring cream
24 tinned snails (see page 209), drained
2 tablespoons finely chopped curly parsley
2 sheets ready-rolled butter puff pastry, thawed
1 egg yolk, beaten

1. Using a mandoline, shave the fennel as thinly as possible.

2. Heat 30 ml of the olive oil and 20 g of the butter in a saucepan over low heat. Add the carrot and fennel, season to taste with salt and pepper, then cover and cook for 5 minutes or until tender. Remove from the heat.

3. Heat another 30 ml of the olive oil and 20 g of the butter in another saucepan over medium heat. Add the eschalot, fennel seeds and half of the garlic and cook, stirring, for 3–4 minutes or until the eschalot is soft but not coloured. Add the white wine, then bring to the boil and simmer for 5 minutes or until reduced by half. Add the stock and cream and simmer for 5 minutes or until reduced by two-thirds. Puree the sauce in a blender until smooth. Press through a fine-mesh sieve over a bowl and set aside to cool.

4. Pat the snails dry with paper towel, then season to taste with salt and pepper. Heat the remaining olive oil and butter in a large frying pan over medium heat. Add the snails and cook, stirring, for 4 minutes. Add the remaining garlic and cook for another 2–3 minutes or until fragrant. Remove the pan from the heat.

5. Preheat the oven to 200°C.

6. Divide the carrot and fennel mixture among four 150 ml capacity ramekins (mine are 9 cm diameter). Top with the snail mixture, then pour over the sauce and scatter with parsley.

7. Using a 12 cm pastry cutter, cut out four rounds of puff pastry and place one over the top of each ramekin, pressing firmly at the edges to seal well. Score a diamond pattern gently on the pastry tops, taking care not to cut through the pastry. Place the ramekins on a baking tray, then brush the pastry tops with the egg yolk and, using a wooden skewer or small sharp knife, pierce a small hole in the centre to allow steam to escape.

8. Bake the pies for 12 minutes or until the pastry is puffed, golden and crisp. Serve.

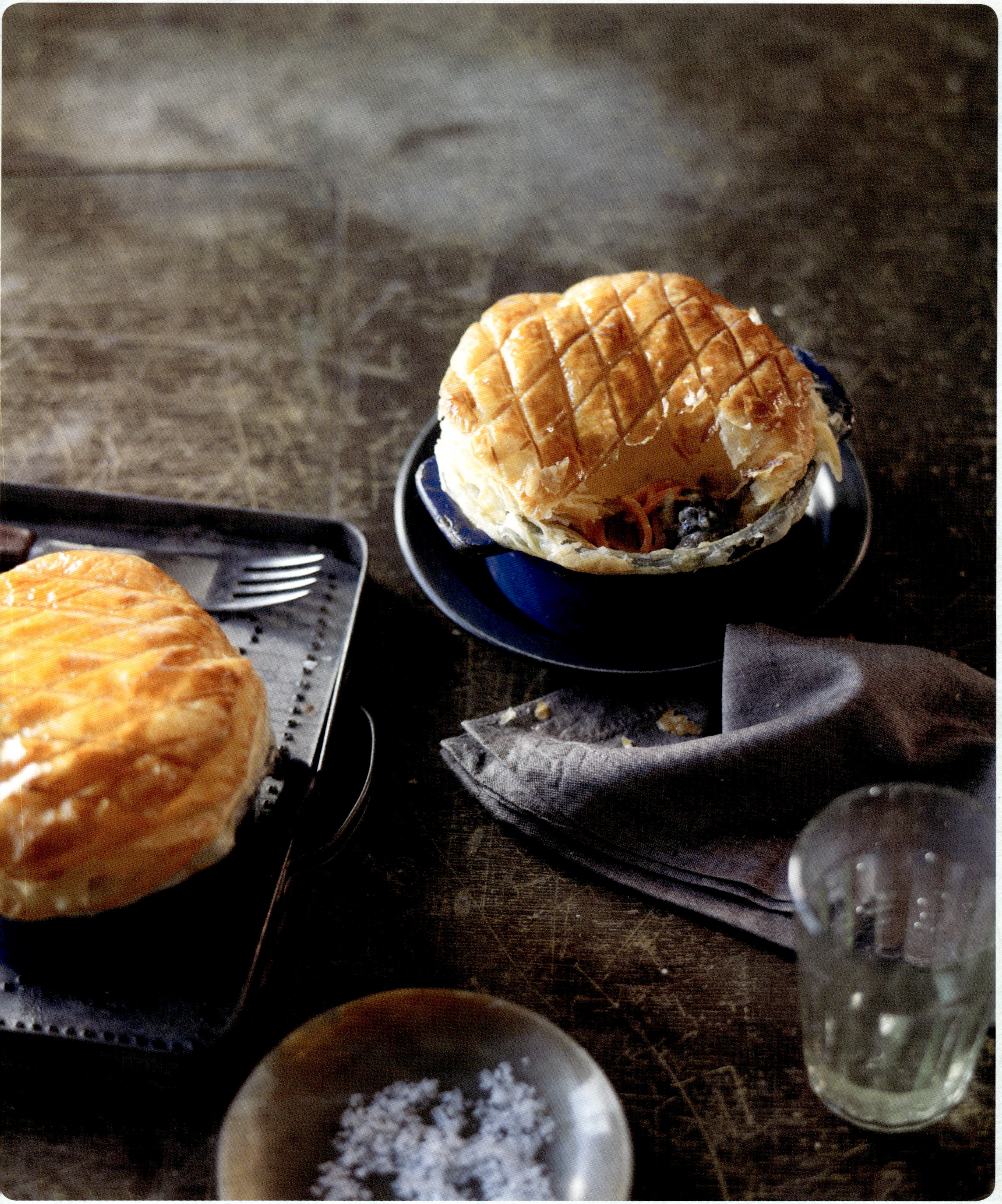

SALADE DE CUISSE DE POULET CONFITE
SALAD OF CHICKEN LEG CONFIT

Confit (poultry or meat cooked and preserved in its own fat) never goes out of fashion, and this beautiful salad proves why. While it is traditional to use duck confit, here I've made it with the chicken leg confit on page 105. The sharpness of the frisee cuts through the richness of the confit, while the crunch of hazelnuts adds an interesting texture. Hazelnut oil can be found at specialty food stores.

SERVES 4

200 g kipfler potatoes, scrubbed
50 g hazelnuts
1 tablespoon olive oil
600 g Chicken Leg Confit (see page 105), shredded
125 g frozen peas, thawed
sea salt and freshly ground black pepper
100 g frisee, washed and dried

HAZELNUT VINAIGRETTE

1 tablespoon wholegrain French Dijon mustard (see page 208)
1 tablespoon red wine vinegar
sea salt and freshly ground black pepper
30 ml hazelnut oil
60 ml vegetable oil
60 ml olive oil

1. Place the potatoes in a large saucepan of lightly salted water, bring to the boil over high heat, then reduce the heat to medium and simmer for 20 minutes or until the potatoes are tender but still firm and not falling apart. Drain, then when cool enough to handle, peel and cut into thick slices. Set aside.

2. Meanwhile, preheat the oven to 180°C. Place the hazelnuts on a baking tray and roast for 5–6 minutes or until golden. Set aside.

3. To make the vinaigrette, place the mustard, vinegar, and salt and pepper to taste in a bowl and whisk to combine well. Whisking continuously, gradually add the oils in a thin steady stream until emulsified. (Makes about 160 ml.)

4. Heat the olive oil in a heavy-based non-stick frying pan over medium heat. Add the potato and cook for 2–3 minutes on each side or until golden all over. Add the shredded chicken and cook, stirring, for 4–5 minutes or until just warmed through. Add the peas and hazelnuts, then season to taste with salt and pepper and continue to cook for 2 minutes or until warmed through.

5. Place the frisee in a bowl, then add 60 ml of the vinaigrette and toss to just coat the leaves.

6. To serve, divide the frisee among plates, top with the chicken and potato mixture, then drizzle with the remaining vinaigrette.

CROQUETTES D'ESCARGOTS AU BEURRE D'AIL
SNAIL CROQUETTES

I wanted to include a really special recipe for snails in this book, and this is one of my favourites. I first cooked this for a Bastille Day feast, and have been developing the idea ever since. The snails are crumbed twice — the first layer locks in the garlicky butter, while the second layer uses panko breadcrumbs (a coarse, packaged Japanese-style breadcrumb available in larger supermarkets and Asian food stores), to make the snails extra-crisp. A perfect and very moreish mouthful — yum!

SERVES 4

250 g unsalted butter, chopped and softened
2 eschalots, finely chopped
3 tablespoons finely chopped flat-leaf parsley
4 cloves garlic, finely chopped
sea salt and freshly ground black pepper
24 tinned snails (see page 209), drained
6 eggs
250 g plain flour
250 g fine breadcrumbs
250 g panko breadcrumbs
500 ml sunflower oil, for deep-frying

TOMATO FONDUE

500 g tomatoes, coarsely chopped
2 cloves garlic, crushed
2 tablespoons extra virgin olive oil
sea salt and freshly ground black pepper
2 fresh bay leaves
4 sprigs thyme

1. Preheat the oven to 120°C.

2. To make the tomato fondue, puree the tomato in a food processor. Add the garlic and olive oil and season with salt and pepper, then blitz again. Transfer the mixture to a deep baking dish (mine is 1.5 litre capacity). Tie the bay leaves and thyme together with kitchen twine, then add to the puree. Bake for 2 hours or until the tomato fondue is deep red and the liquid has evaporated. Discard the bouquet garni. Press the fondue through a fine-mesh sieve into a bowl. Set aside.

3. Meanwhile, combine the butter, eschalot, parsley, garlic, and salt and pepper to taste in a bowl and set aside.

4. Pat the snails dry with paper towel, then spread an even amount of the garlic butter around each one. Place the snails on a baking tray, then refrigerate for 15 minutes or until the butter is hard.

5. Crack the eggs into a bowl, then season with salt and pepper and give them a good whisk. Place the flour on one plate, the fine breadcrumbs on another and the panko breadcrumbs on another. Roll each snail in the flour, dip into the beaten egg, then roll in the fine breadcrumbs, making sure that they are well coated. Dip each snail into the beaten egg again, then roll in the panko breadcrumbs, making sure they are completely covered. Return the snails to the baking tray and refrigerate for 1 hour or until set.

6. Heat enough oil for deep-frying in a deep-fryer or heavy-based saucepan until it registers 180°C on a sugar/deep-fry thermometer, then, working in batches, deep-fry the snails for 1–2 minutes or until golden brown. Remove with a slotted spoon or wire basket and drain on paper towel. Serve immediately with a bowl of the tomato fondue alongside.

SARDINES À L'ESCABÈCHE
SARDINES ESCABECHE

I love the big, oily flavour of sardines, and they taste fantastic served in this Catalan-style dish. Make it the day before, if you can, to leave plenty of time for the fish to soak up the flavour of the delicious vinegary marinade. It is worth using real sherry vinegar from Jerez in Spain, as it has a touch of sweetness that is a perfect counterpoint to the saltiness of the sardines.

SERVES 4

8 fresh sardine fillets, skin-on
sea salt
50 ml olive oil
1 small red onion, thinly sliced
2 cloves garlic, thinly sliced
1 small carrot, thinly sliced into ribbons with a vegetable peeler
1 small bulb fennel, trimmed and thinly sliced
1 sprig thyme
1 fresh bay leaf
250 ml dry white wine
5 black peppercorns
250 ml sherry vinegar (see page 209)
4 basil leaves
1 lemon, cut into segments (see page 208), then thinly sliced
crusty bread and micro herbs or cress (optional), to serve

1. Season the sardines on both sides with salt. Heat 1 tablespoon of the olive oil in a large frying pan over low heat and, working in batches, cook the sardine fillets, skin-side down, for 20 seconds, then turn and cook for 10 seconds. Remove from the pan and place, skin-side up, on a wire rack.

2. Heat the remaining oil in the pan. Add the onion and garlic and cook, stirring, for 3–4 minutes or until soft but not coloured. Add the carrot, fennel, thyme, bay leaf and wine. Bring to the boil and cook for 5–6 minutes or until the wine has reduced by half. Add the peppercorns, vinegar and basil and simmer for another 5 minutes, then remove from the heat.

3. Place the sardine fillets, skin-side up, in a deep ceramic dish just large enough to hold them snugly in a single layer. Pour the hot vinegar mixture over the top, cover the dish with foil and leave to stand until cooled to room temperature. Refrigerate for 24 hours.

4. To serve, remove the sardines escabeche from the fridge 30 minutes before serving to allow it to come to room temperature. Scatter with the lemon segments and micro herbs or cress, then serve with plenty of crusty bread, if liked.

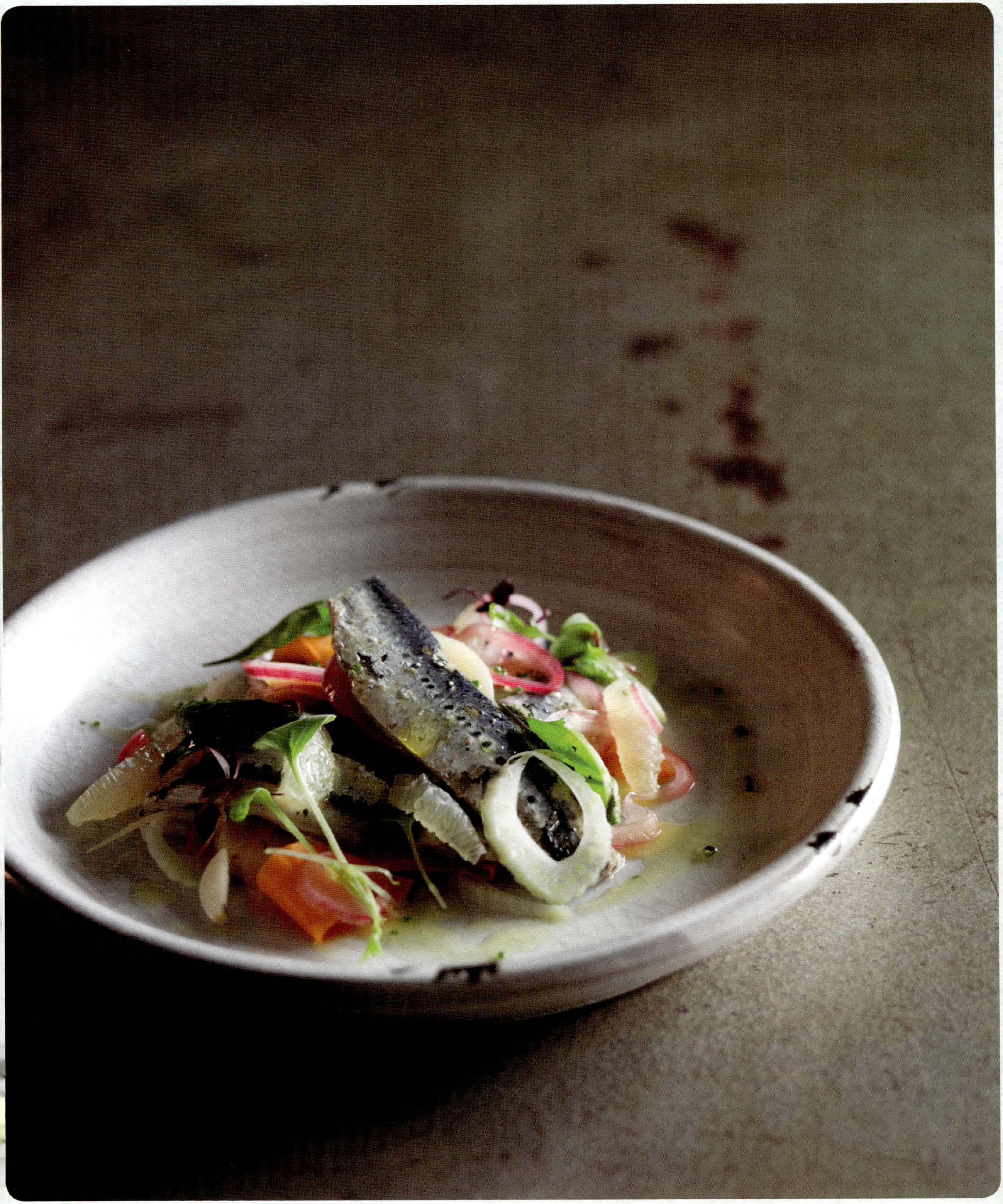

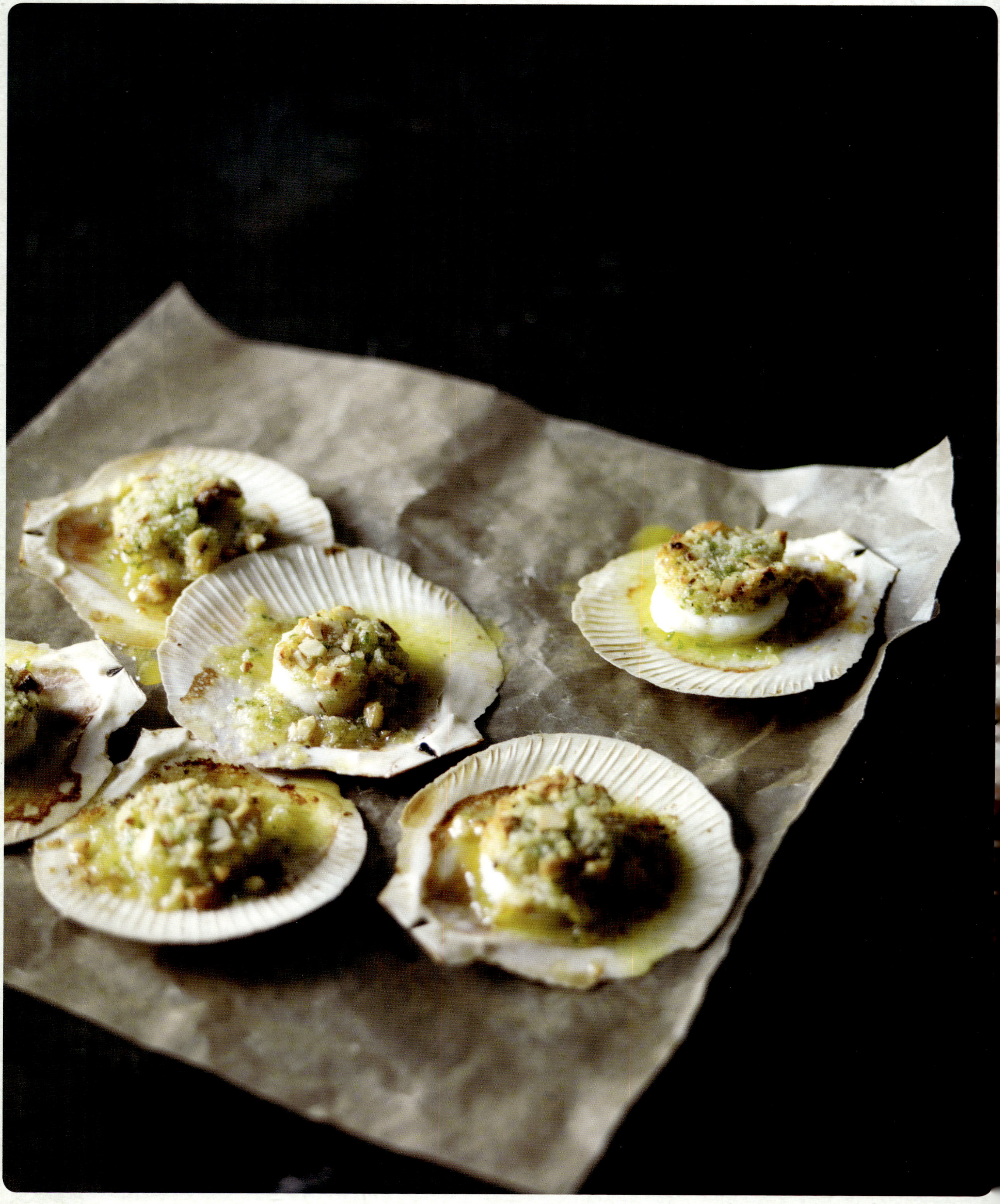

COQUILLES SAINT-JACQUES AU BEURRE DE NOISETTE
SCALLOPS WITH HAZELNUT BUTTER

Whenever I'm asked what the three most important ingredients are in French cooking, I always answer: butter, butter and butter! This recipe is a great way to showcase top-quality fresh scallops – just don't overcook them or they'll be rubbery. You only need a little of the hazelnut butter on each scallop as you don't want to overwhelm their natural flavour. You could easily make double the amount of hazelnut butter and store it in the fridge, wrapped in plastic film, then use it to dress up a simple piece of pan-fried fish.

SERVES 4

100 g unsalted butter, chopped and softened
1 tablespoon finely chopped chives
50 g finely chopped hazelnuts
30 g panko breadcrumbs (see page 45)
juice of ½ lemon
freshly ground black pepper
1 kg rock salt
12 scallops in the half-shell, roe removed
sea salt

1. Place the butter, chives, hazelnuts, breadcrumbs, lemon juice and a pinch of pepper in a bowl and combine well. Have a piece of plastic film ready, then place the butter mixture in a log along the plastic film and roll to wrap well. Wrap with foil, then refrigerate for 30 minutes or until firm.

2. Preheat the oven to 180°C.

3. Spread the rock salt in an even layer on a baking tray lined with baking paper. Place the scallops in their shells on the salt. Unwrap the hazelnut butter, then slice into twelve 5 mm thick discs. Place a disc of hazelnut butter on each scallop.

4. Bake the scallops for 5 minutes or until the butter has melted and the scallops are just cooked through.

5. Season the scallops with sea salt and pepper, then serve immediately.

GNOCCHI À LA PARISIENNE
GNOCCHI PARISIAN-STYLE

Parisian-style gnocchi are made with choux pastry rather than potato. Much lighter than their Italian counterparts, they puff up beautifully when cooked. If you've made Italian-style gnocchi before, then you will notice that the French method is a bit different. Instead of rolling the mixture into logs and cutting it into pieces, you pipe and then cut it directly into the pan of boiling water. Use only the best-quality gruyere cheese in the mornay sauce – do not be tempted to try any other cheese or the flavour just will not be the same.

SERVES 6

250 ml milk
80 g unsalted butter
sea salt
150 g plain flour
4 eggs
50 g grated parmesan
pinch freshly grated nutmeg
ice cubes

MORNAY SAUCE

1 litre milk
1 eschalot, peeled
1 clove garlic, peeled
1 sprig thyme
1 bay leaf
5 black peppercorns
70 g unsalted butter
70 g plain flour
4 egg yolks
200 g grated gruyere cheese
sea salt and freshly ground black pepper

1. Place the milk, butter and a pinch of salt in a large saucepan and bring to the boil over medium heat. Remove the pan from the heat and, using a wooden spoon, stir the flour into the milk mixture until smooth. Stir vigorously over low heat for a few minutes to remove the excess moisture. Remove the pan from the heat again, then add one egg at a time, stirring well after each addition, until a dough forms.

2. Stir in the parmesan and nutmeg. Transfer the dough to a piping bag fitted with a plain 1.5 cm piping nozzle.

3. Bring a large saucepan of salted water to the boil over high heat. Hold the piping bag over the pan of boiling water, squeeze gently and, as the dough is extruded, cut it into 3 cm lengths and let them drop into the pan. Cook the gnocchi in batches for 1–2 minutes or until they rise to the surface.

4. Remove the gnocchi with a slotted spoon and place in a bowl of iced water to stop it cooking immediately. Drain the gnocchi and divide among six 500 ml capacity gratin dishes. Set aside.

5. To make the mornay sauce, place the milk, eschalot, garlic, thyme, bay leaf and peppercorns in a large heavy-based saucepan. Bring to the boil over medium heat, then remove from the heat. Set aside to infuse for 20 minutes. Strain into a clean jug, discarding the solids.

6. Meanwhile, preheat the oven to 200°C.

7. Melt the butter in a saucepan over medium heat. Stir in the flour and cook for 1–2 minutes (this is called a roux). Gradually whisk in the infused milk until the sauce is smooth. Cook, stirring continuously, for 1–2 minutes or until the sauce has thickened. Remove from the heat and stir in the egg yolks and 80 g of the gruyere, then season to taste with salt and pepper.

8. Spoon the sauce over the gnocchi and top with the remaining gruyere. Bake for 30 minutes or until golden brown. Serve.

COQUILLES SAINT-JACQUES AU FONDUE DE POIREAUX
SCALLOPS WITH LEEK FONDUE

This simple yet elegant dish can be prepared and finished with a moment's notice, making it perfect for last-minute entertaining. The leek fondue is so simple to prepare, and works equally well with a perfectly cooked piece of ocean trout (see page 90), or, if you are feeling extravagant, grilled lobster halves.

SERVES 4

2 tablespoons olive oil
20 g unsalted butter
2 small leeks, white part only, well washed and cut into julienne (see page 208)
1 tablespoon finely chopped French tarragon (see page 208)
100 ml pouring cream
12 scallops in the half-shell, roe removed, shells well washed, dried and reserved
sea salt and freshly ground black pepper

1. Heat 1 tablespoon of the olive oil in a frying pan over low heat, then add half of the butter. When the butter starts to foam, add the leek and cook for 5 minutes or until it has softened but not taken on any colour. Add the tarragon and cream and simmer for 3–4 minutes or until thickened slightly, then stir well and set aside.

2. Preheat the oven to 180°C.

3. Place the reserved cleaned scallop shells (not the scallops) on a baking tray in the oven for 2 minutes or until warmed through. Remove from the oven and place a spoonful of leek fondue in each shell.

4. Heat the remaining olive oil in a heavy-based frying pan over medium heat. Season the scallops with salt and pepper, then pan-fry for 30 seconds. Add the remaining butter to the pan. When the butter turns nut-brown, carefully turn each scallop over and cook for another 30 seconds; they should still be just translucent in the centre.

5. To serve, top the leek fondue nest in each scallop shell with a scallop.

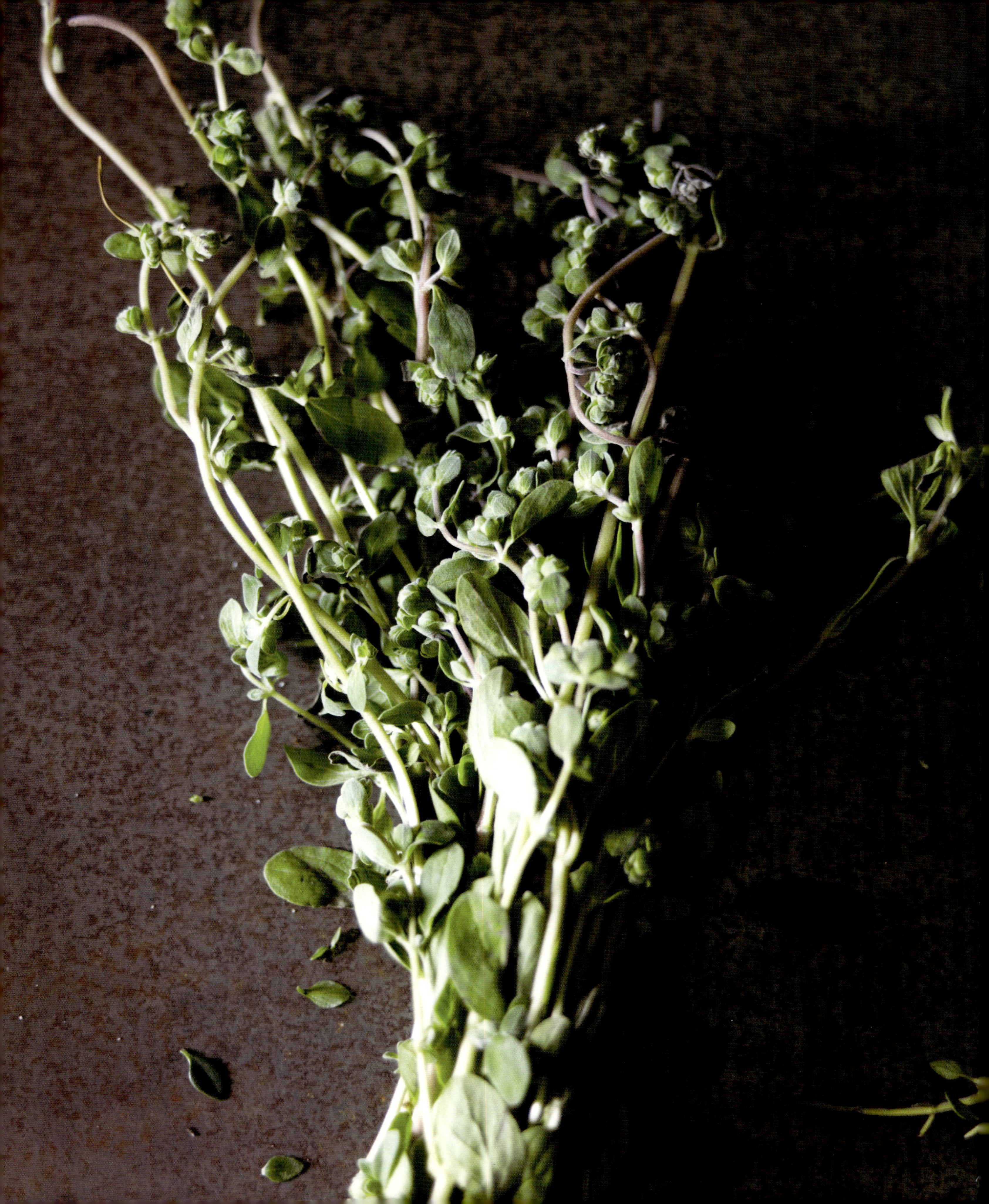

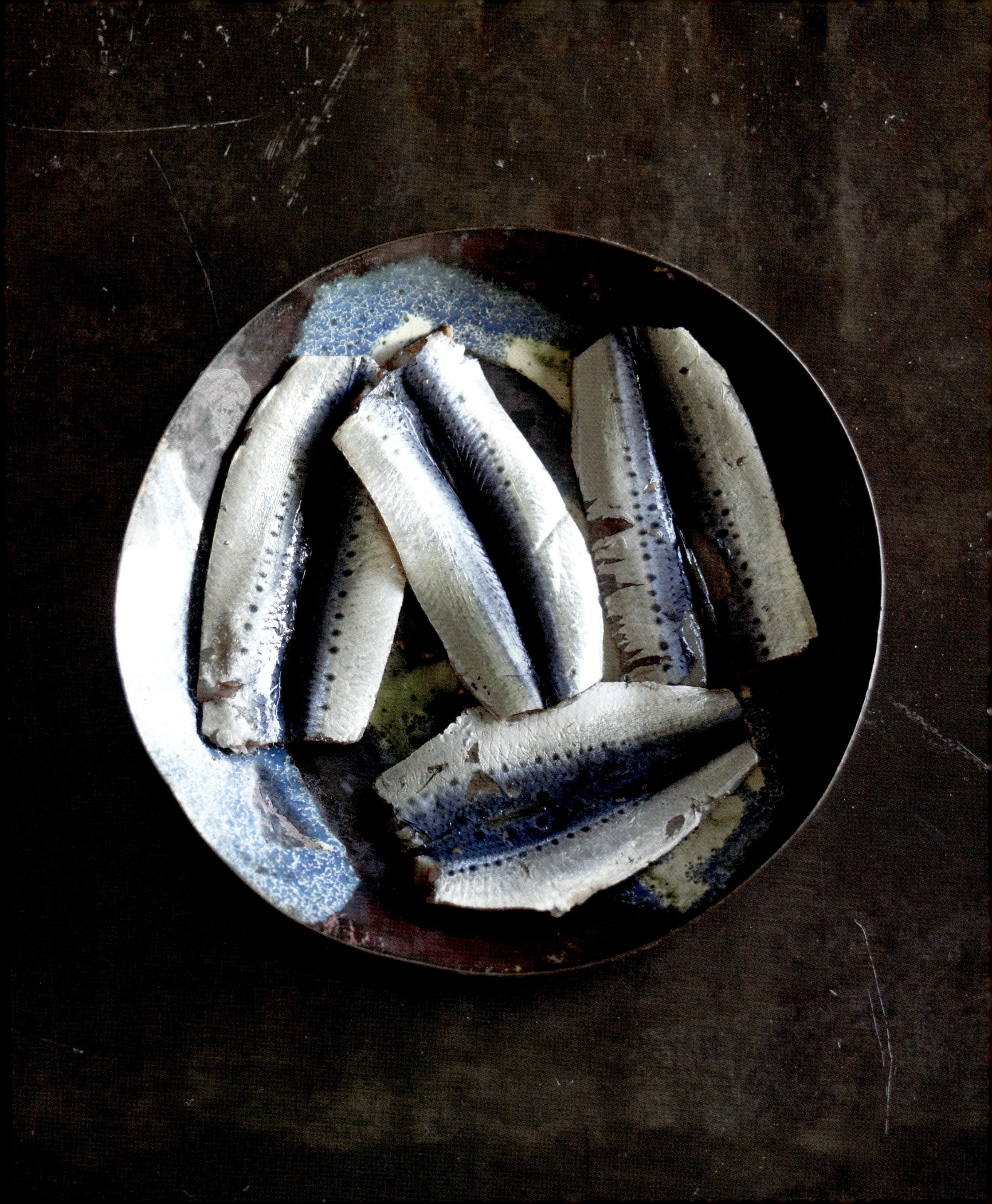

CANNELLONI DE THON ET DE CRABE ET CRÈME D'AVOCAT
TUNA & CRAB 'CANNELLONI' WITH AVOCADO CREAM

I only call these crab-filled tuna rolls 'cannelloni' because of their shape. This dish is not as complicated as it looks, and can be prepared in advance, then served up to look quite spectacular, making it a perfect dinner-party starter for when you really want to impress.

SERVES 4

1 baguette, thinly sliced on the diagonal
60 ml olive oil
1 small head celeriac
250 g cooked crab meat, picked over to remove any shell
2 tablespoons finely chopped chives
60 ml Mayonnaise (see page 202)
1 tablespoon lemon juice
sea salt and freshly ground black pepper
1 × 500 g piece sashimi-grade tuna loin, cut lengthways into 5 mm thick slices
baby coriander sprigs (optional), edible flowers (optional) and extra virgin olive oil, to serve

AVOCADO CREAM
2 avocados
1 tablespoon lime juice
180 ml pouring cream
sea salt and freshly ground black pepper

1. Preheat the oven to 180°C. Place the baguette slices on a baking tray and brush each side with olive oil. Bake for 5–6 minutes or until golden. Set aside.

2. To make the avocado cream, process the avocado flesh in a food processor with the lime juice until smooth, then transfer to a bowl and set aside. Using hand-held beaters, whip the cream until soft peaks form, then fold into the pureed avocado. Season to taste with salt and pepper, then cover closely with plastic film and refrigerate until needed. (Makes about 250 ml.)

3. Trim, peel and quarter the celeriac, then cut into thin strips (julienne, see page 208), using a mandoline or very sharp knife. Place the celeriac, crab, chives, mayonnaise and lemon juice in a bowl and mix gently. Season to taste with salt and pepper.

4. Place a 30 cm × 30 cm piece of plastic film on a clean work surface and lay a tuna slice on top. Spoon some of the crab mixture in a line down the centre, then roll the tuna over to form a cannelloni-like log, enclosing the crab mixture (the plastic film simply helps to hold the rolls or 'cannelloni' in place). Repeat with extra sheets of plastic film and the remaining crab mixture and tuna slices. Cut each tuna 'cannelloni' into 3 even pieces. Discard the plastic film.

5. To serve, place a spoonful or two of avocado cream on each plate. Arrange three pieces of the tuna 'cannelloni' on each plate, then add baby coriander (if using) and edible flowers (if using) and drizzle with olive oil. Serve with the toasted baguette.

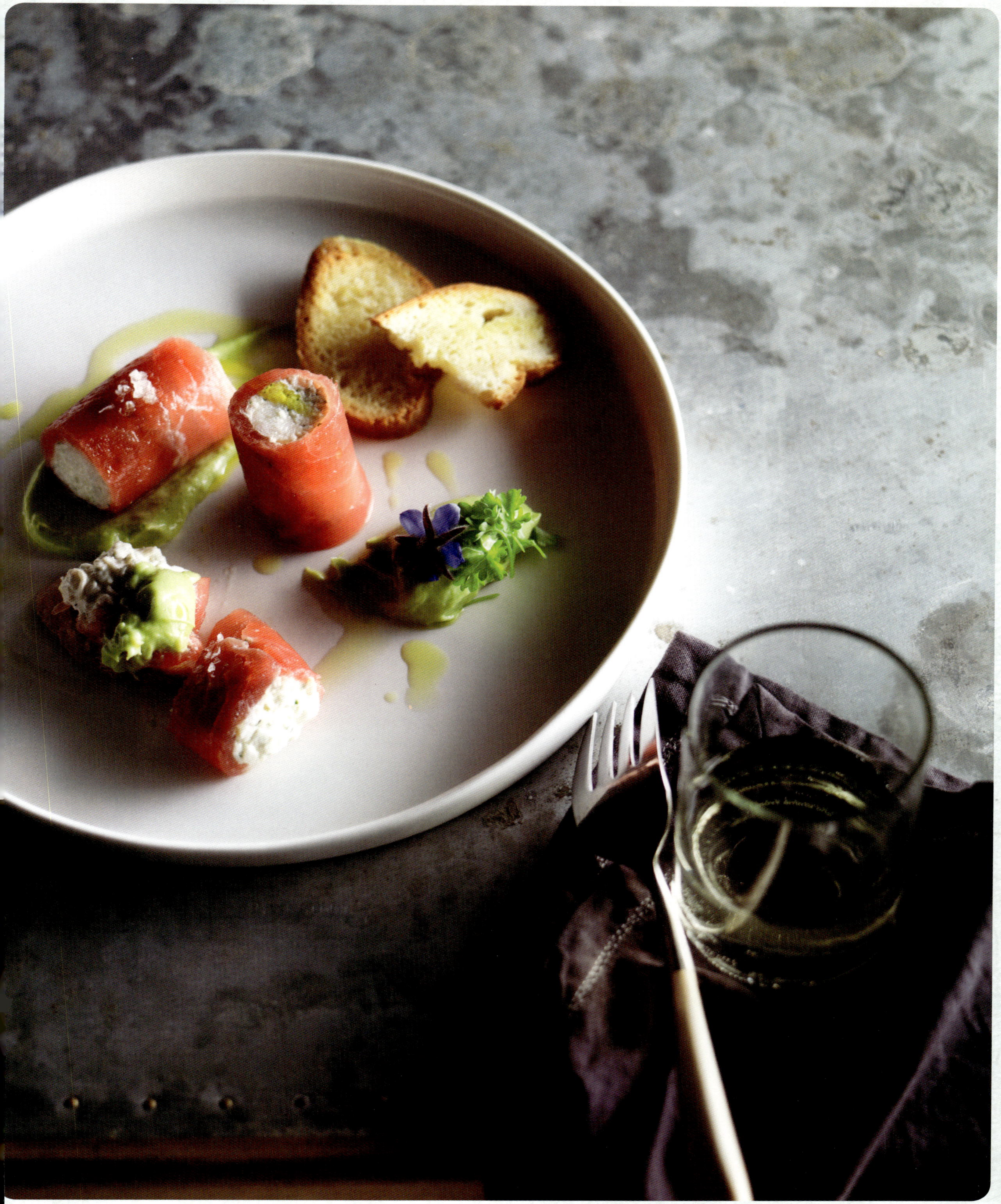

MOUSSE DE FOIE DE VOLAILLE
CHICKEN LIVER PARFAIT

Old-fashioned French fare such as this reminds me of my uncle, a *charcutier* (charcuterie maker) from near Angers in western France. I used to spend my school holidays helping him in the kitchen of his charcuterie business, smelling and tasting the different kinds of products he made by hand. If you can manage it, the foie gras adds a truly decadent touch. You will need to use a meat thermometer to check that the parfait is cooked.

SERVES 8

125 ml port
2 eschalots, finely chopped
1 clove garlic, crushed
1 sprig thyme
450 g unsalted butter, chopped, plus extra for greasing
250 g duck livers, trimmed, membrane removed and livers cut into 2.5 cm pieces
250 g chicken livers, trimmed, membrane removed and livers cut into 2.5 cm pieces
1 egg, beaten
100 g foie gras (optional), cut into 1 cm pieces
sea salt and freshly ground black pepper
crusty bread, cornichons (see page 208) and mixed salad leaves, to serve

1. Preheat the oven to 150°C.

2. Place the port, eschalot, garlic and thyme in a saucepan and bring to the boil. Simmer over medium heat for 8–10 minutes or until it has reduced to a thick, syrupy glaze. Remove from the heat and discard the thyme.

3. Heat 50 g of the butter in a large heavy-based frying pan over medium heat, then add the livers and cook, turning often, for 3–4 minutes or until golden and still a little pink in the centre; do not overcook or the parfait will be grainy. Meanwhile, melt 200 g of the butter in a small saucepan and set aside.

4. Transfer the livers and glaze to a food processor and process until smooth. Add the melted butter and pulse to combine, then add the egg and continue to process until smooth. Press the liver mixture through a fine-mesh sieve into a bowl (this greatly improves the texture of the finished parfait), then stir in the foie gras (if using).

5. Grease a 700 ml capacity (mine is 25 cm × 8 cm) terrine mould with extra butter, then line with two layers of baking paper. Add the liver mixture and smooth the surface with the back of a large metal spoon.

6. Place the terrine mould in a large roasting pan, then add enough boiling water to the pan to come halfway up the sides of the mould. Bake for 30–35 minutes or until the internal temperature of the parfait registers 64°C on a meat thermometer; the parfait should be firm but still a little wobbly in the middle. Remove the terrine mould from the roasting pan, then leave to cool to room temperature. Cover with plastic film and refrigerate for at least 2–3 hours.

7. Meanwhile, soften the remaining 200 g butter at room temperature. Unwrap the parfait and place it on a baking tray. Using a pastry brush, paint the top, ends, and sides of the parfait with a thick layer of softened butter and refrigerate for 1 hour or until the butter has hardened. Turn the parfait over and paint the bottom with a thick layer of butter. Return to the fridge to set for 1 hour, or overnight, if time permits.

8. Serve slices of the parfait seasoned with salt and pepper, with crusty bread, cornichons and mixed salad leaves alongside. (Leftover parfait can be stored in the fridge for up to 4 days.)

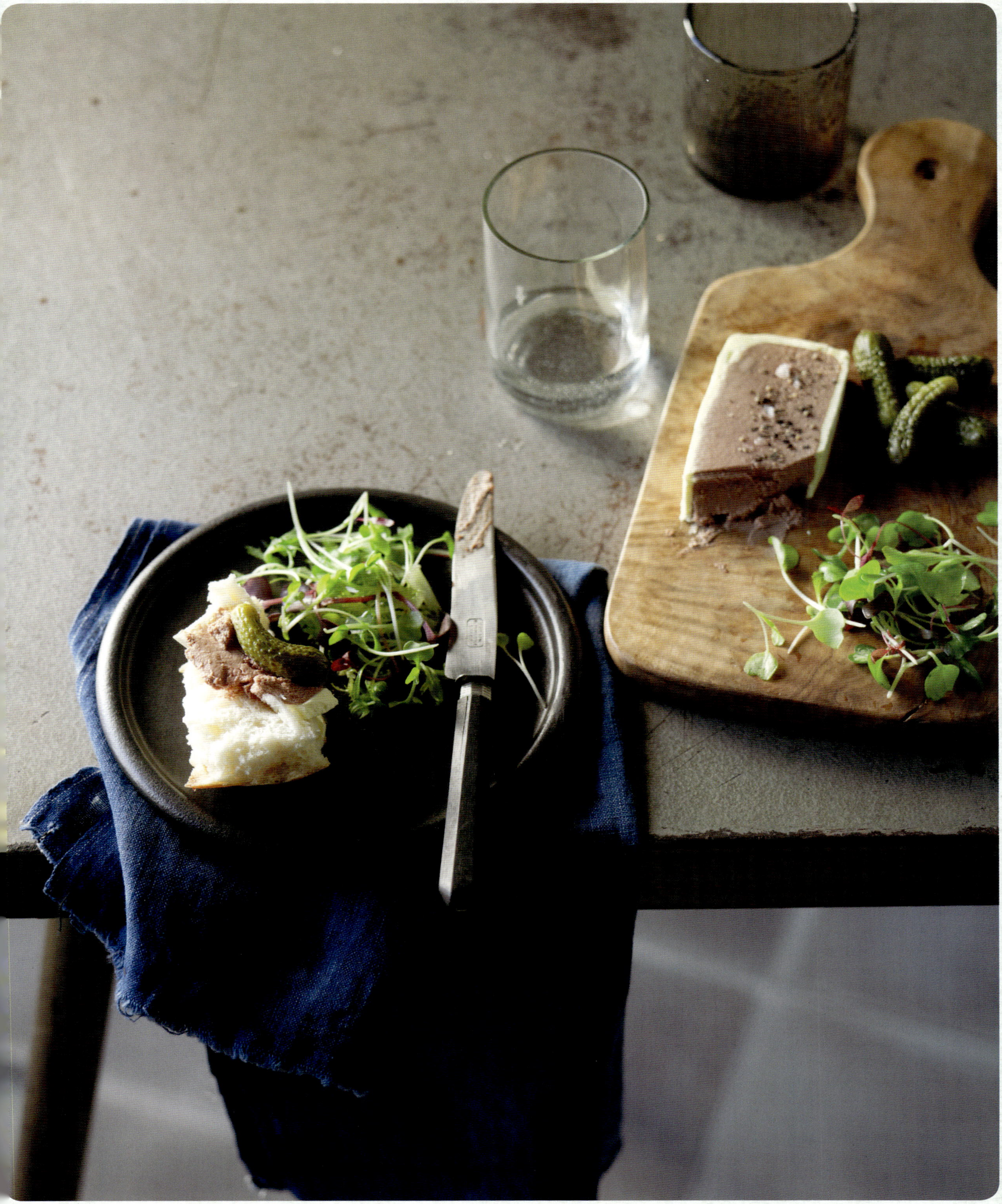

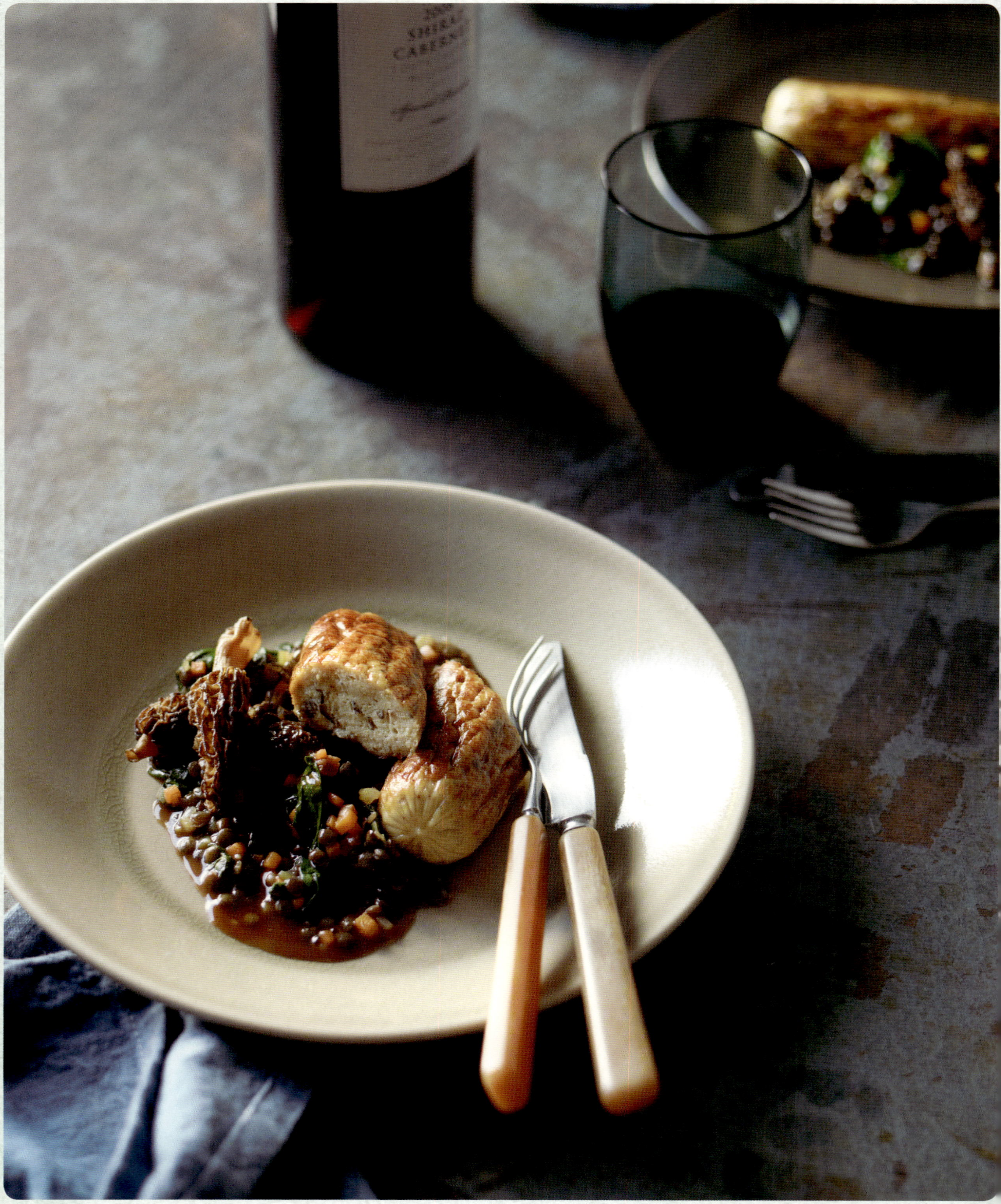

BOUDIN BLANC DE VOLAILLE AUX MORILLES
CHICKEN & MOREL MUSHROOM SAUSAGES

Making your own sausages is a lot of fun – try it and see. I love morel mushrooms, and their distinctive, strong flavour goes beautifully with chicken. They are usually only available fresh in Australia during August and September, so if you can't get them, rehydrated dried ones work just as well. (To rehydrate, just soak in warm water for 15 minutes, then drain and rinse to remove any remaining grit.) I was able to find beautiful fresh morels when I cooked this for the photograph, so I sauteed them in butter and served them alongside.

SERVES 4

300 ml milk
1/2 fresh or 1 dried bay leaf
1 onion, very thinly sliced
3 slices white bread, crusts removed, chopped
2 × 180 g chicken breast fillet halves, chopped into 4 cm pieces
100 g foie gras (optional)
80 g morel mushrooms (see page 209)
1/2 teaspoon freshly grated nutmeg
sea salt and freshly ground black pepper
3 eggs, at room temperature
300 ml double cream
ice cubes
2 tablespoons vegetable oil
50 g unsalted butter
Braised Lentils (see page 112), to serve

1. Put the milk, bay leaf and onion into a saucepan. Bring to the boil, then reduce the heat to low and simmer for 30 minutes or until the milk has reduced and only 60 ml remains. Remove from the heat and add the white bread. Mix with a wooden spoon until the bread has absorbed all the liquid and a paste forms (this is called a *panade*).

2. Process the paste with the chicken in a food processor for 2 minutes. Add the foie gras (if using), morel mushrooms, nutmeg, salt and pepper. Process again until very smooth. With the motor running, add one egg at a time, processing well after each addition. Add the cream and pulse to combine.

3. Press the chicken mixture through a fine-mesh sieve into a bowl. Season with 1 teaspoon salt and mix well. Cover with plastic film and refrigerate for 30 minutes.

4. Place a 20 cm × 20 cm sheet of heatproof plastic film on a clean work surface. Place 100 g of the sausage mixture in the centre, roll to form a sausage shape and enclose with the film. Tie a knot at each end and repeat with extra sheets of plastic film and the remaining sausage mixture.

5. Bring a large saucepan of salted water to a simmer over medium heat, then add the sausages and cook gently for 10 minutes. Remove the pan from the heat and leave the sausages to cool in the water for 15 minutes. Plunge the sausages into a bowl of iced water. When they are cool enough to handle, carefully remove the plastic film.

6. Heat the oil in a large heavy-based frying pan over high heat, then cook the sausage for 2 minutes or until browned all over. Add the butter, then reduce the heat to low, cover the pan and cook for 4–5 minutes or until cooked through.

7. Slice the sausages thickly on the diagonal, then serve with the braised lentils.

TERRINE DE CANARD ET CONFITURE DE PRUNEAUX
DUCK TERRINE WITH PRUNE JAM

Probably because of my experience helping in the kitchen of my uncle's charcuterie, I've always loved terrines, and this one is an old favourite. Don't be put off by the thought that terrines are too complicated to make – they really aren't, especially if you ask your butcher to mince the meats for you. You will need to use a meat thermometer to check that the terrine is cooked.

SERVES 12

4 duck marylands, skin and excess fat removed
1 × 500 g piece pork shoulder, cut into 2.5 cm pieces
1 × 300 g piece pork back fat (see page 209), cut into 2.5 cm pieces, plus 300 g very thinly sliced (ask your butcher to do this)
30 g unsalted butter
4 eschalots, finely chopped
2 cloves garlic, finely chopped
3 eggs, beaten
2 tablespoons brandy
4 tablespoons finely chopped flat-leaf parsley
1 tablespoon finely chopped thyme
50 g truffles (optional), finely chopped
125 g foie gras (optional), cut into 1 cm dice
sea salt and freshly ground black pepper
French Dijon mustard (see page 208), flat-leaf parsley leaves, Prune Jam (optional, see page 207) and fruit bread or brioche, to serve

1. Using a boning knife, remove all the meat from the duck marylands, reserving the bones for making stock (if desired). Using the coarse plate of a meat grinder, mince the duck meat, then place in a large bowl. Mince the pork shoulder and chopped pork back fat twice through the meat grinder, then add to the duck meat. (Alternatively, ask your butcher to do this for you.)

2. Preheat the oven to 150°C.

3. Heat the butter in a small frying pan over low heat. When the butter starts to foam, add the eschalot and garlic and stir for 4–5 minutes or until soft but not coloured. Remove from the heat and set aside to cool.

4. Add the cooled eschalot mixture, the egg, brandy, parsley, thyme, truffle (if using), and foie gras (if using) to the meat mixture, then season with 1 tablespoon salt and 1 teaspoon pepper. Using very clean hands, combine the mixture very well until the fat feels sticky and the mixture has amalgamated. (This step is important in making sure the terrine holds together and is not crumbly once cooked.)

5. Line the base and sides of a 2 litre capacity terrine mould or loaf tin with the back fat slices, overlapping them slightly; allow any excess at the edges to overhang the mould (you should have some slices left). Spoon the meat mixture into the mould, smoothing the surface with a large metal spoon. Fold any overhanging pieces of fat over to cover the top. Use any leftover slices of fat to cover the meat mixture completely. Press down firmly to remove any air pockets.

6. Place the terrine mould in a deep roasting pan and pour enough boiling water into the pan to come halfway up the sides of the mould. Bake the terrine for 1½–2 hours or until the internal temperature of the terrine registers 60°C on a meat thermometer. Carefully remove the roasting pan from the oven, then remove the terrine mould and drain off any excess fat. Cover the terrine with heatproof plastic film, then place a smaller baking tin that fits inside the mould on top of the terrine and fill with tins of food to weigh it down. Leave to cool, then refrigerate overnight.

7. Cut the terrine into slices and divide among plates. Top the terrine slices with a spoonful of mustard garnished with flat-leaf parsley, then serve with prune jam (if using) and fruit bread or brioche alongside.

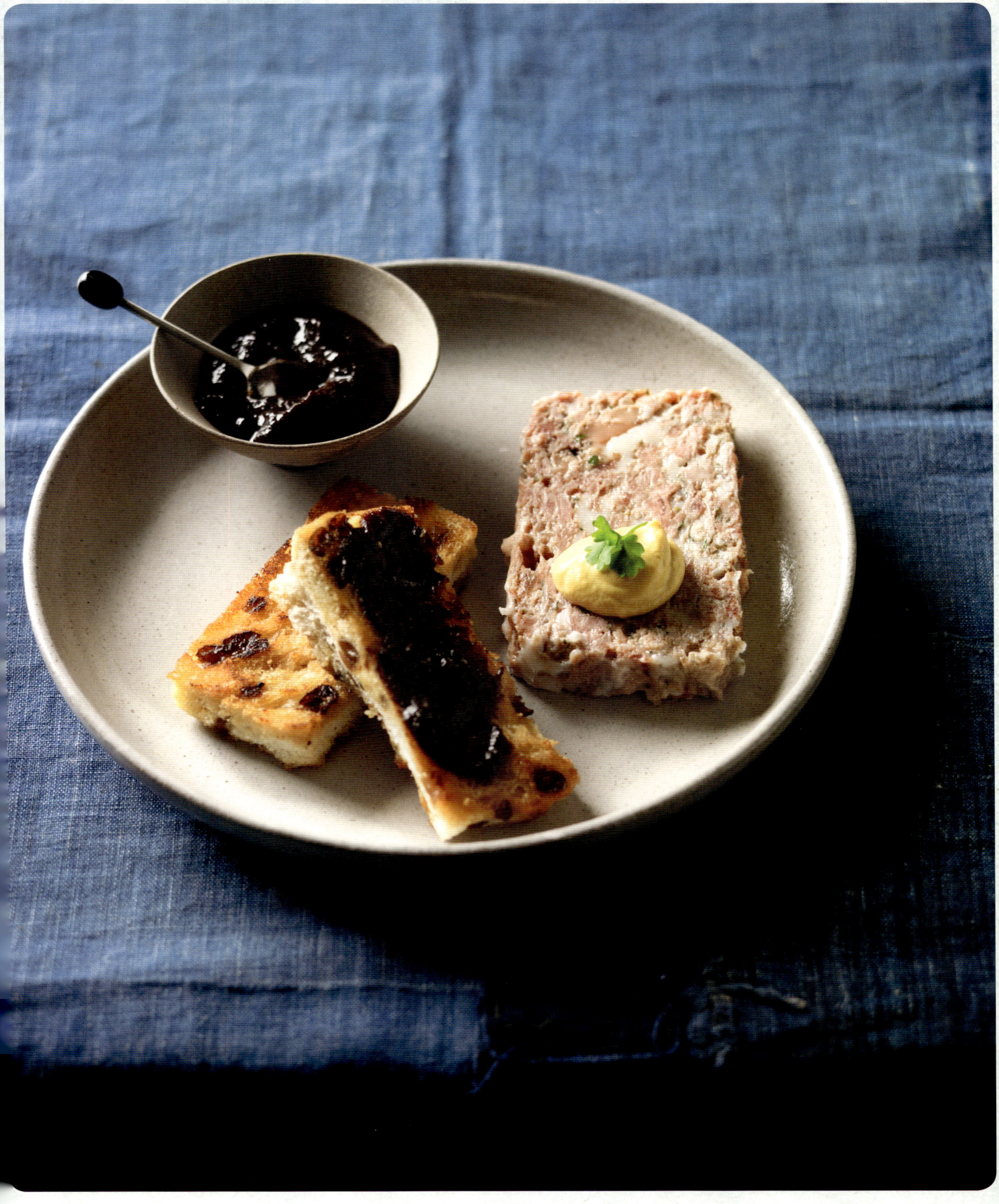

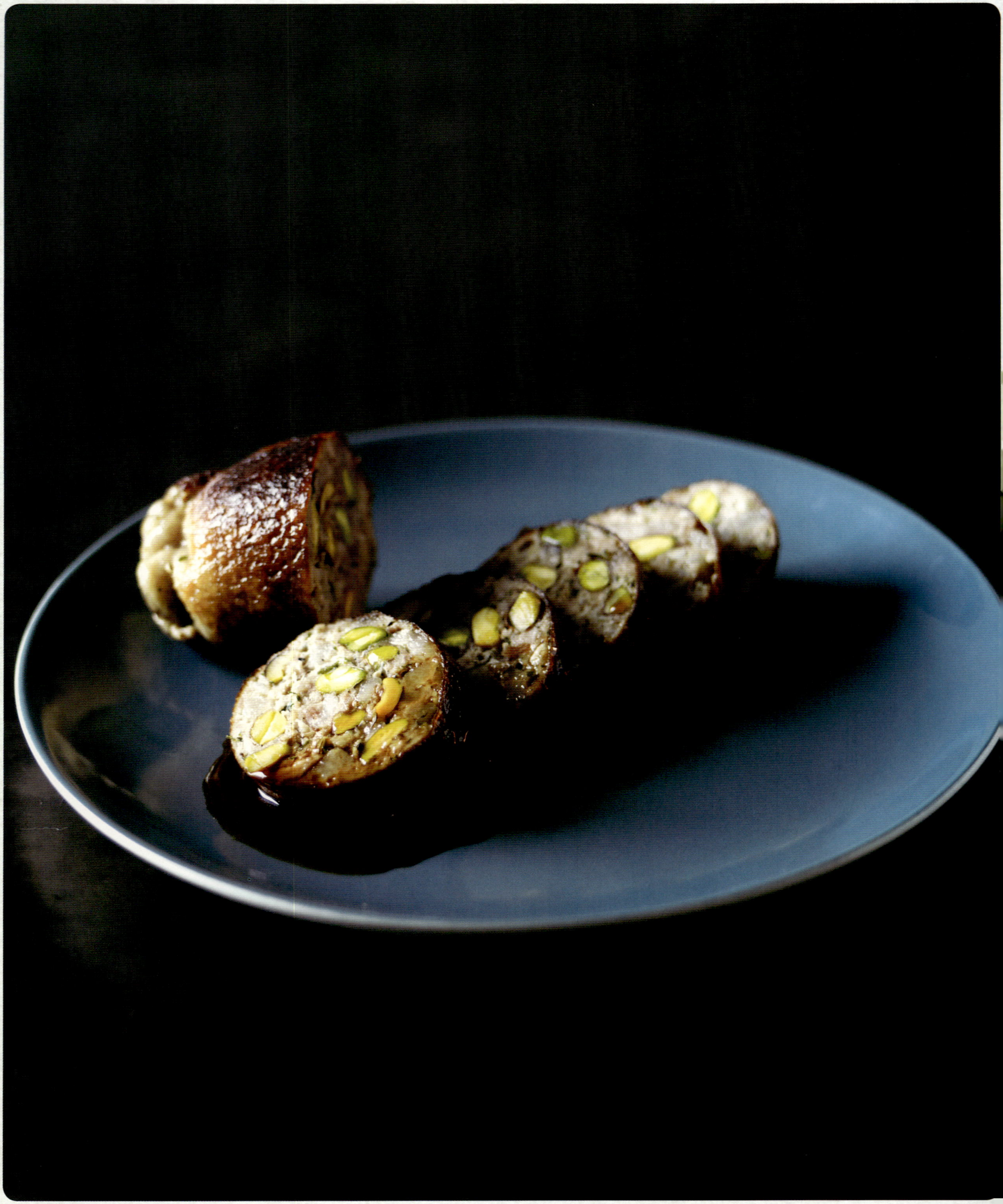

COU DE CANARD FARCI AUX PISTACHES
STUFFED DUCK NECK WITH PISTACHIOS

This cross between a sausage and a terrine makes a very impressive starter, and the duck neck gives it an extra-rich flavour. Ask your butcher to order the duck neck skins, and they can also mince the meats for you if you don't have a meat grinder at home. I find that duck and pistachios go wonderfully well together, but you could use other nuts instead, or leave nuts out altogether.

SERVES 4

3 duck neck skins, cleaned
2 tablespoons olive oil
4 eschalots, finely chopped
2 cloves garlic, crushed
250 g pork shoulder, minced
250 g pork back fat (see page 209), minced
250 g duck leg meat, minced
2 eggs, lightly whisked
125 g raw shelled pistachios
3 tablespoons finely chopped flat-leaf parsley
2 tablespoons thyme leaves, finely chopped
2 tablespoons port or brandy
sea salt and freshly ground black pepper
Duck Jus (optional, see page 206), to serve

1. Preheat the oven to 150°C. Tie one end of each duck neck skin with kitchen twine.

2. Heat the olive oil in a heavy-based frying pan over medium heat. Add the eschalot and garlic and cook for 2–3 minutes or until softened but not coloured.

3. Place the pork and duck meat in a large bowl, then add the eschalot mixture, egg, pistachios, parsley, thyme, port or brandy and salt and pepper. Using very clean hands, mix the ingredients together well.

4. Carefully spoon one-third of the mixture into each duck skin and gently push it down as you go. Tie up the ends with kitchen twine. Tightly wrap each neck in foil and roll into a uniform sausage shape, then wrap in another layer of foil.

5. Place the sausages on a baking tray and cook for 10 minutes. Reduce the oven temperature to 120°C and cook for a further 10–15 minutes or until cooked through. (At this stage you can leave the sausages to cool at room temperature, then refrigerate until needed.)

6. Unwrap the sausages, then cook in a large frying pan over medium heat for 3–4 minutes or until golden brown. Cut into 1.5 cm thick slices, then pan-fry on each side for 1–2 minutes or until golden brown.

7. Spoon some jus onto each place (if using), then top with slices of duck neck sausage. Serve.

RILLETTES DE LAPIN
RABBIT RILLETTES

Rillettes is a type of pate or potted meat. In this case I have used rabbit meat, as its leanness contrasts nicely with the rich pork fat. In the unlikely event that you don't polish this off in one sitting, you can store it, covered in the cooking fat, in the fridge for up to 5 days. It makes for great picnic fare.

SERVES 4

325 g pork back fat (see page 209), coarsely minced (ask your butcher to do this)
500 g rabbit meat (order from your butcher), sinew removed, cut into 4 cm chunks
1 tablespoon thyme leaves
sea salt and freshly ground black pepper
1 onion, peeled and halved
1 carrot, peeled and cut into 3 lengthways
1 stick celery, cut into 4 cm batons (see page 208)
4 cloves garlic, peeled
1 bay leaf
250 ml white wine
500 ml water
50 ml Cognac
100 g foie gras (optional)
1 teaspoon truffle essence (optional, I use Sevarome)
1 teaspoon quatre epices (see page 209)
crusty bread, to serve

1. Place the back fat in a large heavy-based saucepan over medium heat and cook for 5–6 minutes or until melted. Add the rabbit and thyme and season with salt and pepper, then cook for 8–10 minutes. Add the onion, carrot, celery and garlic and cook for another 10 minutes or until the vegetables are tender. Add the bay leaf and white wine, then simmer over medium heat for 3–4 minutes or until the liquid has reduced by half. Add the water and simmer over low heat for 2 hours or until the rabbit is very tender.

2. Remove and discard the vegetables, garlic and bay leaf and leave the rabbit to cool in the cooking liquid. When cooled completely, use a large metal spoon to scrape the layer of fat from the surface and set the fat aside in a bowl.

3. Place the rabbit and its cooking liquid, the Cognac, foie gras (if using), truffle essence (if using) and quatre epices in the bowl of an electric mixer fitted with a dough hook and beat until the rabbit is shredded. Season to taste with salt and pepper. Transfer to four 250 ml capacity ramekins or jars, spoon over a little of the cooled fat and smooth the tops, then cover with a little more of the cooled fat to seal completely. Cover with plastic film or a lid and refrigerate for 2 days before serving.

4. Serve the rillettes with crusty bread. (Leftovers will keep in the fridge for up to 5 days.)

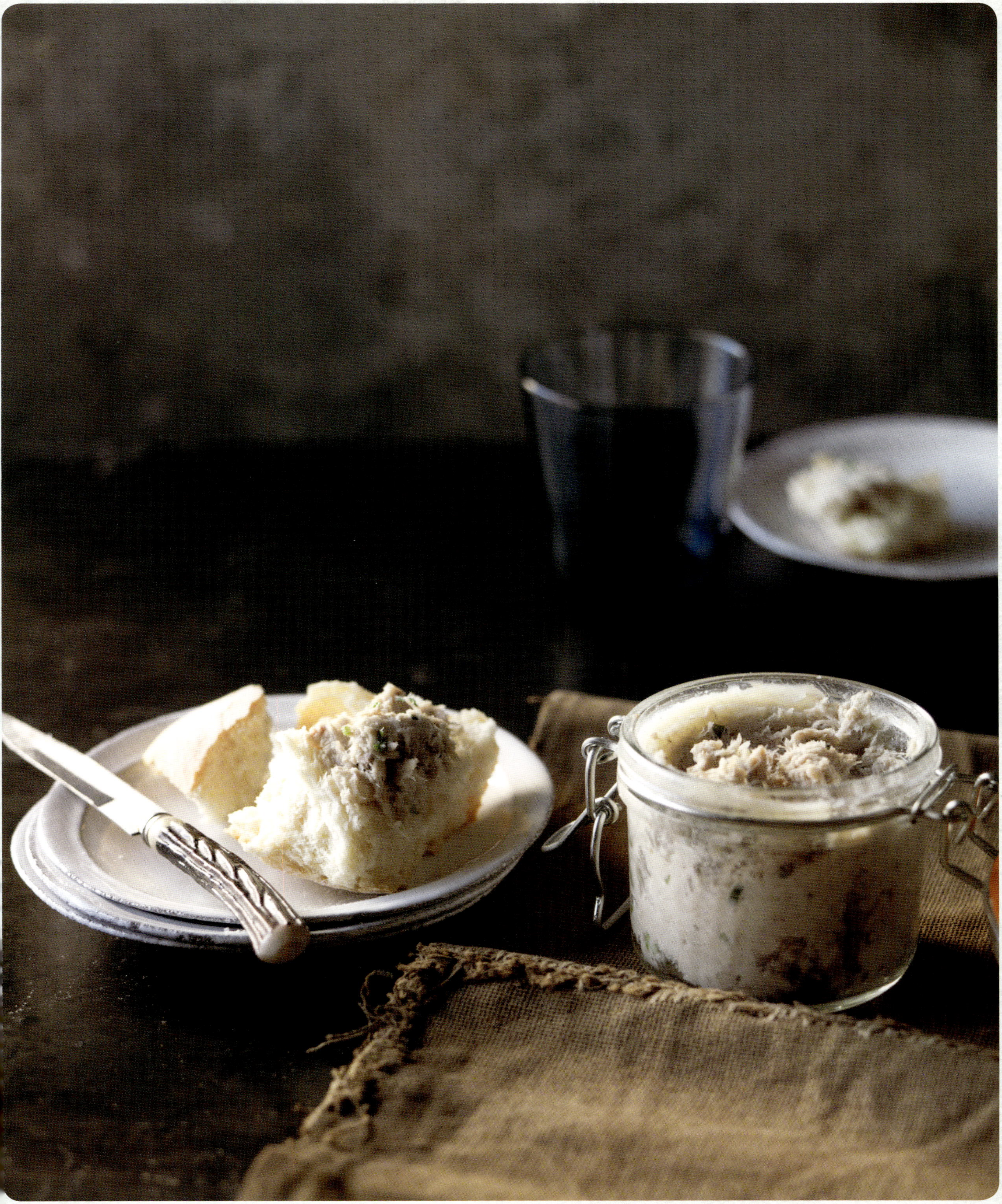

CEVICHE DE 'KINGFISH', VINAIGRETTE À LA CORIANDRE ET AUX PIGNONS
KINGFISH CEVICHE WITH CORIANDER & PINE-NUT DRESSING

Ceviche, originally from South America, is raw fish marinated in lemon or lime juice – the citric acid in the fruit 'cooks' the fish. Here, the citrus taste of the fish is set off perfectly by the roasted pine nuts in the flavoursome dressing. I leave the chilli seeds in to add a little bite, but you can remove them if you prefer. The tomatoes are cooked gently in olive oil, which gives them a luscious texture and concentrates their natural sweetness. This light, summery dish is a great palate-teaser.

SERVES 4

500 g kingfish fillets, skin removed, pin-boned
sea salt
finely grated zest and juice of 3 limes
finely grated zest and juice of 1 lemon
150 ml olive oil
2 roma tomatoes, peeled (see page 209), seeded and cut into quarters
50 ml vegetable oil
2 tablespoons baby salted capers, rinsed very well and drained

CORIANDER & PINE-NUT DRESSING

3 tablespoons coriander leaves, coarsely chopped
60 g pine nuts, roasted (see page 209)
2 teaspoons wholegrain French Dijon mustard (see page 208)
1 small fresh red chilli, thinly sliced
2 tablespoons lemon juice
1 tablespoon lime juice
2 sprigs lemon thyme, leaves picked
100 ml olive oil

1. Place the kingfish fillets in a shallow ceramic dish, season with salt and add the lime and lemon zest and juice, turning the fish to coat evenly. Cover with plastic film and refrigerate for 3 hours.

2. Meanwhile, to make the dressing, combine the coriander, pine nuts, mustard, chilli, lemon juice, lime juice and lemon thyme in a bowl. Gradually add the olive oil and whisk until emulsified. Set aside. (Makes about 160 ml.)

3. Heat the olive oil in a large heavy-based saucepan over medium heat, then add the tomato and cook for 10 minutes or until soft. Remove from the heat and set aside.

4. Heat the vegetable oil in a small heavy-based frying pan over medium heat, then fry the capers for 2–3 minutes or until crisp. Remove and drain on paper towel.

5. Brush the salt and citrus zest off the fish fillets, then slice against the grain as thinly as possible. Arrange the slices on a plate and spoon over the dressing. Add the tomato quarters. Leave to stand for 20 minutes, then scatter over the crisp capers and serve.

RAVIOLI AU JAUNE D'ŒUF, ASPERGES VERTE ET PARMESAN
EGG-YOLK RAVIOLI WITH GREEN ASPARAGUS & SHAVED PARMESAN

Surprise your guests with this slightly unusual starter. Be careful to keep the egg yolks intact as you make the ravioli. I suggest you use really fresh organic eggs if you can, as their yolks tend to hold their shape better. Once you have cooked the ravioli, the yolks should be warm but not cooked, and should taste like poached eggs. *Magnifique*!

SERVES 4

8 round wonton wrappers (available in the refrigerator section of large supermarkets and Asian food stores)
4 eggs
24 large green asparagus spears, trimmed
olive oil, for drizzling
100 g parmesan, shaved with a vegetable peeler
sea salt and freshly ground black pepper
extra virgin olive oil, for drizzling

1. Place 4 of the wonton wrappers on a lightly floured work surface.

2. Carefully separate each egg, placing the whites in one bowl and each yolk in a separate small bowl; take care not to break the yolks as they are the filling for the ravioli. Gently place one yolk in the middle of each wonton wrapper, then brush the edges with the egg white and carefully top with another wrapper, taking care not to break the yolk. Gently press all around the edge of the yolks to seal and remove any air.

3. Blanch the asparagus in a saucepan of boiling salted water for 3 minutes or until tender but firm-to-the-bite. Place 6 asparagus each on warmed plates.

4. Bring a large saucepan of salted water to the boil and add a drizzle of olive oil. Working in batches, cook the ravioli for 1 minute, then carefully remove with a slotted spoon and drain on paper towel.

5. To serve, place a raviolo on top of the asparagus on each plate. Scatter with the shaved parmesan, then season with salt and pepper and drizzle with extra virgin olive oil.

THON MARINÉ À LA VODKA ET AU CITRON VERT, PETITS LÉGUMES AU VINAIGRE ET CRÈME AU RAIFORT
VODKA & LIME-CURED TUNA WITH PICKLED VEGETABLES & HORSERADISH CREAM

The sweet-and-sour character of the pickled vegetables works a treat with the meaty richness of tuna, and the horseradish cream adds just the right touch of piquancy. To give the baby turnips in the photo their purple colour, I simply added some boiled beetroot juice I happened to have in the restaurant coolroom to the pickling liquid. You could also make this with salmon or ocean trout rather than tuna.

SERVES 4

handful coriander leaves, coarsely chopped
handful dill leaves, coarsely chopped, plus 3 tablespoons extra, finely chopped
1 tablespoon lime juice
2 tablespoons vodka
1 tablespoon olive oil
280 g rock salt
125 g soft brown sugar
100 g caster sugar
4 × 200 g sashimi-grade tuna steaks
3 tablespoons finely chopped chervil
4 tablespoons finely chopped flat-leaf parsley

PICKLED VEGETABLES
375 ml water
80 ml champagne vinegar
100 g caster sugar
1 bay leaf
2 sprigs thyme
1 star anise
1 bunch baby (Dutch) carrots, stalks trimmed leaving 2 cm intact, peeled
8 baby turnips, stalks trimmed leaving 2 cm intact, peeled
1 Lebanese cucumber, thinly sliced with a vegetable peeler

HORSERADISH CREAM
50 g grated horseradish
1 tablespoon creamed horseradish (available from specialty food stores)
200 g creme fraiche
freshly ground black pepper

1. Combine the coriander, coarsely chopped dill, lime juice, vodka, olive oil, rock salt and sugars in a deep ceramic dish, then place the tuna on top. Cover with plastic film and refrigerate for 2 hours, turning every 30 minutes; the tuna should turn deep purple and feel firm to the touch. Rinse under cold running water to wash off excess salt. Discard the salt mixture and wash and dry the dish. Place the finely chopped dill, chervil and parsley in the clean dish and mix to combine. Roll the tuna in herbs to coat and set aside.

2. Meanwhile, to make the pickled vegetables, place the water, vinegar, sugar, bay leaf, thyme and star anise in a heavy-based saucepan and bring to the boil, stirring until the sugar has dissolved. Add the carrots and turnips and cook for 3–4 minutes. Remove from the heat, then leave the carrots and turnips to cool completely in the liquid. Place the cucumber in a small bowl and pour over enough cooled liquid to cover. Allow to pickle for 30 minutes only. Remove the vegetables from the pickling liquid and discard the liquid. Roll the cucumber into cylinders, if desired.

3. To make the horseradish cream, combine the horseradish, creamed horseradish and creme fraiche in a bowl, then season to taste with pepper.

4. Thinly sliced the tuna, then serve with the pickled vegetables and horseradish cream.

ENTREES

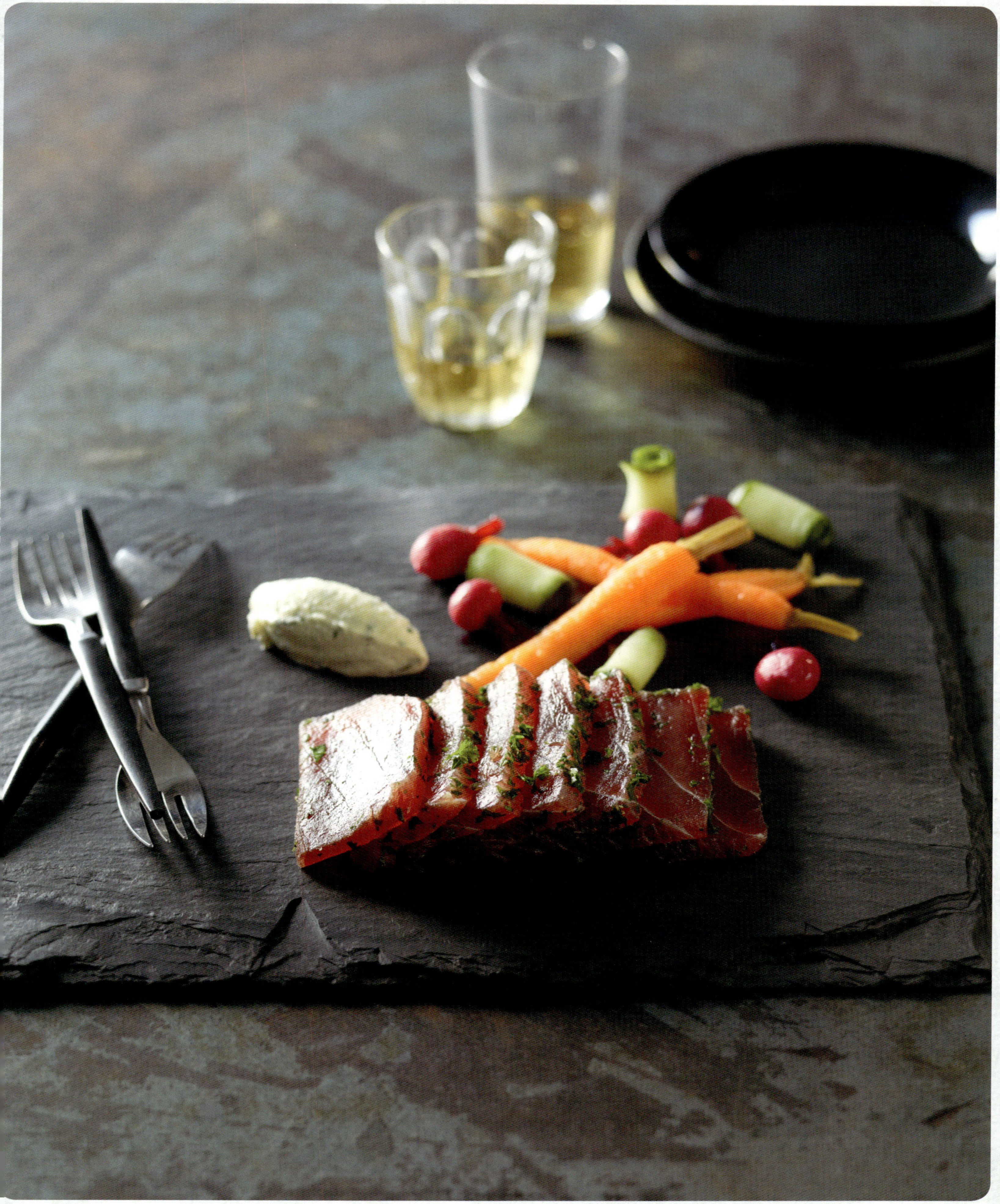

SALADE DE CRABE ET D'ESTRAGON, ASPERGES GRILLÉES ET POMMES DE TERRE NOUVELLES
SPANNER CRAB & TARRAGON SALAD WITH GRILLED ASPARAGUS

I created this simple but stunning recipe especially for this book. I love the combination of flavours – the slight bitterness of the frisee mixed with the sweet crab meat and the kipfler potatoes. It is a wonderful starter for a summer dinner party, or can be a light meal in itself. Cooked and picked crab meat can be purchased from good fishmongers.

SERVES 4

250 g kipfler potatoes, scrubbed
50 g duck fat (see page 105)
16 green asparagus spears, trimmed
sea salt and freshly ground black pepper
250 g frisee, washed and dried
3 tablespoons French tarragon leaves (see page 208)
500 g cooked crab meat (I use spanner crab), picked over to remove any shell

CHAMPAGNE DRESSING

1½ tablespoons French Dijon mustard (see page 208)
1 tablespoon champagne vinegar
¼ teaspoon caster sugar
1 tablespoon lemon juice
sea salt and freshly ground black pepper
100 ml extra virgin olive oil

1. Place the potatoes in a large saucepan of lightly salted water, bring to the boil over high heat, then reduce the heat to medium and simmer for 5 minutes. Remove from the heat and leave the potatoes to cool in the water.

2. When the potatoes are cool enough to handle, thinly slice. Heat the duck fat in a heavy-based frying pan over medium heat, then cook the potato for 3 minutes on each side or until golden and crisp all over. Set aside.

3. Preheat a chargrill pan over high heat and cook the asparagus for 3–4 minutes or until tender but still firm-to-the-bite. Season with salt and pepper and set aside.

4. To make the dressing, place the mustard, vinegar, sugar, lemon juice, and salt and pepper to taste in a bowl and whisk to combine well. Whisking continuously, gradually add the olive oil in a thin steady stream until emulsified. (Makes about 160 ml.)

5. Place the frisee, tarragon and crab in a bowl, then drizzle with enough of the dressing to coat and toss gently to combine. Divide the crab mixture among serving plates, then top with the asparagus and potato. Drizzle with extra dressing. Serve.

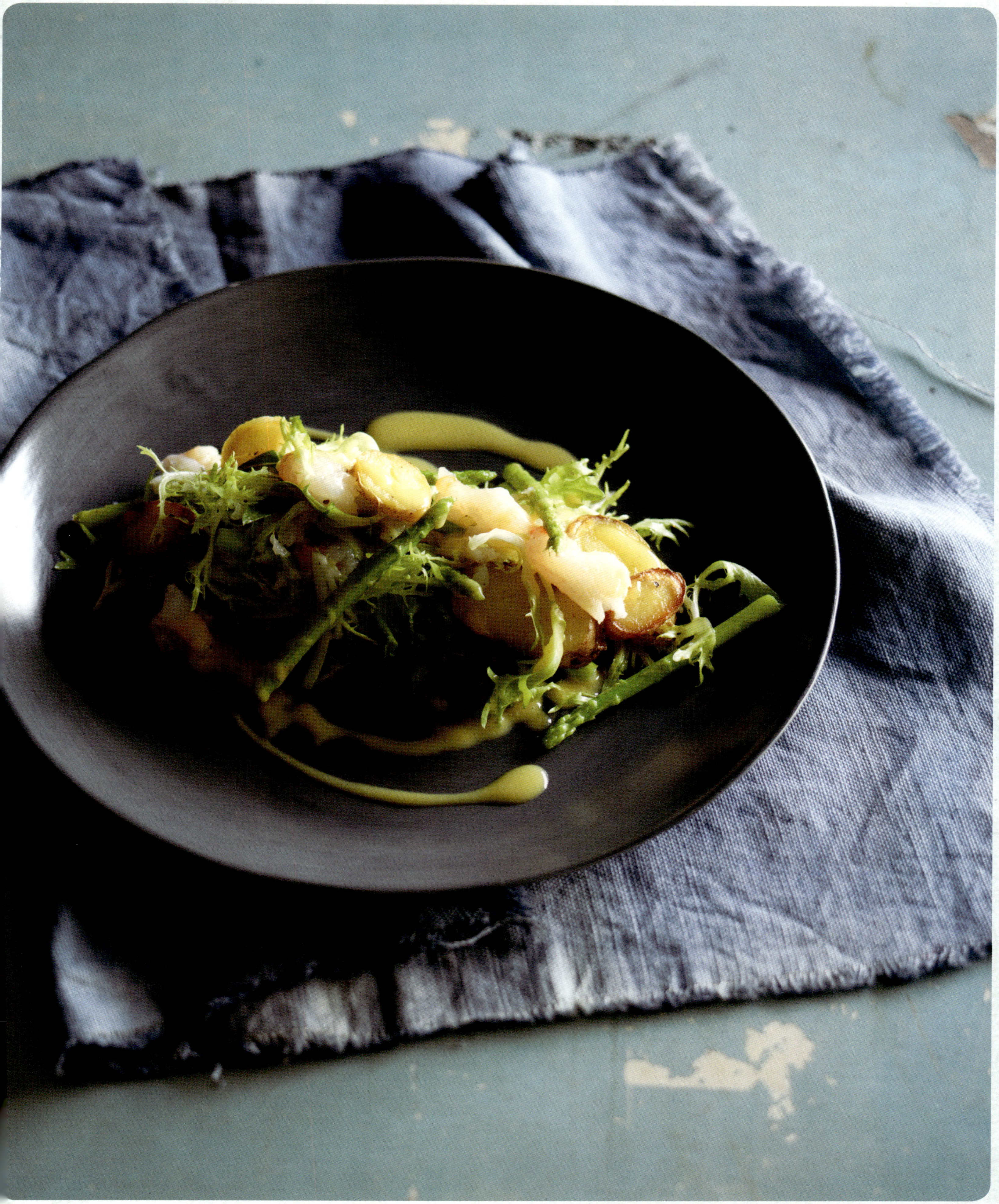

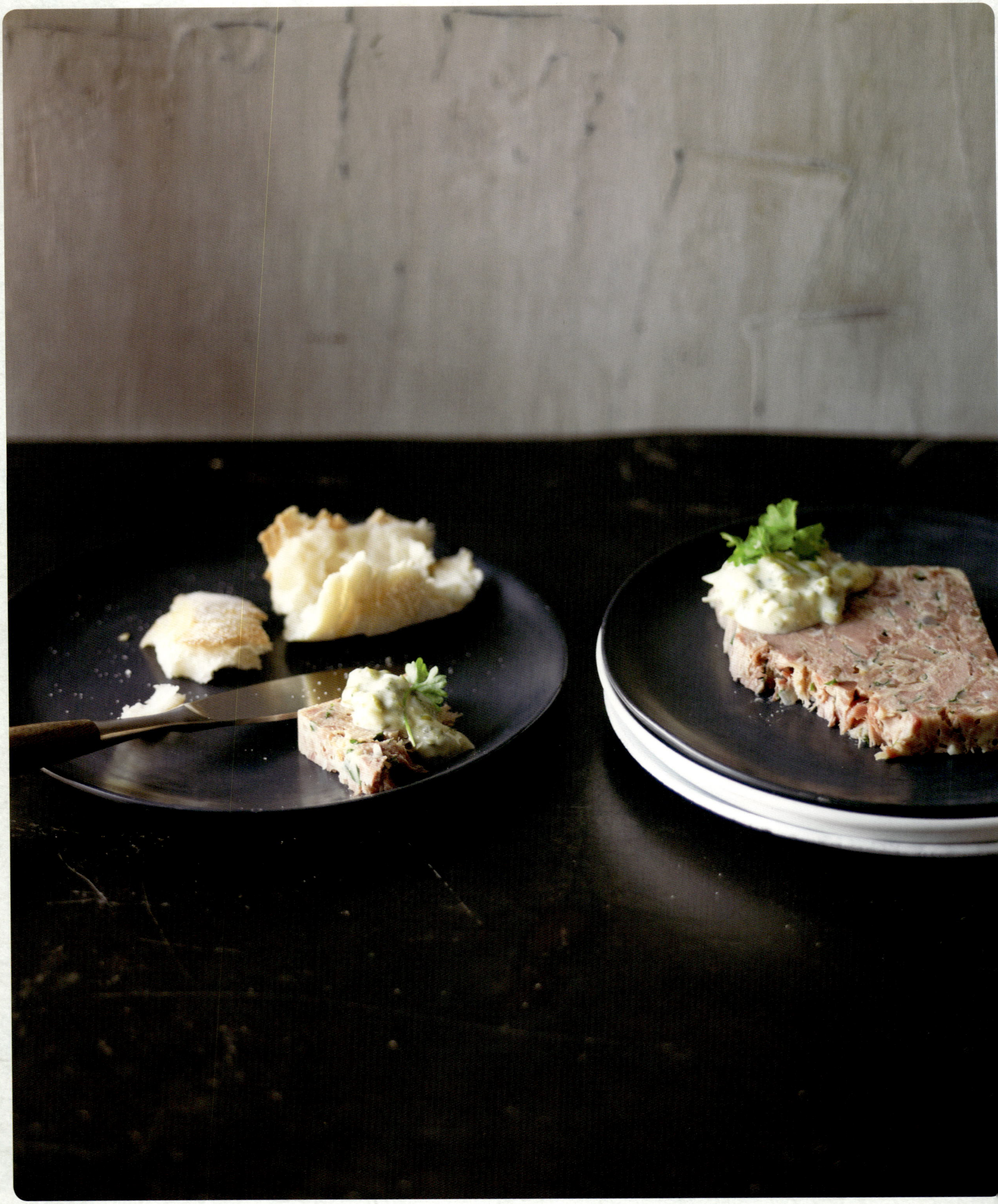

PÂTÉ DE TÊTE AU SAUCE GRIBICHE
SMOKED HAM HOCK TERRINE WITH GRIBICHE SAUCE

This is a variation on a traditional pig's head terrine; however, I prefer to use ham hocks. The terrine needs to set in the fridge overnight, so make sure you start this recipe well in advance. I like to serve it with gribiche sauce, a herb-flecked mayonnaise. I think it's a winning combination – try it and see if you agree.

SERVES 4

4 smoked ham hocks (about 600 g)
1 onion, coarsely chopped
2 sticks celery, 1 coarsely chopped, 1 finely chopped
1½ carrots, 1 finely chopped, ½ coarsely chopped
6 cloves garlic, 3 peeled, 3 finely chopped
4 sprigs thyme
6 black peppercorns
1 bay leaf
1 tablespoon olive oil
4 eschalots, finely chopped
1 tablespoon finely chopped thyme
2 teaspoons wholegrain French Dijon mustard (see page 208)
3 tablespoons finely chopped flat-leaf parsley
sea salt and freshly ground black pepper
crusty bread and flat-leaf parsley leaves, to serve

GRIBICHE SAUCE

4 eggs
100 ml Mayonnaise (see page 202)
50 g baby salted capers, rinsed very well and finely chopped
10 cornichons (see page 208), finely chopped
2 teaspoons finely chopped chervil
2 teaspoons finely chopped flat-leaf parsley
1 teaspoon finely chopped French tarragon (see page 208)
freshly ground black pepper

1. Place the hocks, onion, coarsely chopped celery and carrot, 3 whole garlic cloves, thyme sprigs, black peppercorns and bay leaf in a large saucepan and cover with water. Bring to the boil, then simmer for 3 hours or until the meat falls off the bones. Transfer the hocks with a slotted spoon to a roasting pan. Set aside until cool enough to handle.

2. Strain the reserved cooking liquid through a fine-mesh sieve into a large bowl and set aside, then coarsely shred the meat and discard the bones, skin and fat.

3. Heat the olive oil in a large heavy-based saucepan over medium heat, then add the finely chopped celery, carrot and eschalot and cook for 4–5 minutes or until softened but not coloured. Add the chopped garlic and thyme and cook for another 2 minutes. Place in a large bowl with the shredded meat, mustard and parsley and mix well, taking care not to break up the meat; it should be quite chunky. Season to taste with salt and pepper.

4. Line a 1 litre capacity terrine mould or loaf tin with two layers of plastic film, leaving enough overhanging to help lift the terrine from the tin. Spoon the meat mixture into the mould, pressing down firmly to remove any air pockets. Spoon over 200 ml of the reserved cooking liquid. Fold the overhanging plastic film over to cover the top, then place a weight (such as tins of food) on top and refrigerate overnight to set.

5. To make the sauce, place the eggs in a small saucepan, cover with cold water and bring to the boil over medium heat. Cook for 8 minutes or until hard-boiled, then refresh in cold water. Shell the eggs, then separate the whites and yolks. Place the yolks in a bowl and mash with a fork, then add the mayonnaise, capers, cornichons, herbs and whites and fold gently to mix. Season to taste with pepper. (Makes about 120 ml.)

6. Serve slices of terrine with gribiche sauce, crusty bread and parsley leaves.

ROUGET À L'ESCABÈCHE ET CÉLERI RÉMOULADE
RED MULLET ESCABECHE WITH CELERIAC & APPLE REMOULADE

Escabeche is one of my favourite starters. I've used red mullet (or *barbounia,* as it's known at the fish markets) here, as its lovely, delicate flavour makes it a firm favourite in my kitchen. The fish needs to be really fresh as it is only lightly 'cooked' in the residual heat of the marinade. For something a little different, I've added apple to the classic celeriac remoulade. This has been a big hit at the restaurant.

SERVES 4

1 teaspoon fennel seeds
1 teaspoon coriander seeds
8 × 100 g red mullet fillets, skin-on, scaled and pin-boned
250 ml dry white wine
250 ml champagne vinegar
4 eschalots, thinly sliced
½ small carrot, cut into thin rounds on the diagonal
½ stick celery, thinly sliced
2 cloves garlic, crushed
pinch saffron threads
2 star anise
½ stick cinnamon
1 fresh long red chilli, seeded and thinly sliced
thyme sprigs (optional), to serve

CELERIAC & APPLE REMOULADE
2 tablespoons lemon juice
80 ml Mayonnaise (see page 202)
2 green apples, thinly sliced
1 small celeriac, thinly sliced
3 tablespoons coarsely chopped flat-leaf parsley
sea salt and freshly ground black pepper

1. Heat a small frying pan over medium heat and cook the fennel and coriander seeds for 3–4 minutes or until fragrant. Remove from the heat.

2. Place the red mullet in a deep ceramic dish just large enough to hold it snugly in a single layer.

3. Combine the white wine, vinegar, eschalot, carrot, celery, garlic, saffron, star anise, cinnamon, chilli, fennel and coriander seeds in a large saucepan and bring to the boil. Pour the hot vinegar mixture over the fish, then cover the dish with foil and leave to stand until cooled to room temperature. Refrigerate for 24 hours. Remove the escabeche from the refrigerator 30 minutes before serving to allow it to come to room temperature.

4. Just before serving, make the remoulade. Place the lemon juice and mayonnaise in a bowl and mix well to combine. Add the apple, celeriac and parsley and gently toss to combine. Season to taste with salt and pepper.

5. Divide the escabeche among four bowls, and garnish with thyme sprigs, if desired. Serve with the remoulade alongside.

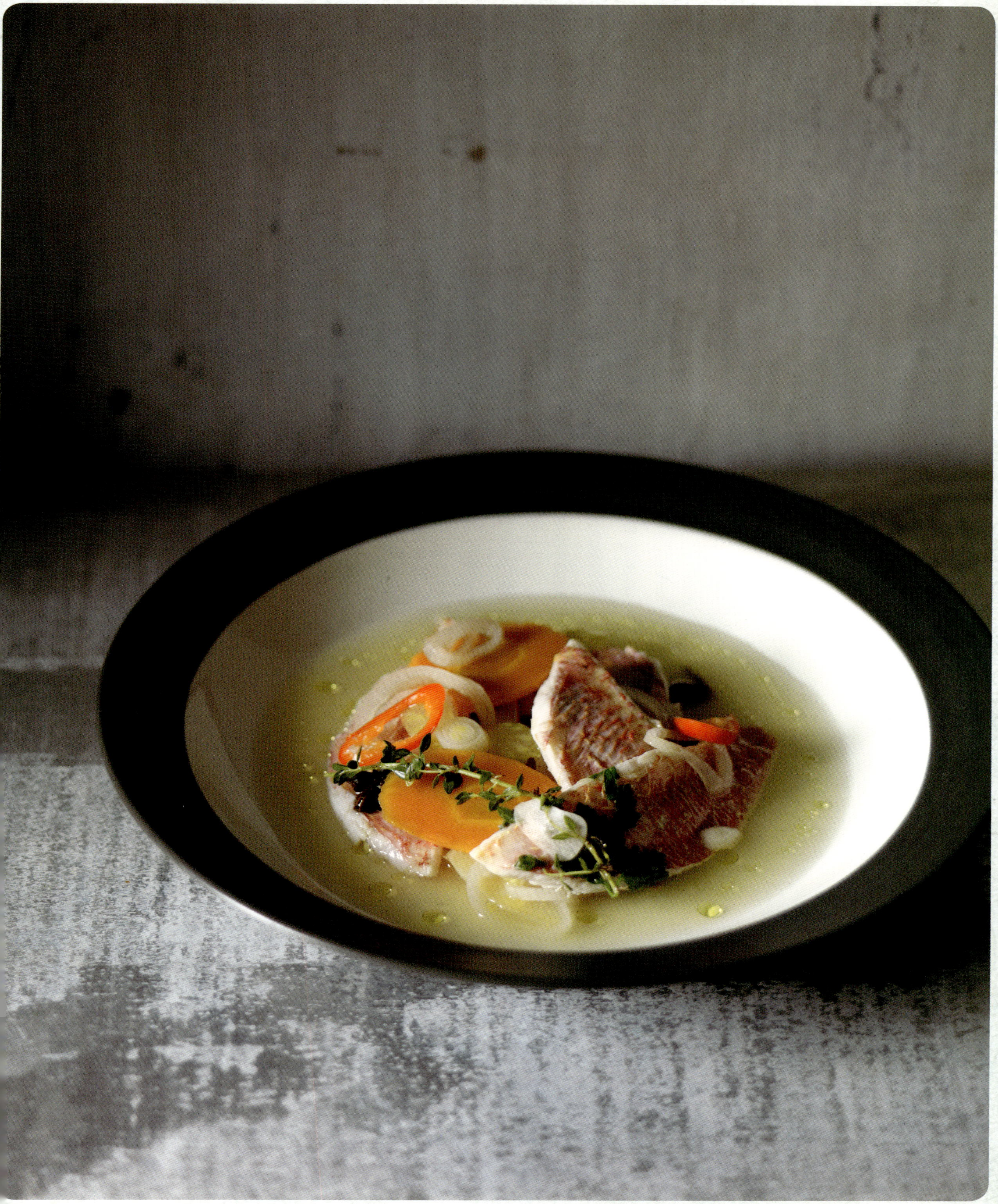

SUMMER

MENU

ENTREES

Ballottine d'aubergines sauce bois boudran
Eggplant rolls with bois boudran dressing 34

Carpaccio noix de Saint-Jacques
Carpaccio of scallop 27

Cannelloni de thon et de crabe et crème d'avocat
Tuna & crab 'cannelloni' with avocado cream 54

Mousse de foie de volaille
Chicken liver parfait 56

Consommé de tomates et salade de crevettes
Chilled tomato consomme with prawn salad 18

MAINS

Pavé de truite de mer et fleurs de courgette farcies au crabe, sauce soubise
Ocean trout with crab-stuffed zucchini flowers & onion soubise 90

Snapper et foie gras 'en papillote'
Papillote of snapper & foie gras 94

Cuisse de poulet confite
Chicken leg confit 105

Selle d'agneau rôtie et panisse
Lamb saddle with chickpea panisse 150

Côte de bœuf sauce béarnaise
Rib-eye of beef with bearnaise sauce 134

DESSERTS

Crème brûlée au chocolat
Chocolate creme brulee 164

Soufflés au nougat glacés
Chilled nougat souffles 183

Tarte aux noix et au caramel mou
Chewy walnut & caramel tart 162

Mousse de fromage blanc et compote de fruits rouge
Fromage blanc mousse with berry compote 174

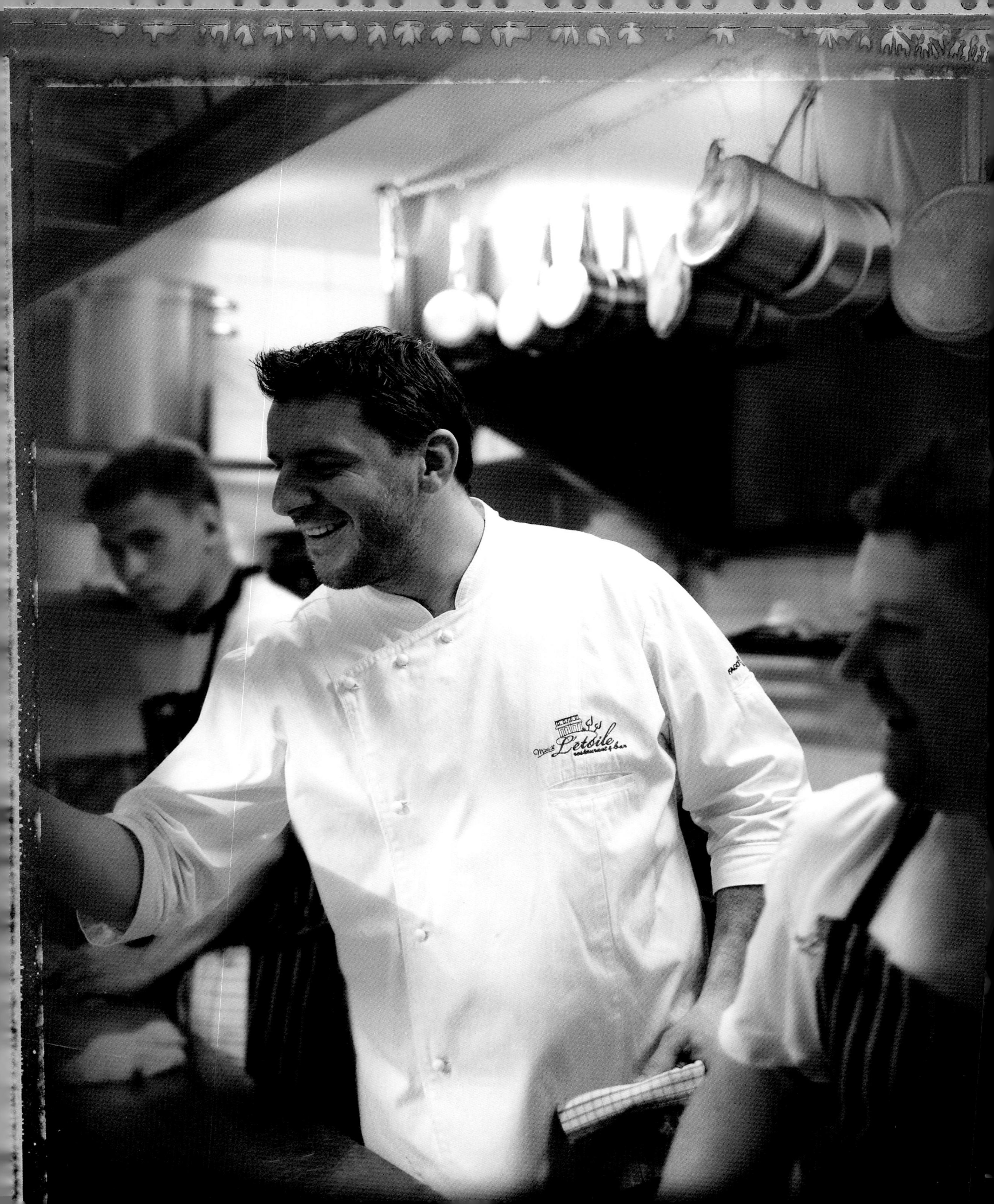

COQ AU VIN
ROAST DUCK WITH SPICED HONEY GLAZE
RIB-EYE OF BEEF WITH BEARNAISE SAUCE

MAINS

FILET DE SAINT-PIERRE, CHOU-FLEUR ET NOISETTE

RAZOR CLAMS MARINIERE

LAMB SADDLE WITH CHICKPEA PANISSE CONFIT
VEAL SWEETBREAD PIE CHICKEN LEG
RIB-EYE OF BEEF WITH BONE MARROW & BORDELAISE SAUCE

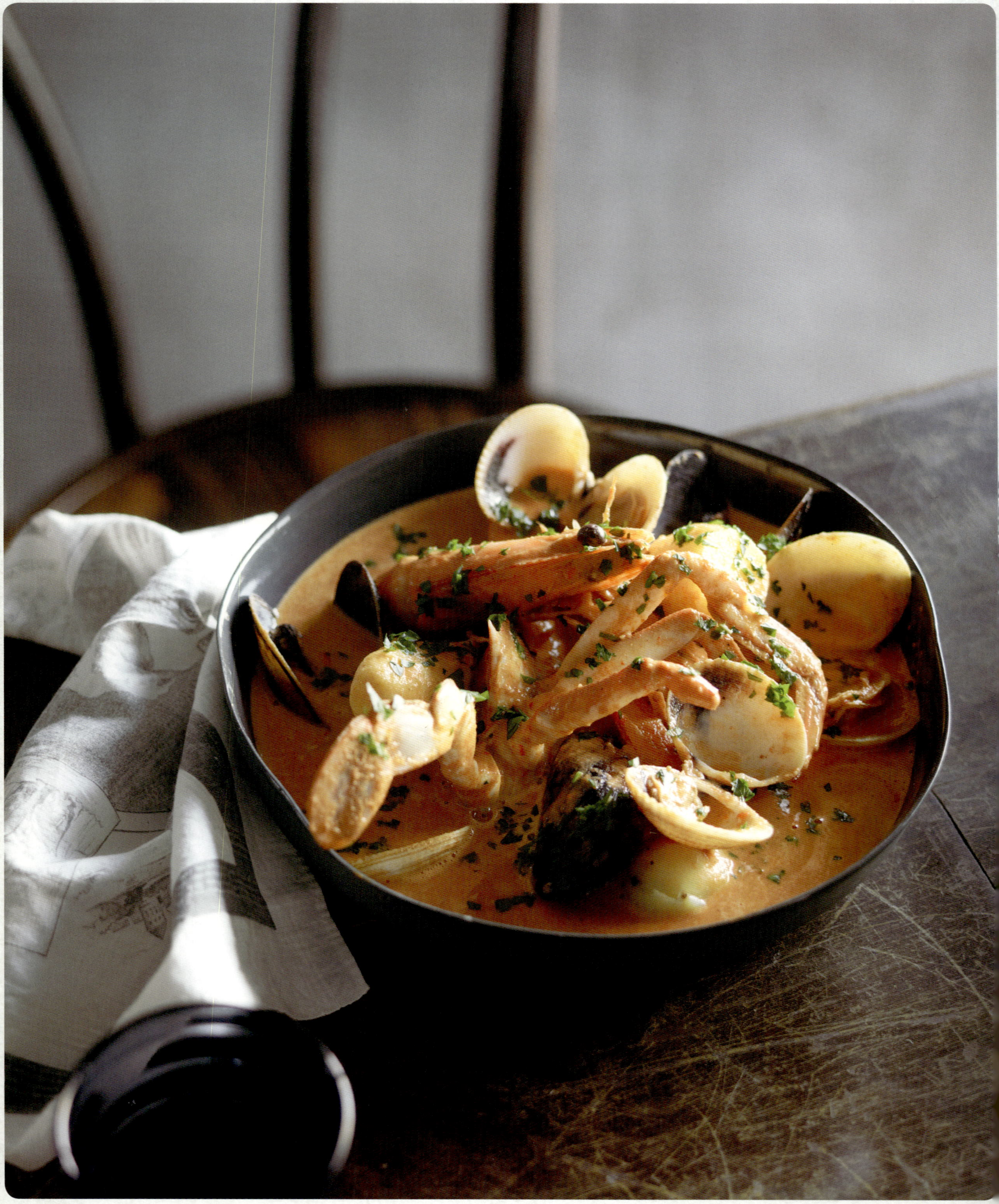

BOURRIDE
SEAFOOD STEW

According to local legend, this traditional Provencal fish stew was so special that the Greek gods would come down to Marseilles to eat it when they were bored with Olympus. This classic winter's dish is always a big hit when it arrives at the table.

SERVES 8

1 teaspoon saffron threads
boiling water
100 ml olive oil
1 leek, white part only, well washed and sliced
1 large onion, sliced
½ head garlic (cut in half widthways)
1 bulb fennel, trimmed and sliced
2½ tablespoons tomato paste
1 teaspoon cumin seeds
3 star anise
3 sprigs thyme
1 bay leaf
1 teaspoon black peppercorns
zest of ½ orange, cut into wide strips, pith removed
3 kg white fish bones (such as rock cod, latchet, snapper, flathead or whiting), cut into small pieces
700 ml dry white wine
1 × 400 g tin chopped tomato
1 litre water
12 kipfler potatoes, scrubbed
pinch cayenne pepper
sea salt and freshly ground black pepper
2 raw blue swimmer crabs, cleaned and cut into small pieces
1 kg black mussels, scrubbed and bearded
500 g clams, soaked in cold water for 20 minutes
500 g white fish fillets, skin removed, pin-boned and cut into 2.5 cm pieces
8 raw king prawns
250 ml Rouille (see page 202)
finely chopped flat-leaf parsley, to serve

1. Place the saffron in a small bowl, cover with boiling water and set aside.

2. Heat the olive oil in a large heavy-based saucepan or stockpot over medium heat. Add the leek, onion, garlic and fennel and cook over medium heat, stirring, for 6–7 minutes or until softened. Add the tomato paste, cumin seeds, star anise, thyme, bay leaf, peppercorns and orange zest and cook, stirring, for 1–2 minutes. Add the fish bones and cook for another 8–10 minutes.

3. Add the wine, then bring to the boil and simmer for 5–6 minutes or until reduced by half. Add the tomato and water and return to the boil, then simmer for at least 1 hour, skimming the surface of the stock as needed to remove any scum.

4. Meanwhile, place the potatoes in a large saucepan of lightly salted water, bring to the boil, then reduce the heat to medium and simmer for 20 minutes or until the potatoes are tender but still firm and not falling apart. Drain, then when cool enough to handle, peel and cut into bite-sized pieces. Set aside.

5. Strain the fish stock, discarding the fish bones. Leave to cool slightly. Transfer the stock to a food processor or blender and process to form a smooth soup. Push the soup through a fine-mesh sieve into a clean saucepan, pressing to extract as much liquid as possible.

6. Add the saffron mixture and cayenne to the soup and season to taste with salt and pepper. (Be generous with the salt – if it is under-salted it won't have the rich flavour of a true bourride.) Bring to the boil over high heat. Reduce the heat to medium, then add the crab, mussels, clams, fish and prawns, and cook for 5–8 minutes or until the fish and seafood are just cooked.

7. Divide the seafood and potato among wide shallow bowls. Whisk half of the rouille into the hot soup, then ladle the soup into the bowls and scatter with parsley. Serve with the remaining rouille to the side.

FILET DE 'KINGFISH', PURÉE DE PANAIS, PETITS OIGNONS AU VINAIGRE ET SPECK
KINGFISH WITH PARSNIP PUREE, PICKLED ONIONS & SPECK

I absolutely love the flavour and texture of kingfish, especially when it's cooked so its skin is really crisp. The saltiness of the speck, sharpness of the pickled onions and subtle sweetness of the kingfish works really well. A new recipe that is well on its way to becoming a favourite at the restaurant, where I like to serve the fish on a bed of wilted spinach or greens for added texture and flavour.

SERVES 4

60 ml olive oil
1 × 250 g piece speck (see page 209) or bacon, cut into 1 cm dice
125 g store-bought baby pickled onions in a jar, drained
250 ml Brown Chicken Stock (see page 204)
4 cloves garlic, crushed
1 tablespoon finely chopped thyme
freshly ground black pepper
3 tablespoons flat-leaf parsley, finely chopped
sea salt
4 × 180 g kingfish fillets, skin-on
50 g unsalted butter, chopped
baby chervil leaves (optional), to serve

PARSNIP PUREE

2 parsnips, peeled and coarsely chopped
100 ml pouring cream
20 g unsalted butter
sea salt and freshly ground black pepper

1. To make the parsnip puree, place the parsnip in a saucepan, cover with cold water, then bring to the boil over high heat. Reduce the heat to medium and cook for 20–25 minutes or until tender. Drain well, then return to the pan and shake over low heat to allow any excess moisture to evaporate. Transfer the parsnip to a food processor, then add the cream and butter and blend until smooth. Return to a clean saucepan, season to taste with salt and pepper and keep warm over low heat.

2. Heat 1 tablespoon of the olive oil in a frying pan over medium heat, add the speck and onions and cook for 5–6 minutes or until golden. Add the stock and simmer for 6–8 minutes or until it has reduced by half and the onions are glossy. Add the garlic, thyme and pepper to taste and cook for 2 minutes or until fragrant. Stir in the parsley. Season to taste with salt and set aside, keeping warm.

3. Heat the remaining olive oil in a heavy-based frying pan over medium heat. Season the fish with salt and pepper, then cook, skin-side down, for 4–5 minutes or until golden. Turn the fish over and cook for another 5 minutes or until just cooked through. Add the butter to the pan and allow to melt, then spoon it over the fish.

4. Serve the fish fillets with the pureed parsnip, and pickled onion and speck mixture, topped with chervil leaves, if desired.

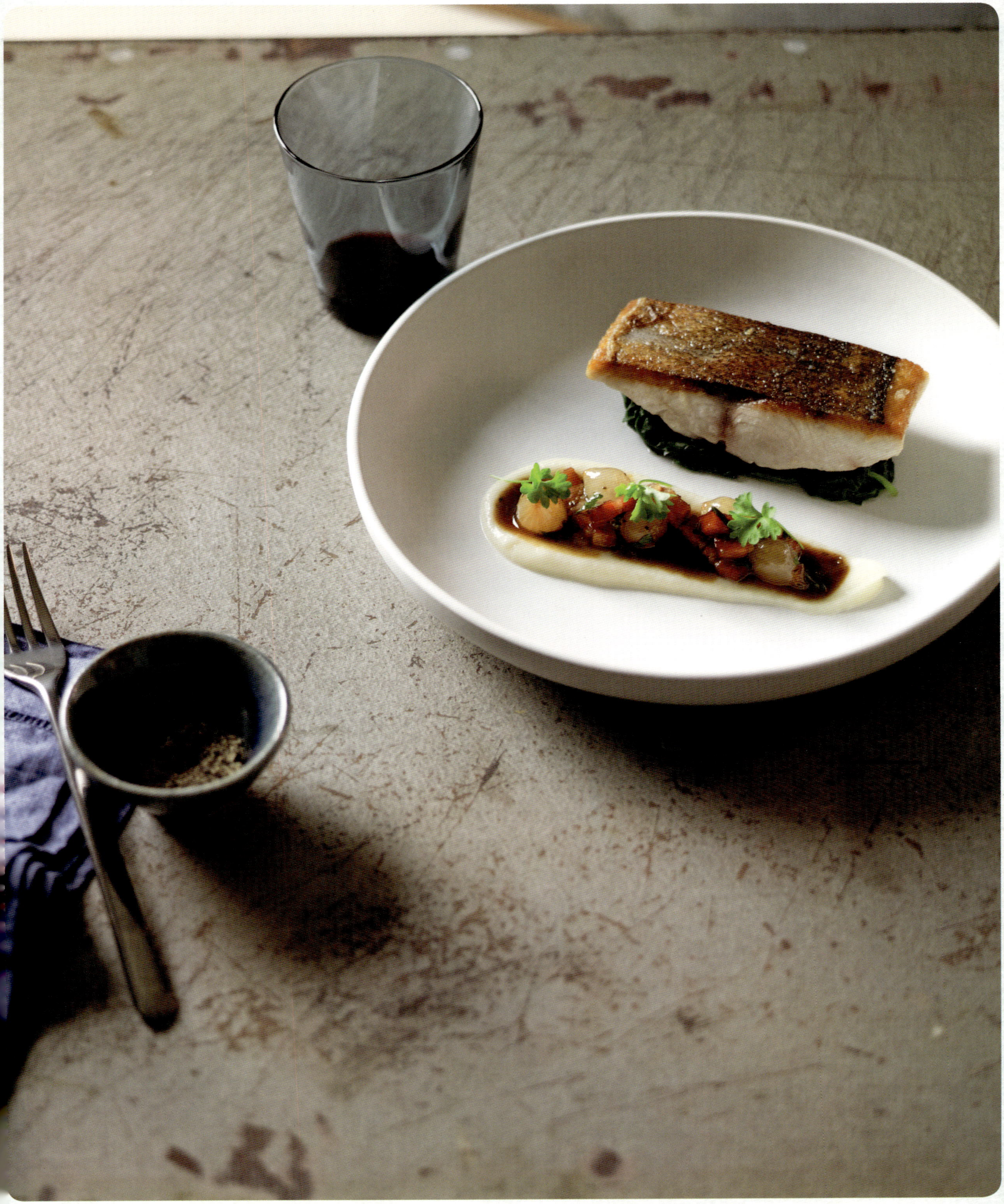

THON FAÇON ROSSINI
TUNA ROSSINI

This is inspired by the timeless dish, Tournedos Rossini, created by the great French chef Escoffier for the famous Italian composer Rossini – my twist is to use tuna instead of beef, which works very well. It's a handy dish to have in your repertoire for special occasions, as it is not difficult, and showcases the superstar ingredients of French cuisine – foie gras and truffles – perfectly.

SERVES 4

60 g unsalted butter, chopped
1 tablespoon olive oil
4 slices white bread, crusts removed, cut into rectangles a little smaller than the tuna steaks
4 × 200 g tuna loin fillet steaks
4 × 50 g slices foie gras (optional)
2 tablespoons port
1 tablespoon brandy
1 tablespoon Madeira
200 ml Brown Veal Stock (see page 205)
2 black truffles (optional), thinly sliced
sea salt and freshly ground black pepper

1. Preheat the oven to 160°C.

2. Heat 20 g of the butter and a little of the olive oil in a large frying pan over medium heat. Add the bread and fry for 3–4 minutes on each side or until golden. Drain on paper towel, then place on a baking tray.

3. Heat another 20 g of the butter and the remaining olive oil in a large heavy-based frying pan over high heat. When the butter starts to foam, add the tuna and cook for 1 minute on each side; the tuna should be rare. Place one piece of tuna on top of each bread slice on the baking tray and top with a slice of foie gras (if using).

4. Add the port, brandy and Madeira to the pan and bring to the boil, scraping to remove any cooked-on bits from the base of the pan. Simmer over high heat for 2 minutes or until reduced by half. Add the stock and sliced truffles (if using) to the pan, then return to the boil and simmer for 5 minutes or until reduced to a sauce consistency. Whisk in the remaining butter to make the sauce glossy, then season to taste with salt and pepper.

5. Transfer the baking tray with the tuna, bread and foie gras to the oven for 1–2 minutes or until warmed through. Spoon some sauce onto each plate, then top with the bread, tuna and foie gras. Serve immediately.

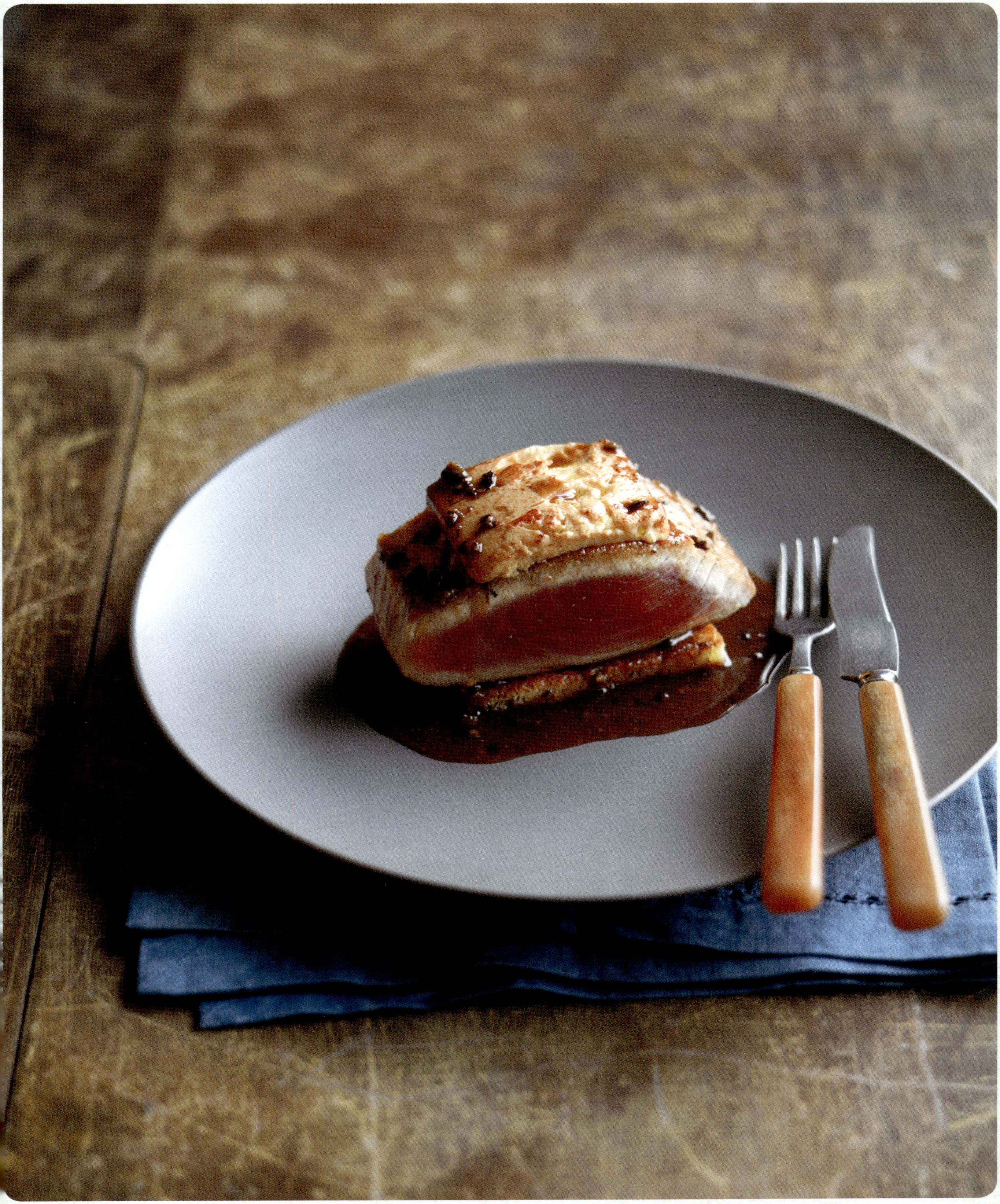

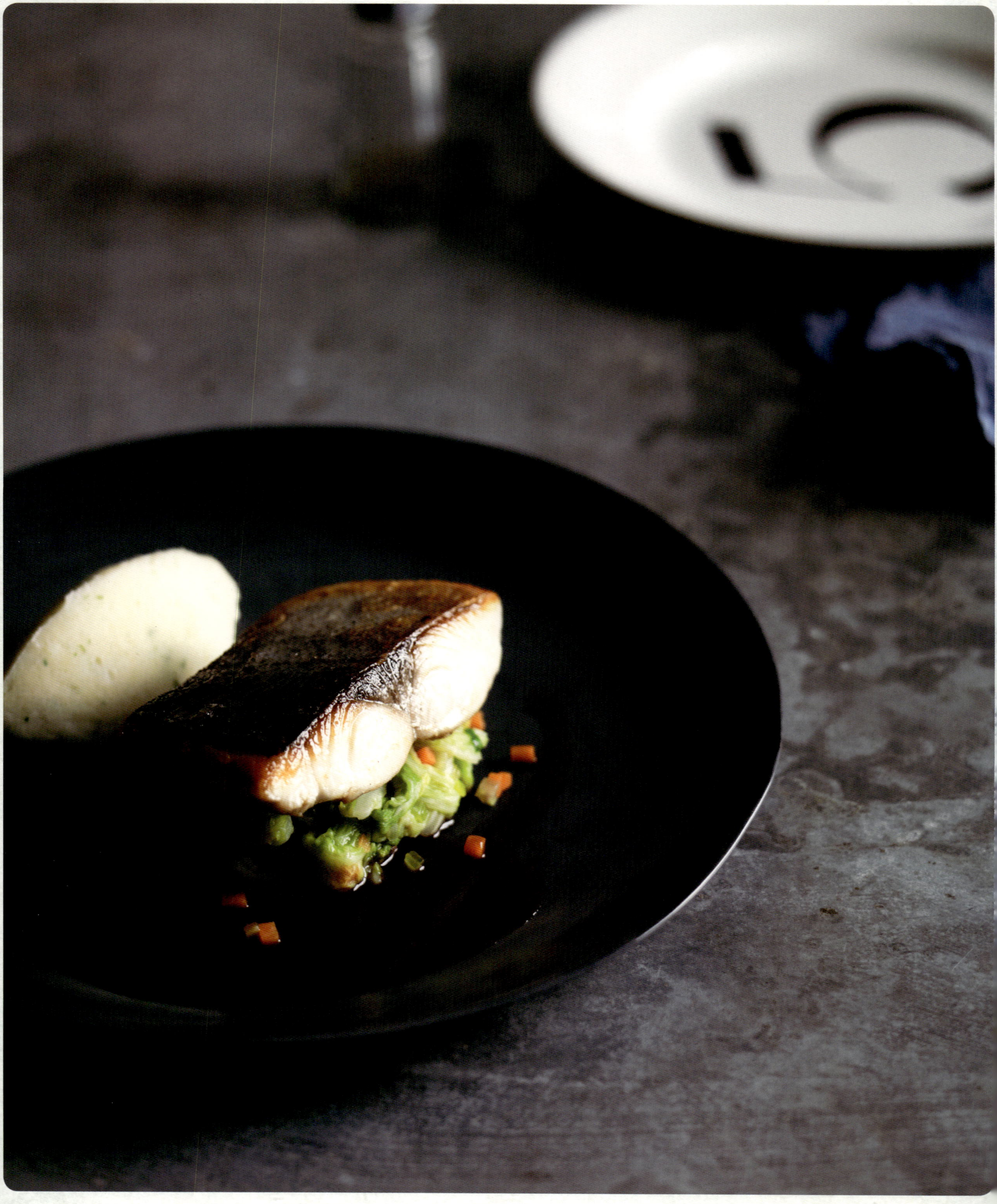

FILET DE 'KINGFISH' ET BRANDADE
KINGFISH WITH BRANDADE

I love how this fabulous wintry dish combines traditional French flavours in a new way. The Provencal staple of brandade is made from salt cod whipped with potatoes and milk, while braised cabbage is a typical vegetable accompaniment found on dinner tables all over France during the winter months. I've matched them with perfectly cooked kingfish fillets to create a dish worthy of any dinner-party table.

SERVES 4

- 1 small Savoy cabbage, cut into quarters, outer leaves discarded, inner leaves separated
- 80 ml olive oil
- 1 small carrot, finely chopped
- 1 stick celery, finely chopped
- 4 eschalots, finely chopped
- 2 cloves garlic, crushed
- 1 tablespoon thyme leaves
- 20 g unsalted butter
- sea salt and freshly ground black pepper
- 4 × 180 g kingfish fillets, skin-on
- extra virgin olive oil (optional), for drizzling

BRANDADE

- 250 g dried salt cod fillets, soaked in cold water for 24 hours (changing the water six times over this period), drained
- 1 sprig thyme
- 1 small bay leaf
- 500 ml milk
- 200 g brushed potatoes, halved
- 2 large cloves garlic, peeled
- 125 ml pouring cream
- 50 ml olive oil, plus extra for drizzling
- sea salt and freshly ground black pepper
- pinch cayenne pepper, or to taste
- lemon juice, to taste

1. To make the brandade, cut the salt cod into 5 cm pieces. Place the salt cod, thyme, bay leaf and half the milk in a saucepan. Bring to the boil over medium heat, then reduce the heat to low and simmer for 10 minutes. Drain the salt cod and discard the milk and herbs. When the salt cod is cool enough to handle, remove and discard the skin and bones and set the flesh aside.

2. Meanwhile, place the potato in a saucepan with the remaining milk, whole garlic cloves and cream. Bring to the boil over medium heat, then reduce the heat to low and simmer for 20 minutes or until the potato is tender. Drain in a colander placed over a bowl and reserve the milk.

3. Using an electric mixer fitted with a paddle attachment, combine the potato, garlic and salt cod. With the motor running, gradually add the olive oil, then add all but 60 ml of the reserved milk and beat until smooth. Adjust the consistency with the remaining milk, if desired. Season to taste with salt, pepper, cayenne and lemon juice. Set aside.

4. Plunge the cabbage leaves into a saucepan of lightly salted boiling water and cook for 1–2 minutes or until soft. Drain on paper towel. Heat 30 ml of the olive oil in a saucepan over medium heat. Add the carrot, celery, eschalot, garlic and thyme and cook for 3–4 minutes or until softened but not coloured. Add the cabbage and butter, then stir to mix and season to taste with salt and pepper. Set aside and keep warm.

5. Preheat the oven to 180°C.

6. Heat the remaining olive oil in a heavy-based ovenproof frying pan over medium heat. Season the kingfish with salt and pepper, then cook, skin-side down, for 4–5 minutes or until golden. Turn the kingfish over, then transfer the pan to the oven and roast for 5 minutes or until just cooked through. Remove from the pan and place on serving plates. Drizzle with extra virgin olive oil, if desired.

7. Serve the kingfish with the braised cabbage and brandade.

FILET DE SAINT-PIERRE, CHOU-FLEUR ET NOISETTE
PAN-FRIED JOHN DORY WITH CAULIFLOWER & HAZELNUTS

This is one of my favourite recipes. I've been building on this dish over many years, experimenting with different combinations of flavours and textures. I love the silkiness of the cauliflower puree, especially when matched with the crunch of the hazelnuts and delicate flavour of the fish. The buttery, star-anise-infused sauce finishes the dish off perfectly.

SERVES 4

50 g hazelnuts
125 ml Fish Stock (see page 205)
1 star anise
150 g unsalted butter, chopped
200 g cauliflower, cut into small florets
1 tablespoon finely chopped chives
4 × 180 g John Dory fillets, skin-on, pin-boned
snipped chives (optional), to serve

CAULIFLOWER PUREE

500 g cauliflower florets
200 ml milk
50 g unsalted butter, chopped
sea salt and freshly ground black pepper

DILL OIL

2 tablespoons finely chopped dill
50 ml extra virgin olive oil

1. Preheat the oven to 180°C. Roast the hazelnuts on a baking tray for 5–6 minutes or until golden, then rub with a clean tea towel to remove the skins. Coarsely chop and set aside.

2. To make the cauliflower puree, place the cauliflower and milk in a large saucepan and bring to the boil. Simmer over medium heat for 8–10 minutes or until the cauliflower is tender, then drain in a colander, discarding the milk. Place the cauliflower, butter and salt and pepper to taste in a food processor and process until a smooth puree forms. Transfer to a clean saucepan and keep warm.

3. To make the dill oil, mix the dill and oil in a small bowl. Cover with plastic film and set aside.

4. Place the fish stock and star anise in a heavy-based saucepan and bring to the boil over medium heat. Gradually whisk in 50 g of the butter until the sauce is thick and glossy. Remove and discard the star anise. Keep warm over low heat.

5. Melt another 50 g of the butter in a large heavy-based frying pan over medium heat. Add the cauliflower florets and cook for 5–6 minutes or until golden and tender. Add the hazelnuts and chives and stir to combine. Transfer to a bowl and keep warm.

6. Melt the remaining butter in the frying pan and cook the fish, skin-side down, for 5–6 minutes or until golden. Carefully turn and cook for another 3–4 minutes or until just cooked through.

7. To serve, place a large spoonful of the cauliflower puree on one side of each plate. Top the puree with the cauliflower and hazelnut mixture and place a fish fillet alongside. Spoon a little of the warm sauce over the fish, then drizzle with the dill oil and top with chives, if desired.

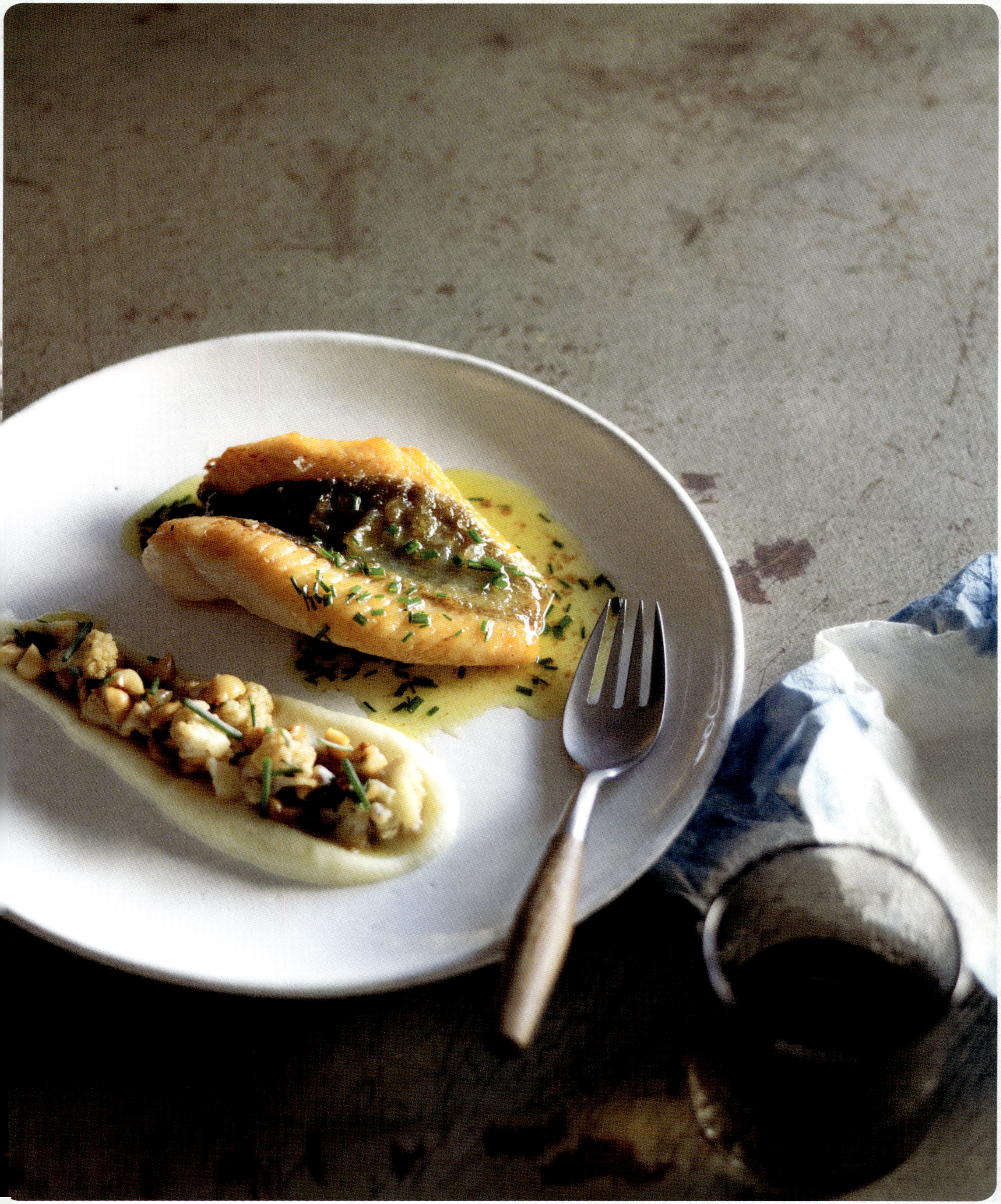

PAVÉ DE TRUITE DE MER ET FLEURS DE COURGETTE FARCIES AU CRABE, SAUCE SOUBISE
OCEAN TROUT WITH CRAB-STUFFED ZUCCHINI FLOWERS & ONION SOUBISE

Here I've paired the classic onion sauce, *soubise*, with the richness of ocean trout rather than the more traditional red meat. I love to cook with zucchini flowers, which, to me, are typically Australian. They taste superb with this light crab filling and crisp beer-batter coating.

SERVES 4

4 × 180 g ocean trout fillets (centre-cut), skin removed and pin-boned
sea salt and freshly ground black pepper
50 ml olive oil
20 g unsalted butter

ONION SOUBISE
80 ml olive oil
2 onions, thinly sliced
½ bay leaf
1 sprig thyme
sea salt
150 ml water
1 tablespoon champagne vinegar
freshly ground black pepper

CRAB-STUFFED ZUCCHINI FLOWERS
200 g self-raising flour
1 egg, lightly whisked
375 ml beer, chilled
125 g cooked crab meat, picked over to remove any shell
1 egg white
2 tablespoons pouring cream
1 tablespoon finely chopped chives
sea salt and freshly ground black pepper
8 zucchini flowers, pistils and stamens removed
vegetable oil, for deep-frying

1. To make the onion soubise, heat the olive oil in a heavy-based saucepan over low heat. Add the onion, bay leaf, thyme and a pinch of salt, then cook for 1 hour or until the onion is translucent; do not allow it to brown. Add the water and vinegar and bring to the boil, then reduce the heat to medium and simmer until the liquid has evaporated. Remove the bay leaf and thyme and transfer the onion mixture to a food processor, then process to form a smooth puree. Press through a fine-mesh sieve into a small saucepan, then season to taste with salt and pepper and keep warm.

2. To make the crab-stuffed zucchini flowers, place the flour, egg and beer in a bowl and stir until well combined, then cover and refrigerate until needed. Place the crab, egg white and cream in a food processor and process until smooth. Add the chives and salt and pepper to taste, then stir until well combined. Transfer the crab mixture to a piping bag fitted with a plain nozzle, then pipe it into the zucchini flowers. Gently twist the tops of the flower petals to enclose the filling.

3. Heat enough oil for deep-frying in a heavy-based saucepan over medium heat until it registers 180°C on a sugar/deep-fry thermometer, then dip the zucchini flowers into the batter, shaking to remove any excess. Working in batches if necessary, deep-fry the zucchini flowers for 2–3 minutes or until golden and crisp, then drain on paper towel.

4. Meanwhile, remove the ocean trout from the fridge and allow it to come to room temperature. Season the skin with salt and pepper.

5. Heat the olive oil in a large heavy-based frying pan over medium heat. Cook the ocean trout, skin-side down, for 4 minutes or until the skin is golden and crisp; do not move the fish during this time or the skin may stick to the pan and tear. Reduce the heat to low, then turn the fish over and add the butter. Cook for another 2–3 minutes or until cooked but still pink in the middle, spooning the golden-brown butter over the skin. Remove the fish from the pan and leave to stand for 5 minutes.

6. Place a generous spoonful of the soubise in the middle of each plate, then top with an ocean trout fillet and add 2 zucchini flowers alongside. Season to taste with salt and pepper. Serve.

MOULES À LA BOURGUIGNONNE
MUSSELS BOURGUIGNON

I called this mussels bourguignon because, like beef bourguignon, it includes speck and red wine, however, it is not traditional at all. The idea came from a dish called *moules à la bretonne* – mussels cooked with cider – which is very popular where I grew up. Using red wine instead of cider gives the dish a richer flavour.

SERVES 4

100 g unsalted butter, chopped
1 × 250 g piece speck (see page 209) or bacon, diced
3 eschalots, finely chopped
1 small onion, finely chopped
1 clove garlic, finely chopped
1 tablespoon thyme leaves
1 bay leaf
2 kg black mussels, scrubbed and bearded
200 ml red wine
200 ml pouring cream
3 tablespoons coarsely chopped flat-leaf parsley
freshly ground black pepper
baguette, to serve

1. Melt the butter in a large saucepan with a tight-fitting lid over medium heat, then add the speck, eschalot, onion, garlic, thyme and bay leaf and cook for 4–5 minutes or until the vegetables are just softened.

2. Discard any broken or open mussels. Place the mussels in the pan and increase the heat to high, then stir well and add the wine. Cover and cook for 5–6 minutes or until the mussel shells open. Add the cream, then bring to the boil, stir in the parsley and season to taste with pepper. Serve immediately with baguette.

RAIE 'EN MATELOTE', CITRON CONFIT ET AMANDE VINAIGRETTE
MATELOTE OF SKATE WING WITH PRESERVED LEMON & ALMOND DRESSING

Matelot means 'sailor' or 'deckhand' in French, and this recipe is based on a traditional dish of eel stewed in red wine that was popular with sailors in Brittany. I have started with this concept and transformed it into an offering worthy of any dinner-party table. Skate is an unusual fish, related to the stingray. Skate wings have no bones, only a central cartilage that can be removed. I found small ones for the photograph, but larger ones will work too; cook them gently or they will be rubbery.

SERVES 6

6 × 180 g skate wings, skin removed
2 bunches green asparagus, trimmed

MATELOTE SAUCE

1 kg white fish bones (such as snapper, John Dory or whiting)
olive oil, for drizzling
1 small leek, white part only, well washed and finely chopped
1 onion, finely chopped
½ small bulb fennel, trimmed and finely chopped
5 cloves garlic, thinly sliced
3 sprigs thyme
1 bay leaf
1.5 litres red wine
200 ml veal demi-glace (available in jars from specialty food stores)
100 g unsalted butter, chopped
sea salt and freshly ground black pepper

PRESERVED LEMON & ALMOND DRESSING

1 preserved lemon quarter, flesh removed and rind thinly sliced
1 tablespoon red wine vinegar
50 ml vegetable oil
50 ml extra virgin olive oil
25 g slivered almonds, roasted (see page 209)
1 tablespoon thinly sliced flat-leaf parsley
sea salt and freshly ground black pepper

1. Preheat the oven to 200°C.

2. To make the matelote sauce, place the fish bones in a roasting pan, drizzle with olive oil and roast for 15 minutes or until golden brown. Meanwhile, heat a drizzle of olive oil in a large heavy-based saucepan over medium heat. Add the leek, onion and fennel and cook for 5–6 minutes or until softened but not coloured. Add the garlic, thyme and bay leaf and cook for a further 1–2 minutes or until golden brown. Add the roasted fish bones to the pan, then cover with the red wine and bring to the boil. Reduce the heat to low and simmer for 1 hour. Strain the stock through a fine-mesh sieve into a clean large heavy-based saucepan, discarding the solids, then add the demi-glace and bring to the boil. Reduce the heat to low and simmer the sauce for 20 minutes or until reduced by half. Whisk in the butter, a little at a time, then season to taste with salt and pepper and set aside.

3. To make the preserved lemon and almond dressing, place the preserved lemon and vinegar in a bowl, then whisk in the vegetable oil and olive oil and add the almonds and parsley. Season to taste and set aside.

4. Return the sauce to a simmer, then add the skate wings and poach for 8 minutes or until opaque and just cooked through.

5. Meanwhile, cook the asparagus in a saucepan of salted boiling water for 2–3 minutes or until tender. Drain.

6. To serve, divide the asparagus among six plates, then top with a skate wing and a little of the sauce. Spoon over the preserved lemon and almond dressing.

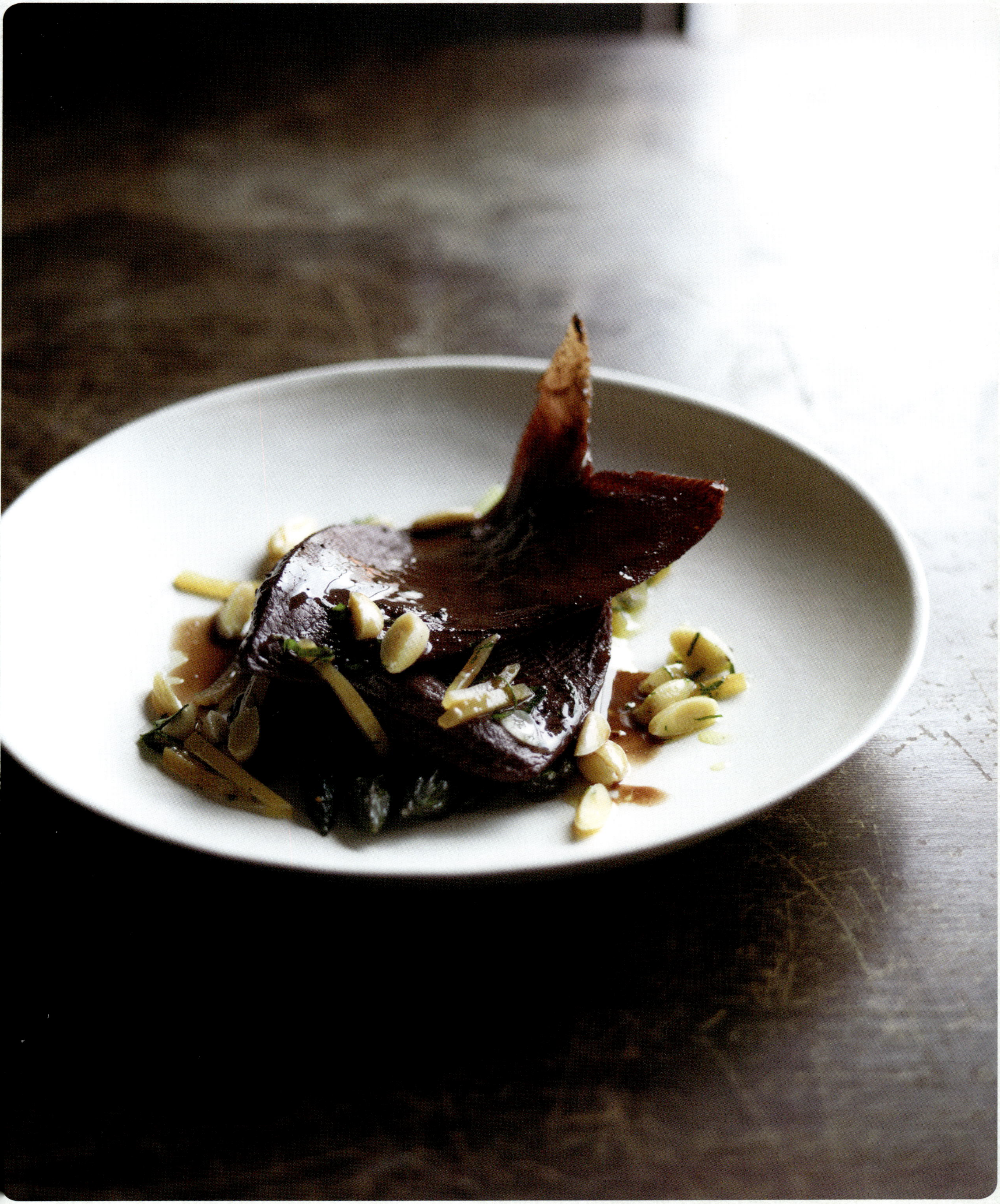

SNAPPER ET FOIE GRAS 'EN PAPILLOTE'
PAPILLOTE OF SNAPPER & FOIE GRAS

I read about the simple French technique of cooking fish in a bag many years ago and was instantly fascinated. It locks in flavour and moisture, and makes it easy to judge when the fish is cooked – just wait until the bag inflates! You could substitute any white fish for the snapper. While you could use a knob of butter instead of the foie gras, using foie gras transforms this from a weeknight dinner to a Saturday-night dinner party.

SERVES 4

60 ml olive oil
2 carrots, thinly sliced
2 leeks, white part only, thinly sliced
4 finger fennel, trimmed, or baby fennel, trimmed and cut into thin wedges
8 zucchini flowers, stamens and pistils removed
3 tablespoons French tarragon leaves (see page 208)
sea salt and freshly ground black pepper
4 × 160 g snapper fillets, skin-on
200 g foie gras (optional), cut into 4 slices
125 ml white wine

1. Preheat the oven to 200°C.

2. Heat 1 tablespoon of the olive oil in a large heavy-based saucepan over medium heat, then add the carrot, leek, fennel and zucchini flowers and cook for 5–6 minutes or until just softened. Stir in the tarragon and season to taste with salt and pepper, then set aside to cool.

3. Cut eight 30 cm squares of baking paper, then place four squares on one or more baking trays. Place one-quarter of the vegetables in the centre of each square of baking paper, then drizzle with the remaining olive oil. Top each one with a snapper fillet, skin-side down, then top with a slice of foie gras (if using) and season with salt and pepper. Pour one-quarter of the wine over each snapper fillet. Place a square of the remaining baking paper over each one, then fold and seal the ends to enclose.

4. Bake the snapper parcels for 15–20 minutes or until the bags have inflated and the fish is cooked through. Serve immediately.

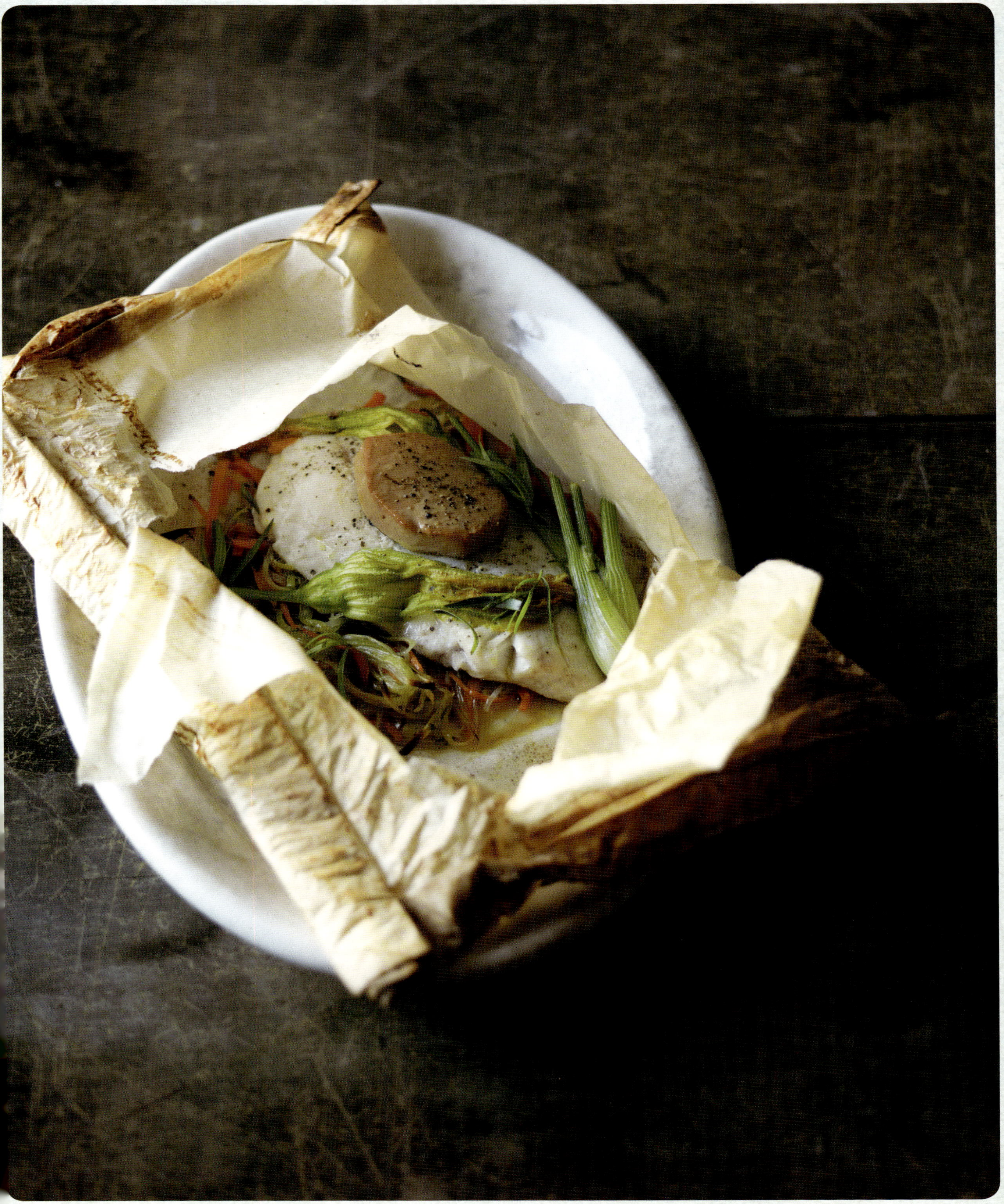

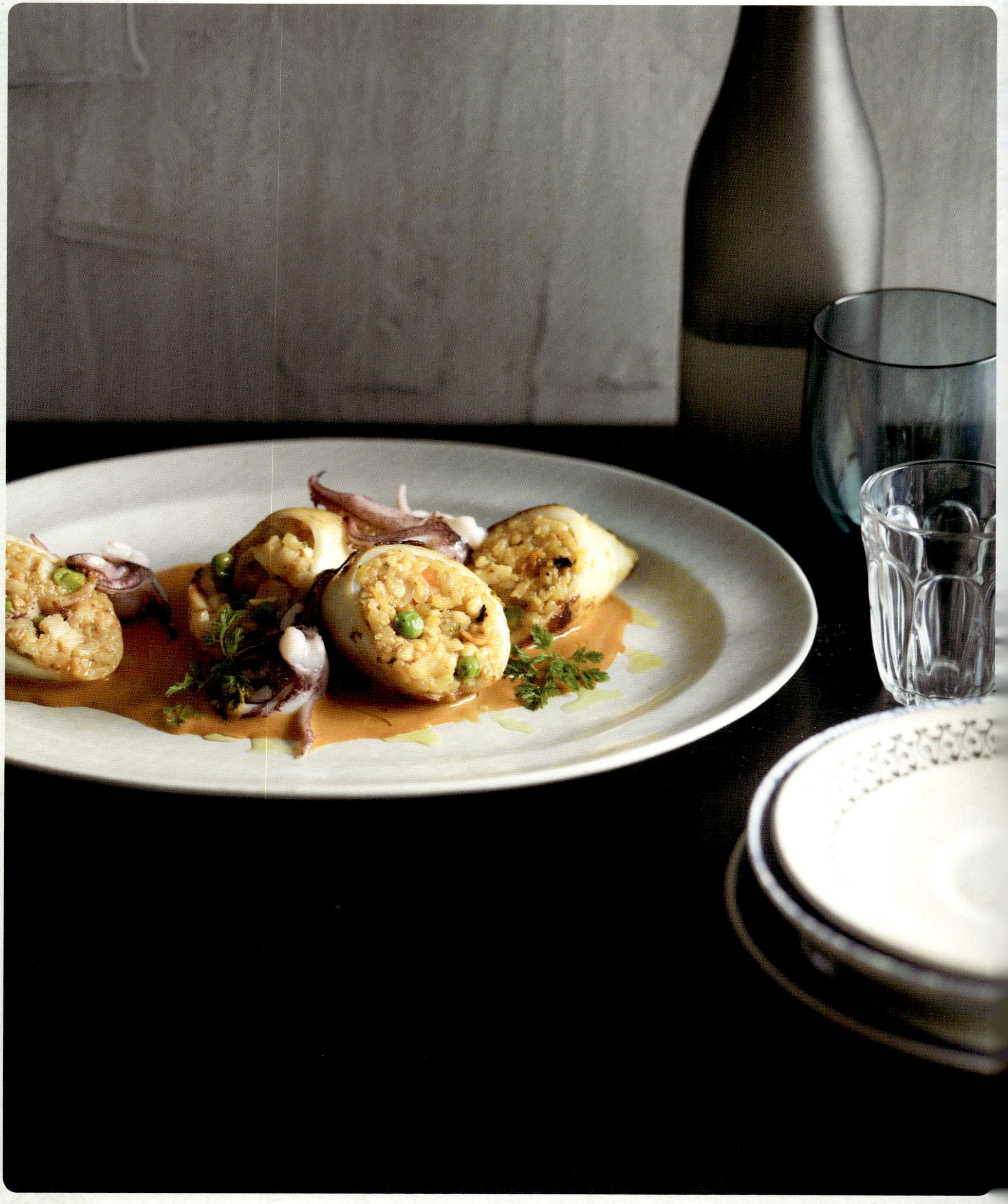

CALMAR FARCI À LA PAELLA
SQUID STUFFED WITH PAELLA

I have had a bit of fun with this – instead of adding squid to paella, I added paella to squid! A soffrito is a combination of aromatic ingredients cooked lightly in olive oil that forms the basis of many savoury recipes. Most paella recipes call for calasparra rice, a short-grain Spanish rice, but you can use arborio rice instead. If you can't find piquillo peppers, substitute roasted red capsicums.

SERVES 4

80 ml olive oil
200 g calasparra or arborio rice
500 g black mussels, scrubbed and bearded
4 raw king prawns, peeled and cleaned, heads and tails intact
500 ml White Chicken Stock (see page 204)
sea salt and freshly ground black pepper
100 g frozen peas, thawed
60 ml lemon juice
4 medium-sized squid, cleaned, tentacles removed and reserved
Bisque Sauce (optional, see page 203), small flat-leaf parsley leaves (optional) and extra virgin olive oil, to serve

SOFFRITO

80 ml olive oil
2 teaspoons sherry vinegar (see page 209)
2 ripe tomatoes
½ chorizo sausage, roughly chopped
3 eschalots, peeled
2 cloves garlic, peeled
2 piquillo peppers (small Spanish capsicums, available tinned from specialty food stores)
1 tablespoon finely chopped thyme
3 tablespoons finely chopped mint
3 tablespoons finely chopped flat-leaf parsley
3 tablespoons finely chopped coriander
1 tablespoon chopped chives
pinch saffron threads
1 teaspoon sweet paprika
1 teaspoon smoked paprika

1. To make the soffrito, place all the ingredients in a food processor and process for 2 minutes or until a smooth puree forms.

2. Heat 60 ml of the olive oil in a large paella pan or wide shallow saucepan. Add the rice and cook, stirring occasionally, for 5 minutes or until translucent. Stir in the soffrito and cook for 3 minutes or until warmed through. Add the mussels and prawns, then pour in the stock and season well with salt and pepper. Cook over medium heat, without stirring, for 25 minutes or until the stock has been absorbed and the rice is almost tender. Add the peas, then remove the pan from the heat. Cover the pan and leave to stand for 5 minutes. Add the lemon juice and stir to combine, then set aside to cool for 30 minutes.

3. When the paella has cooled, pick out the mussels and discard the shells. Remove and discard the heads and tails from the prawns and cut each prawn into four pieces. Return the seafood to the rice mixture.

4. Fill the squid tubes with the paella and seal each end with a toothpick. Heat the remaining olive oil in a heavy-based frying pan over medium heat and cook the squid tubes and tentacles for 2 minutes on each side or until golden brown and just cooked through.

5. Remove the toothpicks and slice the squid tubes into 4 pieces. Serve with the tentacles and bisque sauce (if using), scattered with parsley leaves, if desired, and drizzled with olive oil.

COUTEAUX DE MER MARINIÈRE
RAZOR CLAMS MARINIERE

The long, thin shell of razor clams makes them look like old-fashioned cut-throat razors, hence their name. Known in French as *couteau de mer*, or 'knife of the sea', they are prized for their unusual flavour. They can be hard to find in Australia. If you are lucky, your fishmonger might be able to order some from South Australia. They are also imported from Scotland. Alternatively, use mussels or regular clams instead. *Marinière* means 'mariner's style' — typically, a dish cooked with white wine and herbs.

SERVES 4

200 ml dry white wine
2 eschalots, coarsely chopped
2 sprigs thyme
1 bay leaf
2 cloves garlic, bruised
5 black peppercorns
2 kg razor clams, cleaned
200 ml pouring cream
large handful flat-leaf parsley leaves, coarsely chopped
freshly ground black pepper
crusty bread, to serve

1. Place the wine, eschalot, thyme, bay leaf, garlic and peppercorns in a large deep frying pan. Bring to the boil over high heat and simmer for 2 minutes. Working in batches, add the razor clams, then cover and cook, shaking the pan occasionally, for 5 minutes or just until the shells open. Remove the clams with tongs or a slotted spoon and transfer to a serving dish. Repeat with the remaining clams.

2. Strain the cooking liquor through a fine-mesh sieve into a small saucepan and bring to the boil. Add the cream, then bring to the boil again and simmer for 2 minutes. Stir through the parsley.

3. Check the seasoning (razor clams are quite salty, so you usually only need to season with a little pepper). Pour the sauce over the clams and serve immediately with crusty bread.

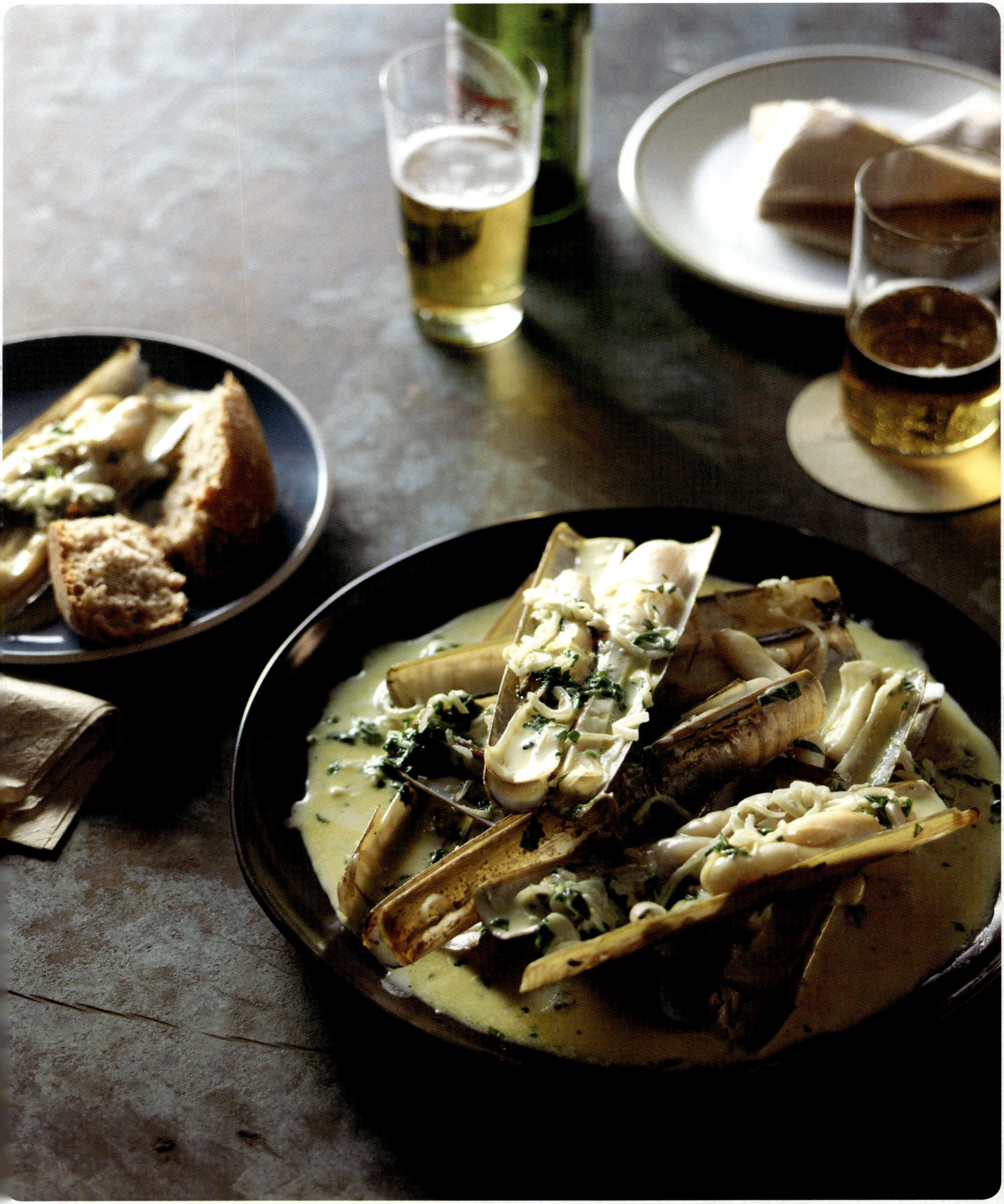

'BLACK FLATHEAD', SALADE TIÈDE DE HARICOTS BLANC VINAIGRETTE
BLACK FLATHEAD WITH WARM WHITE BEAN SALAD

Black flathead are a little hard to find in Australia, so if you ever catch one, don't throw it back! They have quite a different texture and flavour to other flathead, and are delicious. You could use kingfish or regular flathead fillets instead. It's great to have a few ways to dress up a simply cooked piece of beautiful fresh fish, and this white bean salad really does the trick. You'll need to soak the dried beans in water overnight.

SERVES 4

300 ml Brown Chicken Stock (see page 204)
30 g unsalted butter, chopped, plus 20 g extra
30 ml olive oil
4 × 180 g black flathead fillets, skin-on and pin-boned
sea salt and freshly ground black pepper

WHITE BEAN SALAD

200 g dried cannellini beans, soaked in cold water overnight
1 litre White Chicken Stock (see page 204)
½ onion, coarsely chopped
½ carrot, coarsely chopped
1 bouquet garni (see page 208)
2 handfuls baby spinach leaves
3 tablespoons coarsely chopped flat-leaf parsley
sea salt and freshly ground black pepper

FRENCH DRESSING

½ teaspoon French Dijon mustard (see page 208)
30 ml red wine vinegar
sea salt and freshly ground black pepper
100 ml olive oil

1. To make the dressing, place the mustard, vinegar and salt and pepper to taste in a bowl and whisk to combine well. Whisking continuously, gradually add the oil in a thin steady stream until emulsified. Set aside. (Makes about 130 ml.)

2. To make the white bean salad, place the beans, stock, onion, carrot and bouquet garni in a large heavy-based saucepan and bring to the boil. Reduce the heat to low and simmer for 1 hour or until the beans are just tender, stirring halfway through cooking. Drain the beans and discard the liquid and vegetables. Transfer the beans to a large saucepan with the spinach, parsley and dressing and mix over low heat until well combined and the spinach has wilted. Season to taste and set aside.

3. Place the stock in a small saucepan, then bring to the boil. Simmer over medium heat for 5–6 minutes or until reduced to a sauce consistency. Whisk in the butter, one piece at a time; this makes the sauce glossy. Keep warm.

4. Heat the olive oil in a large heavy-based frying pan over medium heat. Season the fish with salt and pepper, then cook, skin-side down, for 4–5 minutes or until golden. Turn the fish over and cook for another 3–4 minutes. Add the extra butter to the pan and cook for 2 minutes or until melted, spooning the melted butter over the fish; the fish should be just cooked through.

5. Place a large spoonful of the bean salad on each plate, then top with a fish fillet and a little of the melted butter. Pour the warm sauce around the beans. Serve.

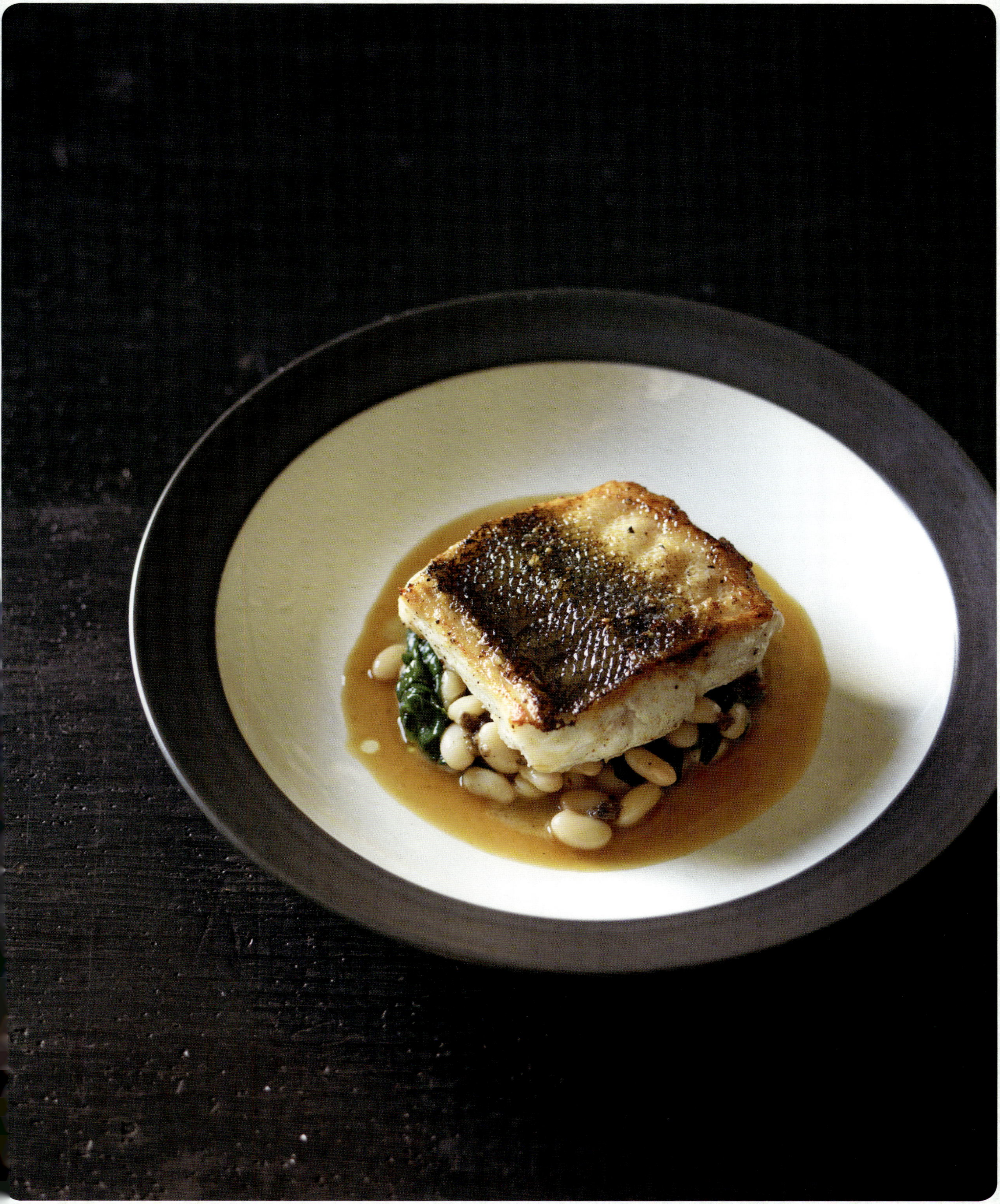

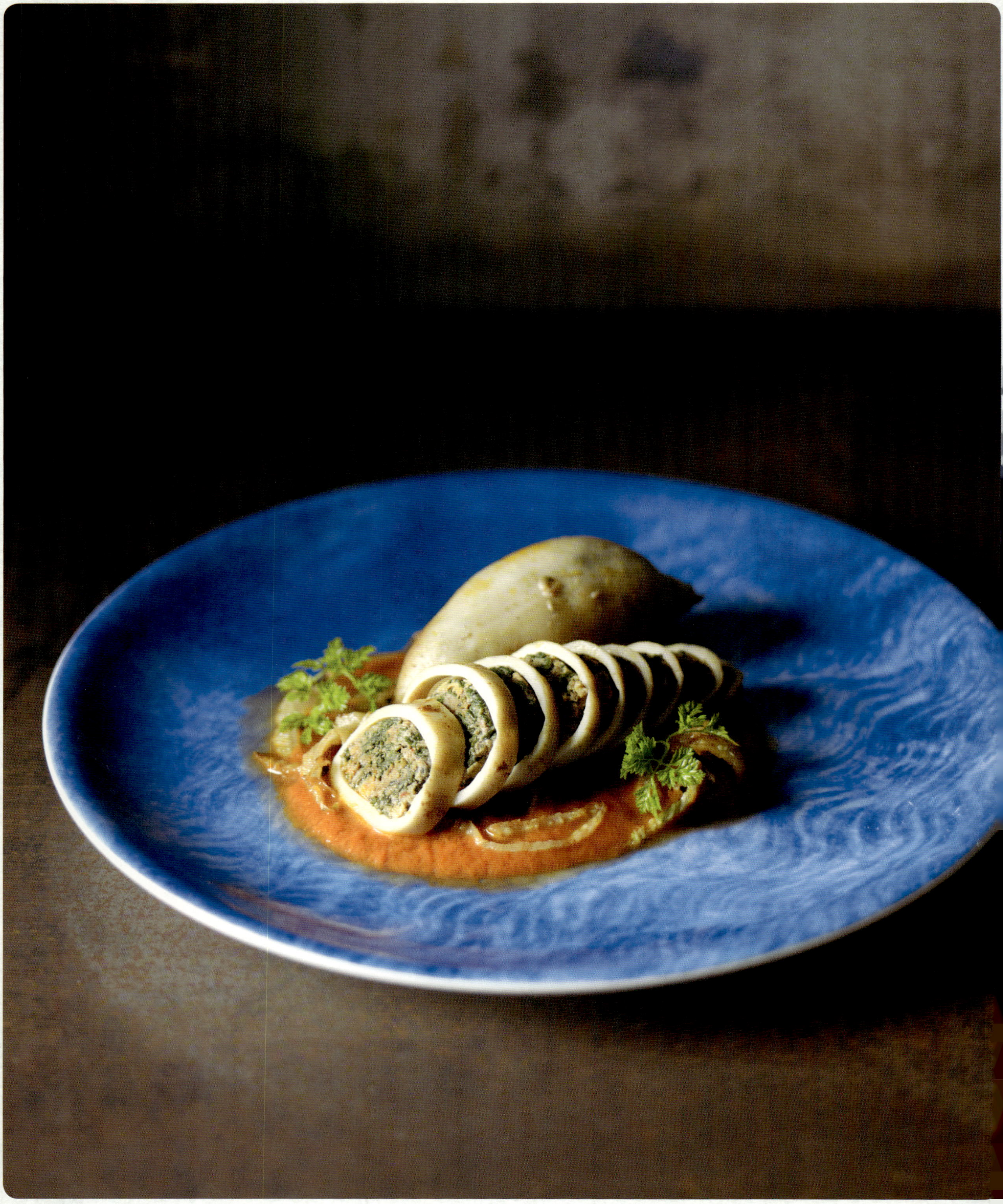

CALMAR FARCI AUX MOULES, MERGUEZ ET ÉPINARDS
SQUID STUFFED WITH MERGUEZ, MUSSELS & SPINACH

I love the combination of squid and sausage. Often squid is paired with chorizo in Spanish cooking, but here I've used North African-style spiced lamb or mutton sausages called merguez. If you can't get merguez, substitute with any spicy lamb sausage.

SERVES 4

250 ml white wine
2 eschalots, finely chopped
1 fresh bay leaf
2 cloves garlic, crushed
2 tablespoons thyme leaves
500 g black mussels, scrubbed and bearded
3 merguez sausages, skin removed
160 g baby spinach leaves, stalks removed
1 tablespoon olive oil
3 tablespoons finely chopped curly parsley
sea salt and freshly ground black pepper
4 medium-sized squid hoods, cleaned
1 quantity Bisque Sauce (see page 203)
small flat-leaf parsley or chervil sprigs, to serve

1. Place the white wine, half of the eschalot, the bay leaf, half of the garlic and half of the thyme leaves in a large heavy-based saucepan over high heat. Bring to the boil and boil for 30 seconds, then add the mussels. Cover and cook for 2–3 minutes or until the mussels open. Remove the mussels as they open and transfer to a bowl. Leave to cool, then remove the mussels from their shells and finely chop. Discard the shells.

2. Place the sausage meat in a bowl and mash with a fork to form a smooth paste. Set aside.

3. Bring a small saucepan of salted water to the boil. Add the spinach and cook for 30 seconds or until just wilted. Drain on a clean tea-towel to absorb any excess moisture. Coarsely chop and set aside.

4. Heat the olive oil in a saucepan over medium heat. Add the remaining eschalot, garlic and thyme and cook for 2–3 minutes or until softened. Transfer to the bowl with the sausage meat and add the mussels, spinach and parsley. Mix well and season to taste with salt and pepper.

5. Spoon one-quarter of the sausage mixture into each squid hood, packing it in until it almost reaches the top; take care not to overfill. Secure the ends with a toothpick and set aside.

6. Place the bisque sauce in a heavy-based saucepan and bring to the boil over high heat. Reduce the heat to low, then add the stuffed squid. Cover and cook for 2 hours or until the squid is tender. Season to taste with salt and pepper.

7. To serve, remove the toothpicks from the squid. Using a sharp knife, slice each squid into eight 1 cm thick slices. Spoon the bisque sauce onto the centre of four plates, then add the squid slices and garnish with parsley or chervil.

POCHOUSE DE SAINT-PIERRE
POCHOUSE OF JOHN DORY WITH MUSSELS

Meaning 'fisherman' in the old Burgundy dialect, *pochouse* is a traditional dish from this land-locked region, usually made with freshwater fish stewed in white wine. It makes a heart-warming dinner-party centrepiece served with crusty bread and a good Chardonnay on a cold winter's night.

SERVES 4

16 pencil leeks, trimmed
16 finger fennel or 8 baby fennel, trimmed and cut into thin wedges
4 × 160 g John Dory fillets, skin removed and flesh pin-boned
1 kg black mussels, scrubbed and bearded
2 preserved lemon quarters, flesh removed, rind rinsed and thinly sliced
50 g semi-dried tomatoes, thinly sliced

POCHOUSE

1 kg white fish bones (such as snapper, John Dory or whiting)
170 ml olive oil
1 small leek, white part only, well washed and diced
1 onion, coarsely chopped
½ small bulb fennel, trimmed and coarsely chopped
5 cloves garlic, peeled
3 sprigs thyme
1 bay leaf
700 ml dry white wine
sea salt and freshly ground black pepper

1. Preheat the oven to 200°C.

2. To prepare the pochouse, place the fish bones in a roasting pan and roast for 10–12 minutes or until golden brown. Heat 1 tablespoon of the olive oil in a large heavy-based saucepan over medium–high heat, then add the leek, onion, fennel, garlic, thyme and bay leaf and cook for 5–6 minutes or until the vegetables are just golden. Transfer the fish bones to the saucepan, then cover with the white wine and bring to the boil. Reduce the heat to low and simmer for 1 hour. Strain the stock through a fine-mesh sieve into a clean saucepan, discarding the solids, then bring to the boil. Simmer over medium heat for 25–30 minutes or until reduced by half. Using a stick blender, blitz in the remaining olive oil and season with salt and pepper.

3. Transfer the pochouse sauce to a large deep frying pan and bring to the simmer over medium heat. Add the leeks and fennel and cook for 4–5 minutes. Add the fish and mussels and continue to cook for 8–10 minutes or until the fish has cooked through and the mussels have opened.

4. Divide the fish, mussels and vegetables among shallow bowls, then spoon about 100 ml of the sauce into each one. Top with the preserved lemon and tomato. Serve immediately.

CUISSE DE POULET CONFITE
CHICKEN LEG CONFIT

'Confit' comes from the French word *confire*, meaning 'to preserve'. It is one of those fabulous French dishes that makes a big impression yet is pretty straightforward to make, provided you leave yourself a good half-day to cook it. You can buy duck fat from specialty food stores, and the great thing about it is you can reuse it – just drain off and discard the cooking juices, then store the fat in the fridge and use it when you roast potatoes. It is actually more traditional to confit duck legs, so if you want to try this, simply add a star anise and the finely grated zest of an orange to the food processor with the salt and other ingredients, then proceed with the recipe.

SERVES 4

200 g sea salt
1 clove garlic, crushed
2 cloves
5 black peppercorns
1 tablespoon thyme leaves, plus extra (optional), to serve
4 chicken marylands (leg and thigh joints)
1 fresh bay leaf
1 kg duck fat

1. Place the salt, garlic, cloves, peppercorns and thyme in a food processor and process until a coarse paste forms.

2. Place the chicken marylands, bay leaf and salt mixture in a deep baking dish and toss to coat well. Cover with plastic film and refrigerate for at least 3 hours.

3. Remove the chicken legs from the salt mixture, wiping away the excess with paper towel. Rinse well under cold running water, then pat dry with a clean tea towel.

4. Place the duck fat in a large enamelled cast-iron casserole and heat over very low heat until melted. Add the chicken marylands and cook for 2 hours or until the meat is very tender and starting to come away from the bone. (It is important to cook the chicken as slowly as possible – the temperature of the fat should not exceed 80°C on a sugar/deep-fry thermometer.)

5. Preheat the oven to 200°C.

6. Remove the chicken from the fat, then place, skin-side up, on a wire rack sitting over a deep baking dish. Roast the chicken for 10 minutes or until the skin is golden and crisp.

7. Scatter the chicken with thyme (if desired). Serve.

CANARD RÔTI AU MIEL ET AUX ÉPICES
ROAST DUCK WITH SPICED HONEY GLAZE

In my opinion, no one cooks crispy spiced duck as well as the Chinese, but here is my version and, I have to say, it is pretty special. The combination of the spices and honey is hard to beat, and the flavours really develop if you have time to marinate the duck in the fridge overnight. I based this on a recipe from a famous old Parisian Michelin-starred restaurant called Lucas Carton, which has since changed hands.

SERVES 4

3 teaspoons coriander seeds
3 teaspoons fennel seeds
3 teaspoons cumin seeds
1 teaspoon black peppercorns, cracked
200 ml white wine
80 g honey
1 × 1.8 kg duck
olive oil, for cooking
sea salt

GLAZED CARROTS & PARSNIP

12 baby (Dutch) carrots, stalks trimmed leaving 2 cm intact, peeled
3 parsnips, peeled and quartered lengthways
50 ml olive oil
1 tablespoon finely chopped thyme
30 g unsalted butter
30 g honey
sea salt and freshly ground black pepper

1. Place the coriander seeds, fennel seeds, cumin seeds and pepper in a small dry frying pan and toast over medium heat for 4–6 minutes or until fragrant. Set aside. In a large bowl, combine the white wine, honey and spices. Place the duck, breast-side down, in the marinade, then cover the bowl with plastic film and marinate in the fridge overnight.

2. The next day, take the duck out of the marinade and pat dry with paper towel. Transfer the marinade to a small saucepan and bring to the boil over high heat. Reduce the heat to medium and simmer for 10–12 minutes or until the sauce has thickened, then set aside and keep warm.

3. Preheat the oven to 180°C.

4. Heat a splash of olive oil in a flameproof roasting pan over medium heat. Season the duck with salt, then cook for 1–2 minutes on each side or until browned, taking care not to burn the skin – it may burn easily as it has been marinated in honey.

5. Cover the duck with foil, then transfer the pan to the oven and roast for 1 hour. Remove the foil from the duck and roast for a further 35–40 minutes or until golden and cooked through. Brush the duck with the reserved sauce and leave to rest for 15 minutes before serving.

6. Meanwhile, to make the glazed carrots and parsnip, place the carrots, parsnip, olive oil and thyme in a shallow roasting pan and toss to combine. Roast for 20–25 minutes or until tender. Add the butter and honey and toss well to combine, then season to taste with salt and pepper.

7. Serve the roast duck with the glazed carrots and parsnip alongside.

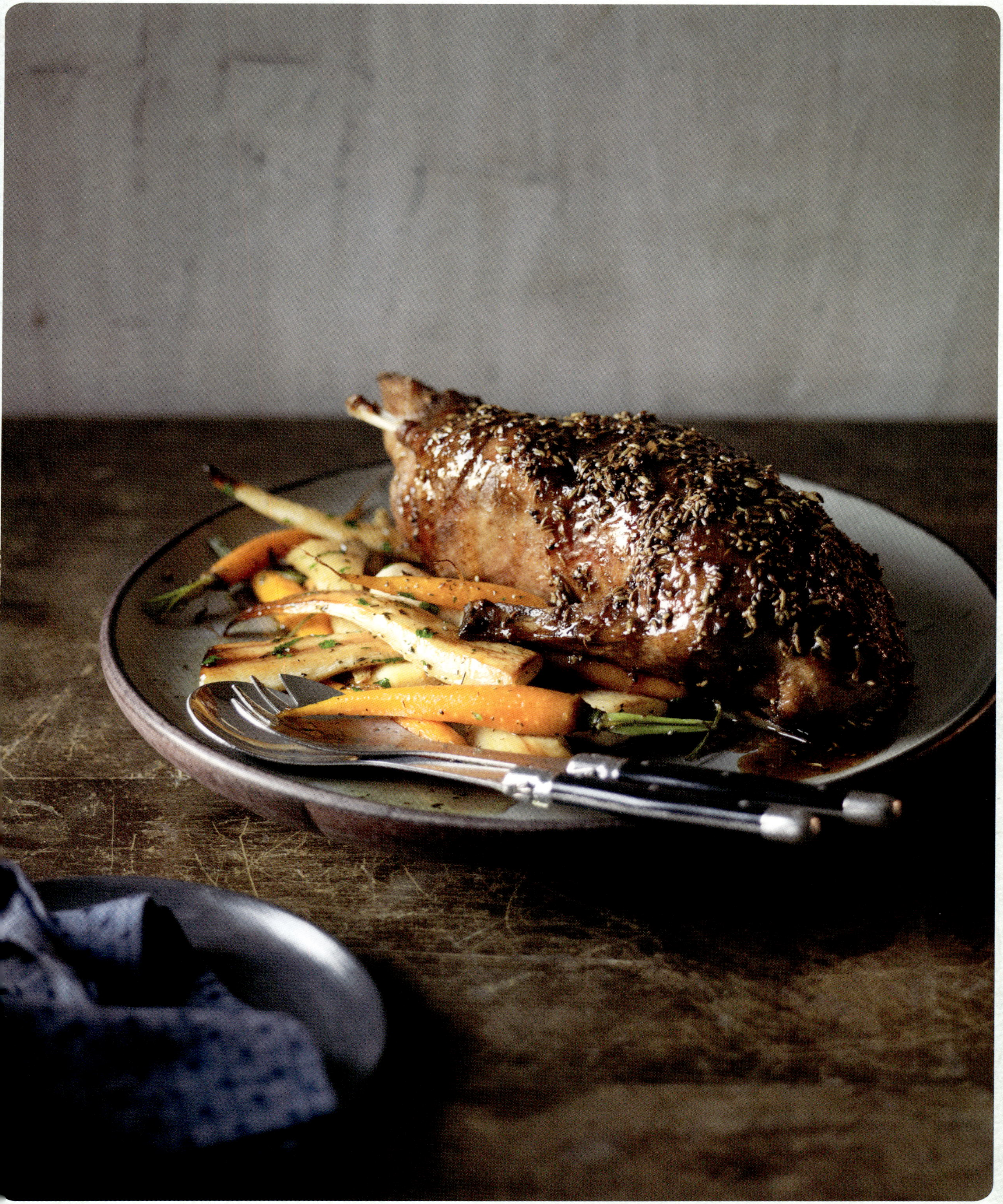

COQ AU VIN

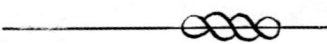

I first learnt how to make this timeless dish when I was an apprentice chef. The head chef, who liked a drink or three, used to drink half the wine himself, so always used half-water, half-wine in the recipe. The first time he let me make it myself, he was furious when I used three whole bottles of wine – but it tasted sublime. Ideally, you should start this one the day before you wish to serve it.

SERVES 6

1.5 litres red wine
1 carrot, sliced
1 onion, sliced
6 cloves garlic, 3 crushed and 3 finely chopped
12 black peppercorns
3 sprigs thyme
1 small fresh bay leaf
6 chicken marylands (leg and thigh joints, about 375 g each)
80 ml vegetable oil
125 ml brandy
60 g unsalted butter
200 g speck (see page 209) or bacon, cut into 3 × 1 cm strips (lardons, see page 208)
12 pearl onions or spring onions with bulbs, peeled
3 eschalots, thinly sliced
500 g small button mushrooms, trimmed
75 g plain flour
1 bouquet garni (see page 208)
coarsely chopped flat-leaf parsley and Potato Puree (see page 152), to serve

1. Place the wine, carrot, onion, crushed garlic, peppercorns, thyme sprigs and bay leaf in a large bowl. Add the chicken, then cover with plastic film and refrigerate for 2 hours or overnight, if time permits.

2. Drain the chicken, reserving the wine and discarding the vegetables and herbs. Pat the chicken dry with paper towel.

3. Heat half the oil in a large heavy-based frying pan over medium heat, then, working in batches, cook the chicken, turning once, for 6–7 minutes or until golden all over. Return all the chicken to the pan, add the brandy and carefully light it with a long match, then, when the flames die down, remove the pan from the heat and set aside.

4. Heat the butter and remaining oil in an enamelled cast-iron casserole over medium heat. Add the speck and pearl onions and cook, stirring, for 5 minutes or until the onions are light golden. Add the eschalot, finely chopped garlic and mushrooms and cook, stirring, over medium heat for 6–7 minutes or until light golden. Add the flour and stir to combine well, then cook, stirring, over medium heat for 2 minutes. Gradually add the reserved wine, stirring continuously to prevent lumps forming. Bring the mixture to a simmer, then add the bouquet garni and the browned chicken pieces and any pan juices. Cover the chicken and cook over low heat for 1¼ hours or until tender.

5. Scatter the chicken with parsley, then serve with potato puree.

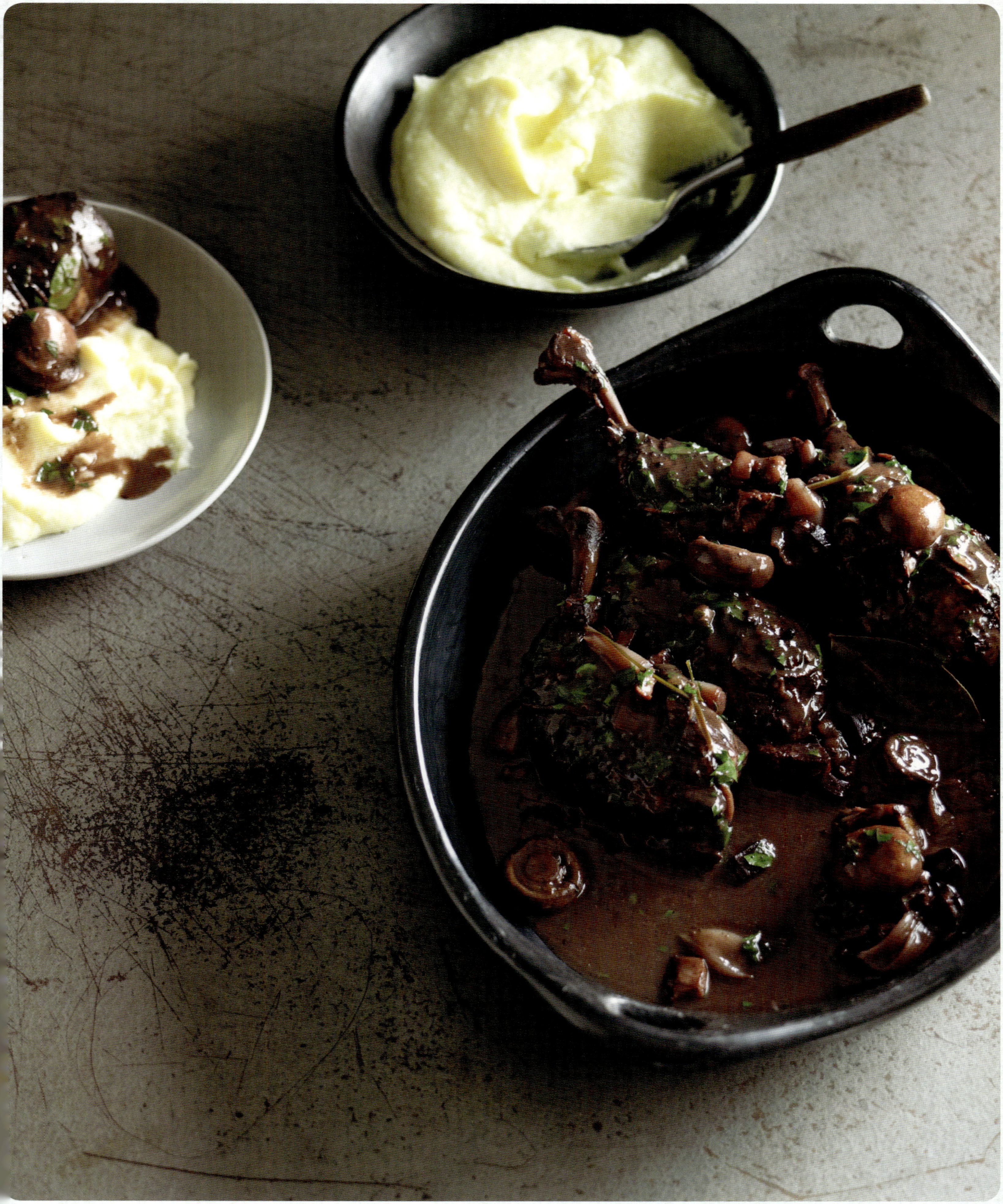

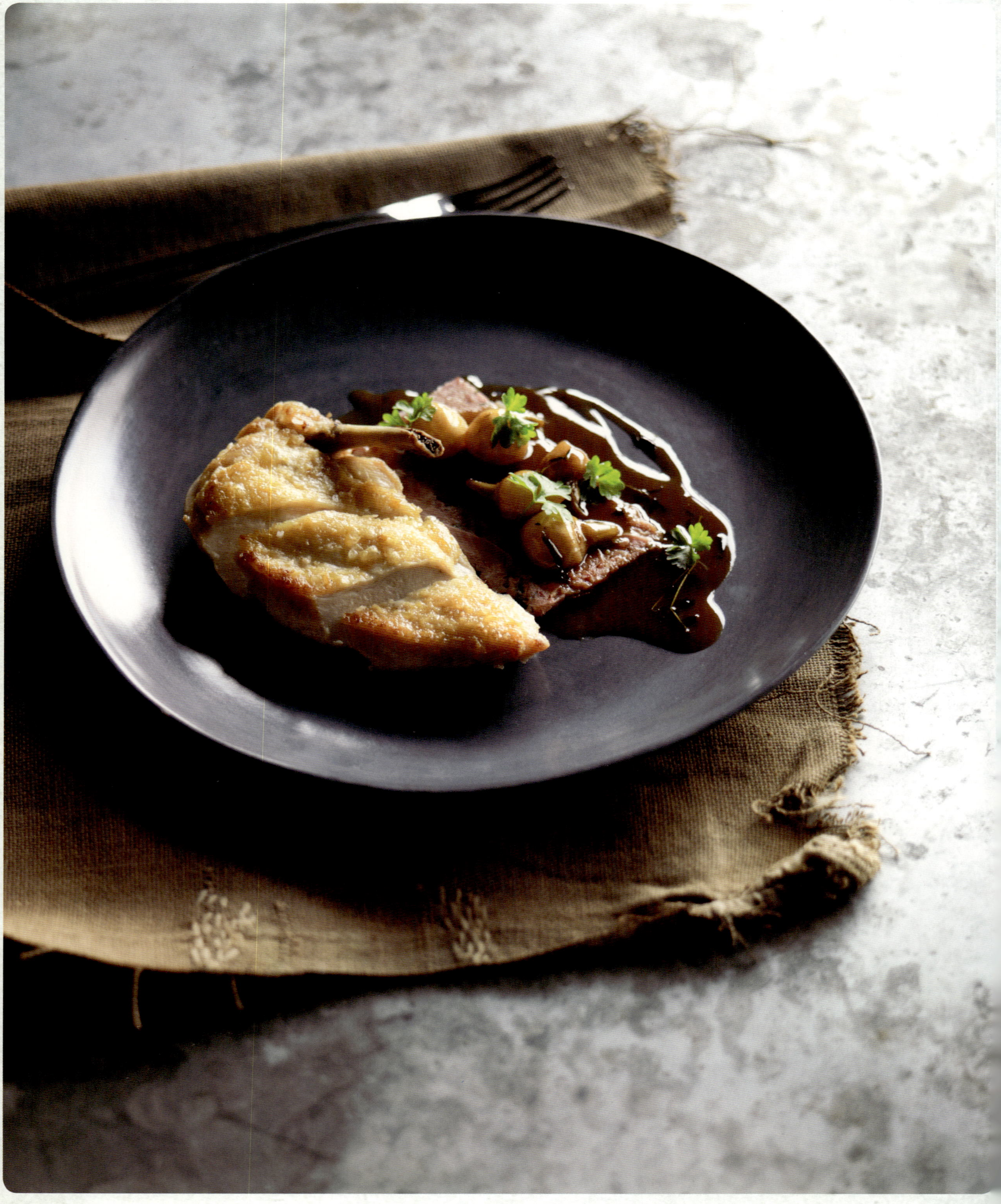

SUPREME DE VOLAILLE, PETITS NAVETS GLACÉS ET PARFUMÉ À L'ESTRAGON
PAN-ROASTED CHICKEN BREASTS WITH BABY TURNIPS

―⦿―

These simply roasted chicken breasts are transformed into a restaurant-quality dish when accompanied by turnips glazed with Chicken and Tarragon Jus (see page 206). This jus takes time to make, but it is worth the effort. (If you're short of time, you could glaze the turnips in chicken stock and butter instead.) When this dish was photographed, I served it with a slice of the ham hock terrine on page 73, but this is purely optional.

SERVES 4

- 12 baby turnips, peeled and trimmed, leaving 1 cm stalk intact
- 4 chicken breasts supremes/kievs (breast portions with wing attached), skin-on, sinew and excess skin removed
- sea salt and freshly ground black pepper
- 2 tablespoons olive oil
- 250 ml Chicken and Tarragon Jus (see page 206) or 250 ml White Chicken Stock (see page 204) with 20 g unsalted butter added
- 20 g unsalted butter
- small flat-leaf parsley leaves (optional), to serve

1. Cook the turnips in a saucepan of lightly salted simmering water for 25 minutes or until the tip of a sharp knife can be inserted without any resistance. Drain and set aside to cool.

2. Preheat the oven to 200°C.

3. Season the chicken skin with salt and pepper. Heat the olive oil in a large ovenproof frying pan over high heat, then cook the chicken breasts, skin-side down, for 5–6 minutes or until golden. Turn over, then transfer to the oven to roast for 7 minutes or until just cooked through; cut a breast open to check and continue cooking if necessary. Transfer to a plate.

4. Place the turnips and the jus or stock and butter in a small saucepan and bring to the boil, then reduce the heat to medium and cook for 5 minutes or until warmed through.

5. Slice each chicken breast into three pieces on the diagonal, then transfer to a plate. Add the turnips, then spoon a little of the remaining warm jus or stock over and scatter with parsley.

CAILLES FARCIES AUX RAISINS ET AU THYM, LENTILS BRAISÉES
GRAPE & THYME-STUFFED QUAIL WITH BRAISED LENTILS

This impressive dish is perfect for autumn, when grapes are at their seasonal best. While it's a little on the challenging side, you'll be thrilled with the result. The sweetness of the grapes, richness of the lentils and tartness of the pickled onions is simply irresistible.

SERVES 4

60 g unsalted butter, chopped
1 eschalot, finely chopped
1 tablespoon finely chopped thyme
125 g green or red grapes
1 small clove garlic, crushed
200 g brioche or sliced white bread, crusts removed, cut into 1 cm dice
sea salt and freshly ground black pepper
4 quails, butterflied (ask your butcher to do this)
2 tablespoons olive oil, plus extra for brushing

BRAISED LENTILS

125 g green Puy-style lentils
½ carrot, cut into 3 lengthways
½ stick celery, cut into 2 pieces
12 pickling onions, peeled, root ends intact
2 cloves
1 bay leaf
5 sprigs thyme
3 cloves garlic, bruised
3 flat-leaf parsley stalks (optional)
1 litre White Chicken Stock (see page 204) or Vegetable Stock (see page 205)
2 handfuls baby spinach leaves (optional)
sea salt and freshly ground black pepper

1. To make the braised lentils, place the lentils, carrot, celery, pickling onions, cloves, bay leaf, thyme, garlic, parsley stalks (if using) and stock in a large heavy-based saucepan and bring to the boil over medium heat. Simmer over medium heat for 25–30 minutes or until the lentils are just tender and still hold their shape. Remove the carrot, celery, cloves, bay leaf and parsley stalks. Stir through the spinach (if using), then season to taste with salt and pepper and keep warm.

2. Meanwhile, heat a large frying pan over medium heat, then add the butter. When the butter starts to foam, add the eschalot and thyme and cook for 2–3 minutes. Add the grapes and garlic and cook for another minute, then add the brioche or bread. Gently stir to mix well, taking care not to crush the grapes. Season to taste with salt and pepper. Set aside to cool.

3. Place the butterflied quails skin-side down on a work surface, then brush with olive oil and season with salt and pepper. Place one-quarter of the bread and grape stuffing mixture along the centre of each quail, then roll one side over to enclose the stuffing. Tie each quail with kitchen twine to secure.

4. Preheat the oven to 200°C.

5. Heat the olive oil in a large ovenproof frying pan over high heat, then add the quail and cook for 5 minutes on each side or until golden. Transfer the pan to the oven and roast the quail for 10 minutes or until golden and cooked through.

6. Serve the quail with the braised lentils.

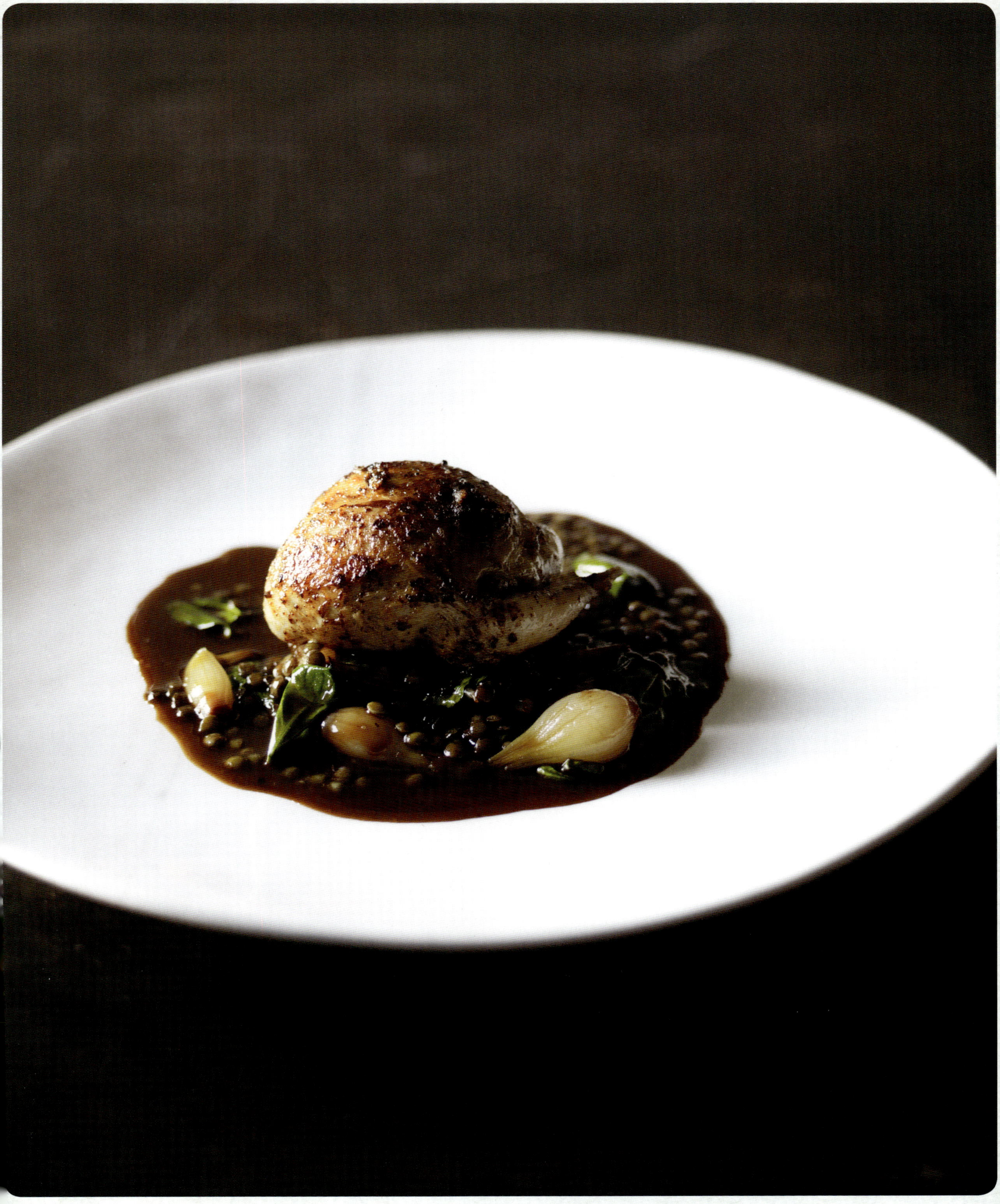

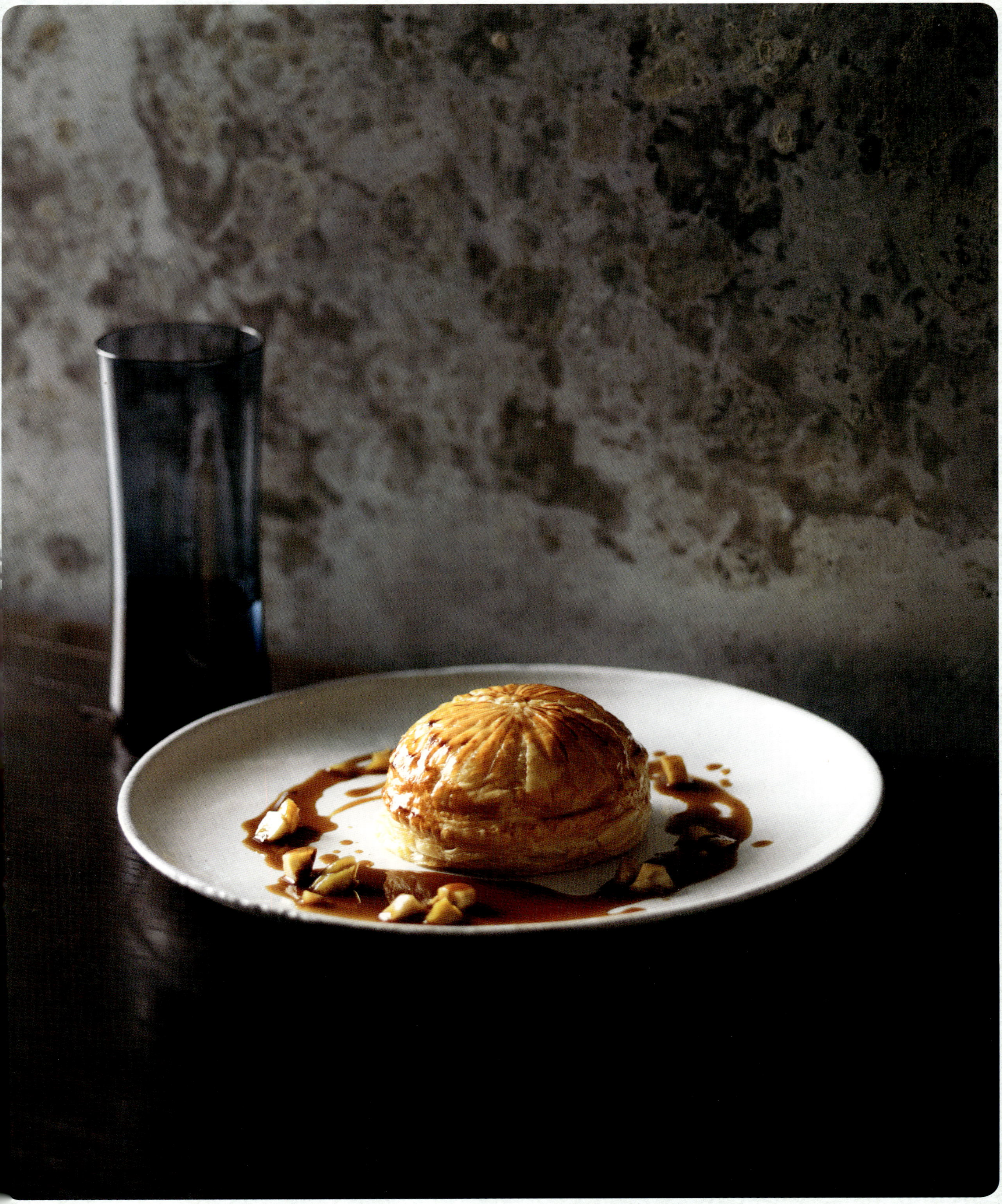

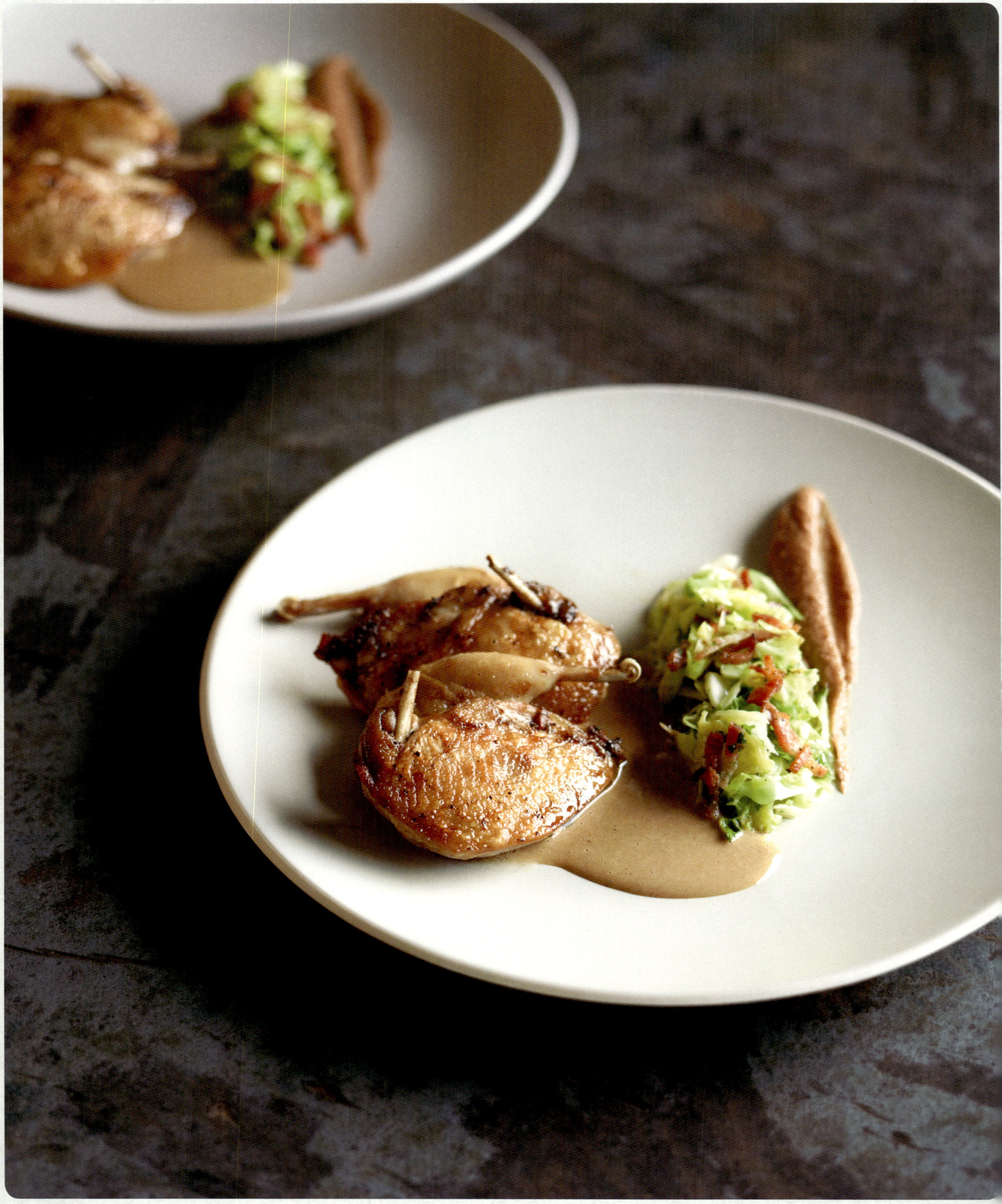

PERDRIX RÔTIE EN SALMIS
ROAST PARTRIDGE 'EN SALMIS'

Roast partridge is quite a common dish in France, although the hunting of game birds is only permitted during a short period each year. In Australia, you should be able to buy partridge from a growers' market, or ask your butcher to order them from a specialist game supplier. This is quite a complex recipe that comes from a time when large households had staff to prepare dishes such as this for them.

SERVES 4

4 partridges, breast (with wing tip attached) and legs removed, carcasses and livers reserved for the jus (ask your butcher to do this)
90 g unsalted butter, chopped
7 cloves garlic, 6 peeled, 1 crushed
6 sprigs thyme
200 g speck (see page 209) or bacon, thinly sliced
100 g morel mushrooms (optional, see page 209), chopped
150 g Savoy cabbage, thinly sliced

PARTRIDGE JUS (OPTIONAL)
60 ml vegetable oil
reserved partridge carcasses, coarsely chopped
10 eschalots, peeled
4 cloves garlic, peeled
8 sprigs thyme
1 fresh bay leaf
250 ml white wine
500 ml White Chicken Stock (see page 204)
100 g duck foie gras
reserved partridge livers
2 teaspoons sherry vinegar (see page 209)
sea salt and freshly ground black pepper

CHESTNUT PUREE
1 × 200 g tin unsweetened chestnut puree (available from specialty food stores)
60 ml White Chicken Stock (see page 204)
20 g unsalted butter, melted

1. To make the jus, if using, heat the oil in a large saucepan over high heat, then add the chopped carcass and cook for 6 minutes or until browned. Add the eschalots, garlic, thyme and bay leaf and cook for 3 minutes or until fragrant. Pour in the wine, then bring to the boil, stirring and scraping the base of the pan to remove any cooked-on bits. Add the stock and bring to the boil, then simmer for 20 minutes or until reduced by half. Strain through a fine-mesh sieve into a clean saucepan, discarding the solids, then bring to the boil and simmer for 10 minutes or until reduced by half. Add the foie gras and livers and blend with a stick blender until smooth. Stir over low heat until heated through. Add the vinegar and season to taste with salt and pepper. Keep warm. (Makes about 350 ml.)

2. To make the puree, place the tinned puree, stock and melted butter in a food processor and blend until smooth. Transfer to a small saucepan, then stir over low heat until heated through. Keep warm.

3. Preheat the oven to 180°C.

4. Heat 70 g of the butter in a large heavy-based frying pan over high heat. When the butter starts to foam, add the peeled garlic and thyme and stir. Add the partridge breasts, skin-side down, and cook for 5 minutes or until golden, then transfer to a baking tray. Cook the legs on each side for 3 minutes or until golden. Transfer to the baking tray, then brush all the meat with melted butter from the pan and top with the garlic and thyme from the pan. Roast for 5–7 minutes or until cooked through.

5. Meanwhile, heat a large frying pan over medium heat, then add the speck and cook for 3 minutes or until browned. Add the remaining butter and crushed garlic and stir until well combined. Add the mushrooms (if using) and cook for 2 minutes or until softened, then add the cabbage and stir for 3–4 minutes or until wilted.

6. Serve the partridge with the jus, chestnut puree and braised cabbage.

RISOTTO D'ORGE PERLÉ AUX CHAMPIGNONS SAUVAGES
PEARL BARLEY RISOTTO WITH WILD MUSHROOMS

As a French man, I don't usually like to recommend vegetarian dishes, but I love this one. You could always serve it with meat – the braised beef cheeks on page 142 would be perfect. For a really deep flavour, use a mixture of different mushrooms. I suggest morels, chanterelles, oysters, enokis and chestnuts, but see what you can find. Pearl barley is a nutritious alternative to arborio rice; however, it does take a bit longer to cook.

SERVES 4

100 ml extra virgin olive oil
4 eschalots, finely chopped
200 g pearl barley
150 ml dry white wine
1 litre White Chicken Stock (see page 204)
sea salt and freshly ground black pepper
400 g mixed mushrooms (such as morels, chanterelles, oysters, shimejis, enokis or chestnuts), cleaned and cut into bite-sized pieces if large
3 cloves garlic, finely chopped
3 tablespoons finely chopped flat-leaf parsley
25 g grated parmesan, plus extra to serve
80 g unsalted butter, chopped

1. Heat 50 ml of the olive oil in a large heavy-based saucepan over medium heat. Add the eschalot and cook, stirring, for 2–3 minutes or until soft but not coloured. Add the pearl barley and cook, stirring, for 3 minutes or until warmed through and coated in the oil mixture. Pour in the wine, then increase the heat to high and bring to the boil. Reduce heat to medium and simmer for 3–4 minutes or until the wine has reduced by two-thirds.

2. Meanwhile, place the chicken stock in a saucepan and bring to the simmer. Season the barley mixture to taste with salt and pepper, then add half of the chicken stock, stirring constantly. Add the remaining stock gradually, stirring, for 25–30 minutes or until the pearl barley is tender.

3. Heat the remaining olive oil in a large heavy-based frying pan over medium heat. Add the mushrooms and cook for 5–6 minutes or until golden. Stir in the garlic and parsley and cook for 1 minute. Add the mushroom mixture to the pearl barley. Taste and adjust the seasoning if necessary. Stir in the parmesan and butter; the result should not be too soupy or dry but just wet enough to ooze a little on the plate (similar to the consistency of porridge).

4. To serve, divide among plates or bowls, then top with a little extra parmesan and voila!

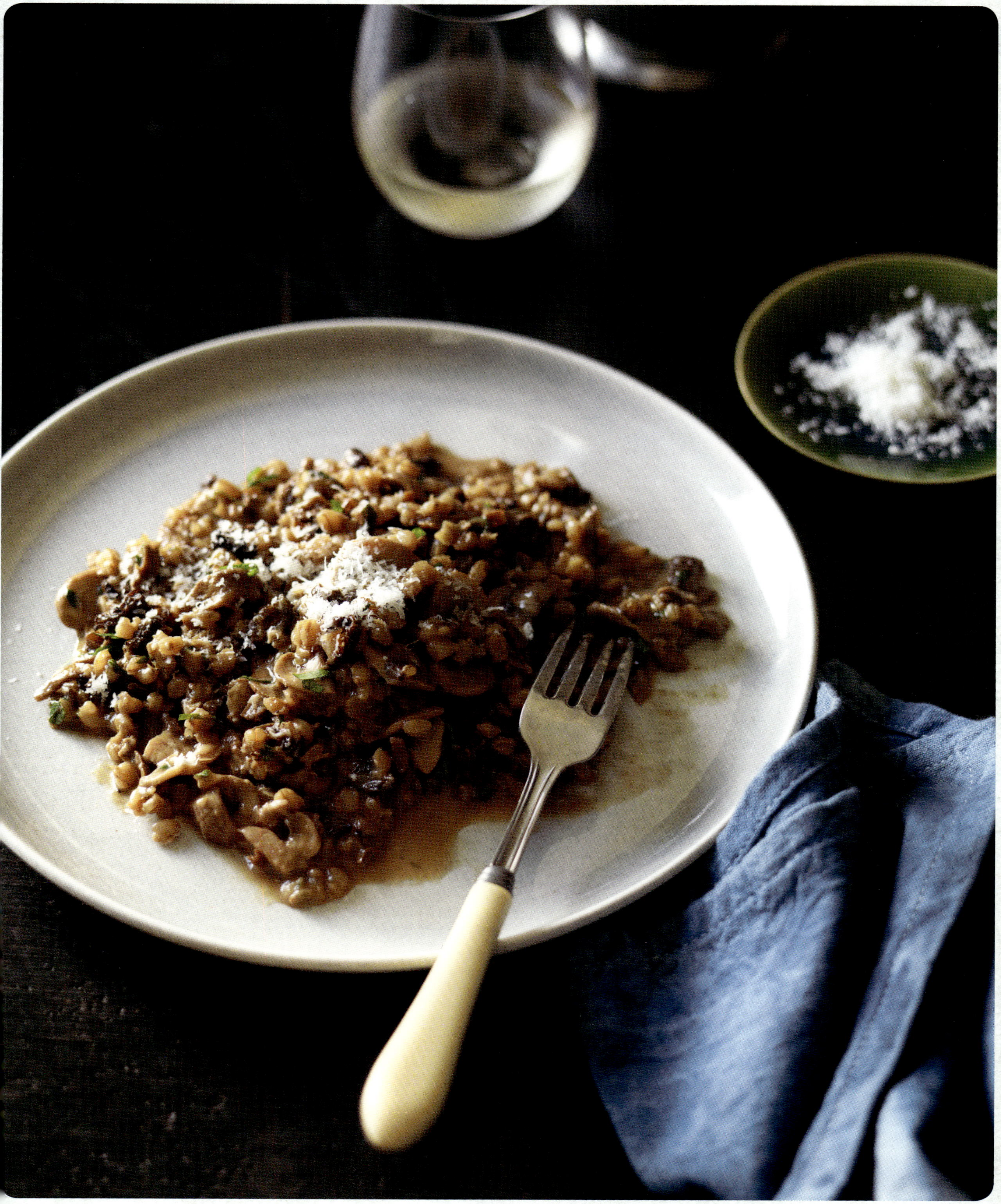

PARMENTIER DE LIÈVRE
FRENCH-STYLE HARE PIE

This is a more sophisticated version of the French comfort-food dish, *hachis parmentier*, France's answer to England's cottage pie. I have used stainless-steel ring moulds to give the 'pies' their shape. Hare is usually only available during winter, and you will probably need to ask your butcher to order it. The meat is dark and has a strong gamey flavour. If you can't find hare, then use another game meat such as venison or boar, rather than rabbit, with which hare is sometimes confused. For best results, the hare will need to be marinated in the fridge overnight, or for at least three hours.

SERVES 4

6 juniper berries
1 clove
1 hare, jointed into pieces, silver skin removed (order from your butcher)
1 carrot, coarsely chopped
1 onion, coarsely chopped
1 stick celery, coarsely chopped
700 ml red wine
2 tablespoons olive oil
120 g unsalted butter, chopped, plus 20 g extra, melted
1 litre Brown Veal Stock (see page 205)
sea salt and freshly ground black pepper
1 kg desiree potatoes, peeled and halved
200 ml milk
1 egg yolk
80 g breadcrumbs, made from day-old bread
1 tablespoon finely chopped thyme
thyme sprigs (optional), to serve

1. Finely crush the juniper berries and cloves with a mortar and pestle. Place the hare in a large baking dish, then rub with the juniper berry mixture. Add the carrot, onion, celery and wine, then cover with plastic film and refrigerate for 3 hours, or overnight if time permits.

2. Remove the hare from the baking dish and pat dry with paper towel. Reserve the marinade.

3. Heat the olive oil and 20 g of the butter in a large enamelled cast-iron casserole over high heat. When the butter starts to foam, add the hare and cook for 5–6 minutes, turning until browned all over. Add the reserved marinade and veal stock and bring to the boil. Season to taste with salt and pepper. Cover, then reduce the heat to medium and cook for 1½ hours or until the hare is tender.

4. Place the potato in a large saucepan of lightly salted water and bring to the boil over high heat, then reduce the heat to low and simmer for 25–30 minutes or until tender. Drain well, then return to the pan and shake over low heat to allow any excess moisture to evaporate. Add the milk, remaining butter and the egg yolk and mash until smooth (or press through a potato ricer or fine-mesh sieve). Season to taste with salt and pepper. Set aside.

5. Remove the hare from the pan and set aside on a plate until cool enough to handle. Strain the cooking liquid through a fine-mesh sieve into a small clean saucepan and discard the vegetables. Shred the hare meat and add it to the pan of liquid. Bring to the boil, then simmer for 30 minutes or until the sauce has reduced and thickened.

6. Preheat the oven to 180°C.

7. Place four lightly greased 10 cm stainless-steel ring moulds on a baking tray. Use a slotted spoon to remove the hare meat from the sauce, keeping the sauce warm over low heat. Spoon the meat evenly into the metal rings, then top with the mashed potato. Brush the potato with melted butter, then sprinkle with breadcrumbs and thyme. Bake for 10–15 minutes or until golden.

8. Serve at once with sauce spooned onto each plate and a thyme sprig to the side, if desired.

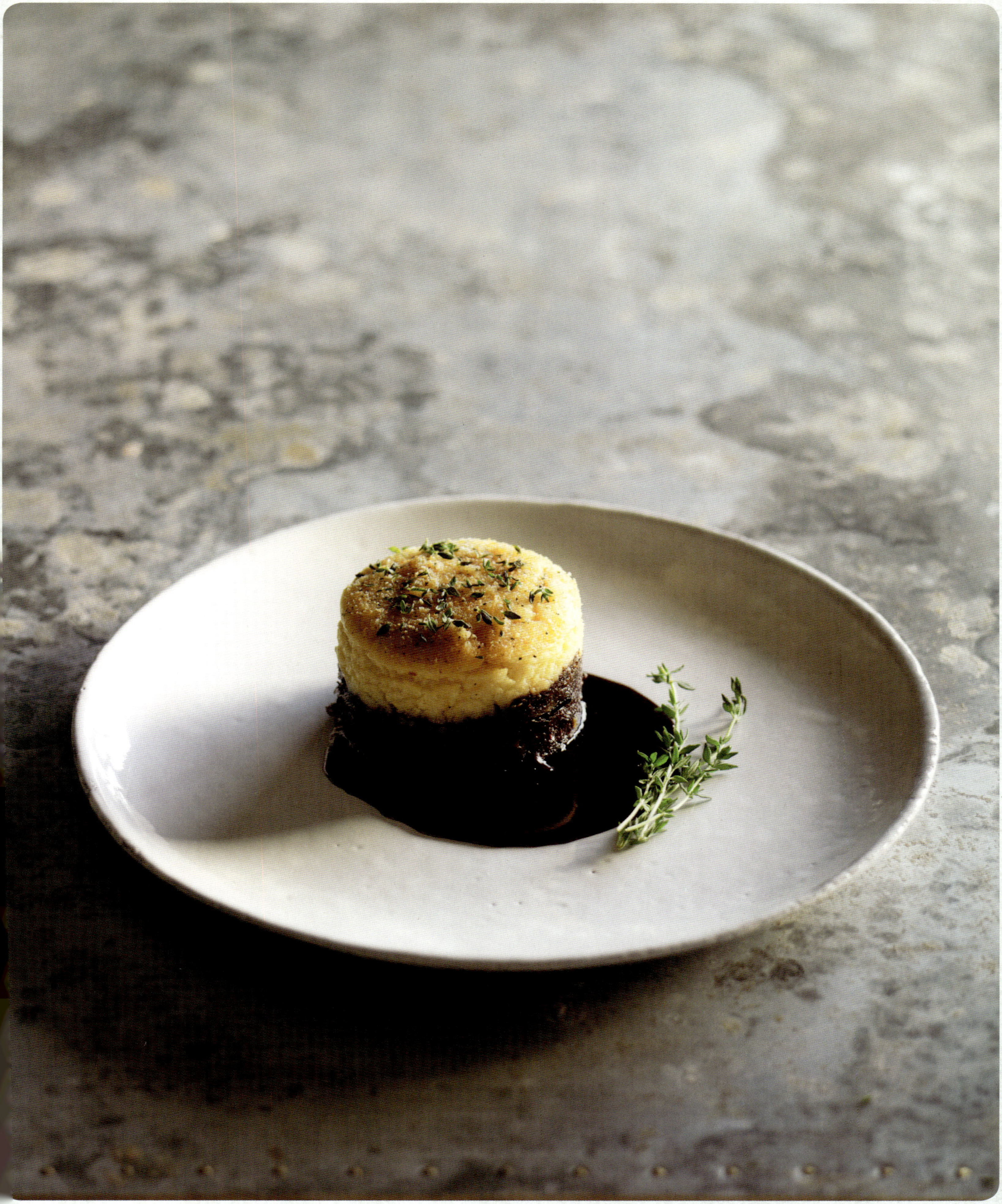

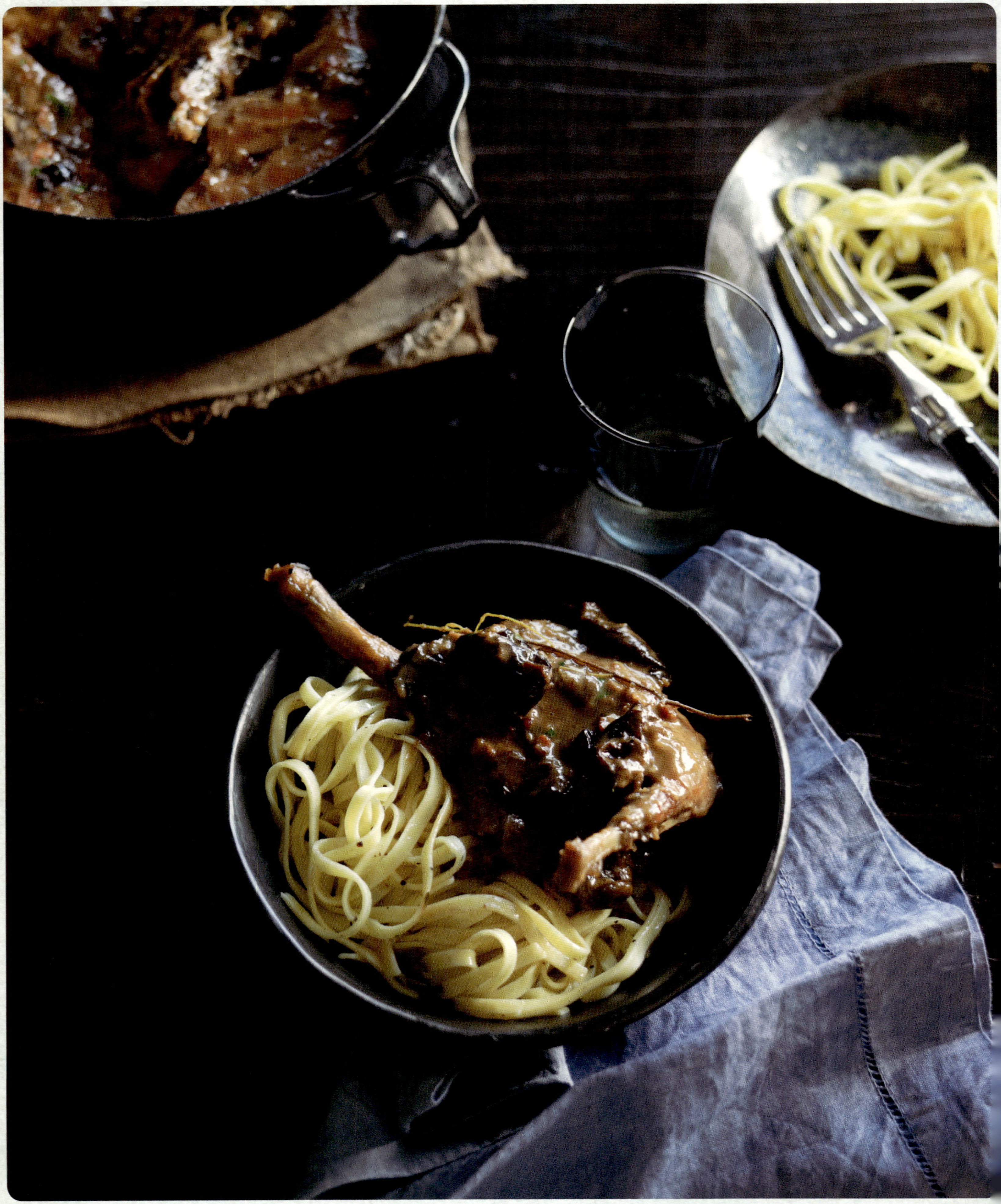

LAPIN AUX PRUNEAUX
RABBIT STEW WITH PRUNES

I love the leanness of rabbit. It combines beautifully with prunes and white wine to produce a rich, satisfying stew that's perfect for a winter dinner party. This is French bistro-style cooking at its best.

SERVES 4

50 g plain flour
sea salt and freshly ground black pepper
4 rabbit hind legs (order from your butcher), sinew removed
60 ml olive oil
50 g unsalted butter
100 g speck (see page 209) or bacon, finely chopped
12 pearl onions, peeled
4 eschalots, finely chopped
4 cloves garlic, finely chopped
3 sprigs thyme
60 ml Armagnac or brandy
100 ml dry white wine
200 g pitted prunes
750 ml White Chicken Stock (see page 204)
100 ml double cream
tagliatelle and finely chopped chives (optional), to serve

1. Season the flour with salt and pepper, then lightly dust the rabbit legs with the seasoned flour, shaking off any excess. Heat 2 tablespoons of the olive oil and all of the butter in a large enamelled cast-iron casserole over medium heat. When the butter starts to foam, add the rabbit legs and cook for 3 minutes on each side or until golden. Remove the rabbit from the pan and set aside. Add the remaining oil and speck and stir for 4–5 minutes or until golden, then remove from the pan. Add the pearl onions and cook, stirring, for 3–4 minutes or until light golden, then add the eschalot, garlic and thyme and cook, stirring, for 1–2 minutes or until fragrant.

2. Return the rabbit to the pan, then add the Armagnac or brandy and carefully tilt the pan towards the flame to ignite the alcohol (or carefully use a long match if necessary). When the flames have subsided, add the wine and prunes and simmer for 3 minutes or until reduced by half, stirring to remove any cooked-on bits from the base of the pan. Add the stock and bring to the boil, then reduce the heat to low, cover closely with a piece of baking paper (called a cartouche, see page 208), then a lid and simmer over very low heat (use a simmer mat if necessary) for 45 minutes or until the rabbit is tender. Remove the rabbit and prunes from the pan and set aside.

3. Strain the cooking liquid through a fine-mesh sieve into a large saucepan, discarding the solids, and simmer over medium heat for 10 minutes or until reduced by half. Add the cream and simmer for 5 minutes or until thickened slightly. Return the rabbit and prunes to the pan, then season to taste and simmer for 1–2 minutes or until just warmed through.

4. Serve the rabbit with tagliatelle, scattered with chives, if desired.

CARRÉ DE PORC RÔTI
ROASTED PORK RACK

Just about everybody loves roast pork. I have added my own touch by using three of my favourite spices: star anise, juniper berries and cloves. You need to salt the pork for four hours, so start this in advance of when you plan to serve it.

SERVES 4

2 star anise
6 juniper berries
3 cloves
8 black peppercorns
2 teaspoons fennel seeds
250 g rock salt
1 × 2 kg pork rack, skin-on and rind scored (ask your butcher to do this)
125 ml olive oil
4 cloves garlic, lightly crushed
6 sprigs thyme
2 fresh bay leaves
freshly ground black pepper
preserved artichoke hearts (optional), to serve

BRAISED LETTUCE

100 ml olive oil
5 eschalots, finely chopped
1 carrot, finely chopped
1 stick celery, finely chopped
50 g unsalted butter, chopped
3 cloves garlic, crushed
4 baby gem lettuces, washed and coarsely chopped
4 sprigs thyme
1 bay leaf
500 ml White Chicken Stock (see page 204) or Vegetable Stock (see page 205)

1. Place the star anise, juniper berries, cloves, peppercorns and fennel seeds in a small frying pan and cook over medium heat for 4–5 minutes or until fragrant. Leave to cool slightly, then transfer to a food processor with the salt and process until finely ground.

2. Place the pork in a baking dish, then rub the rind with 60 ml of the olive oil and rub in the spiced salt mixture. Add the garlic, thyme and bay leaves to the dish, then cover with plastic film and refrigerate for 4 hours.

3. Preheat the oven to 220°C.

4. Wipe the salt mixture off the pork rind, then rinse well under cold running water and pat dry with paper towel. Place the pork in a large roasting pan, drizzle with the remaining olive oil and season with pepper.

5. Roast the pork for 1 hour. Reduce the oven temperature to 180°C and roast for a further 30 minutes or until cooked through. Cover loosely with foil and leave to rest for 20 minutes.

6. Meanwhile, to make the braised lettuce, heat the olive oil in a large heavy-based saucepan over medium heat. Add the eschalot, carrot and celery and cook for 6–8 minutes or until the vegetables just start to brown. Add the butter and garlic and cook for a further 3–4 minutes. Add the lettuce, thyme and bay leaf and cover with stock. Bring to the boil, then reduce the heat to low and simmer for 45 minutes or until the lettuce is soft. Drain the vegetables and discard the liquid.

7. Serve the pork with any pan juices, braised lettuce and artichokes alongside, if desired.

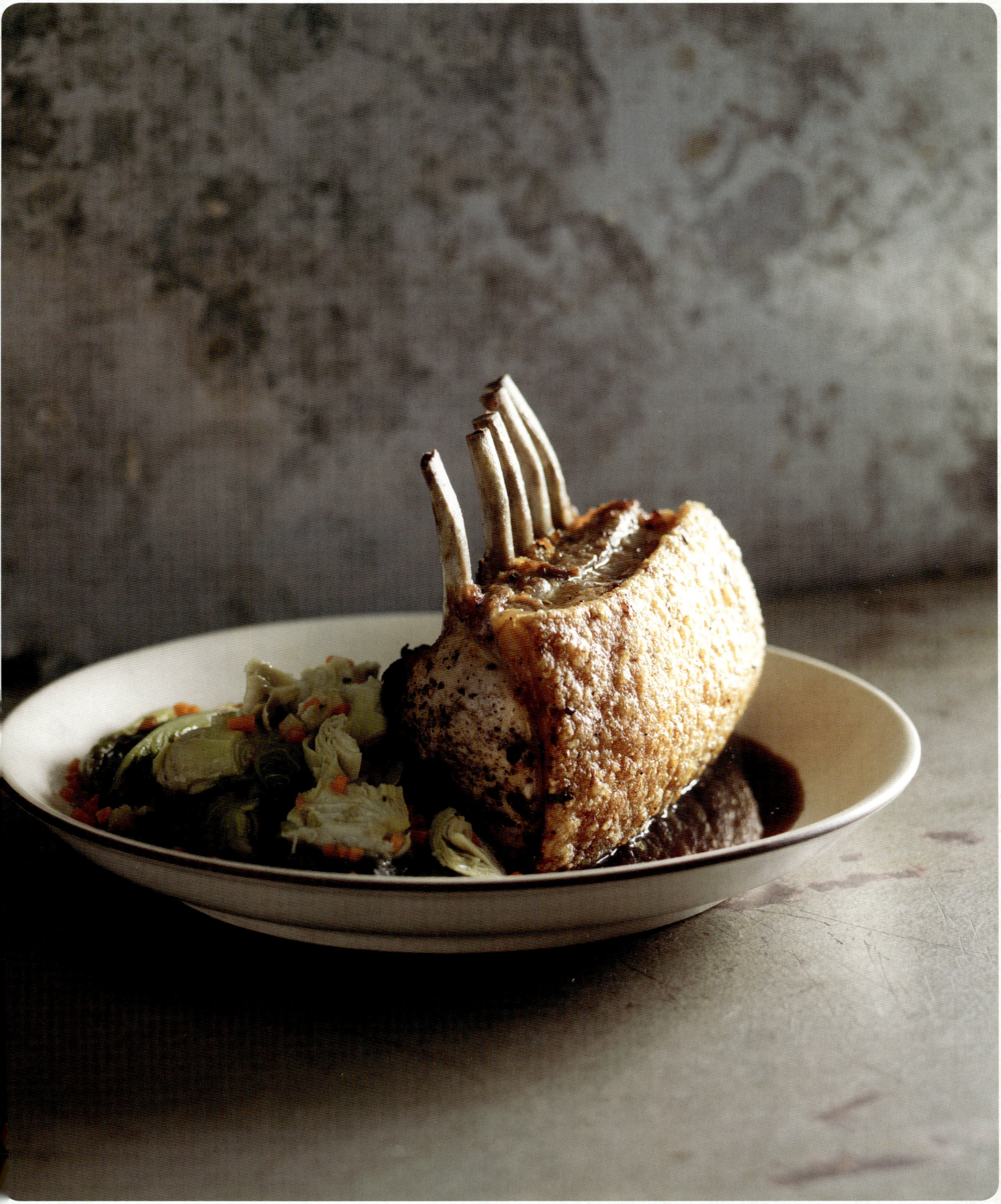

BOUDIN NOIR AUX POMMES
BLACK PUDDING WITH CARAMELISED APPLE

Some of you may be thinking, 'Yuck, black pudding', but I'm sure there are others who think, 'Yum, I want to try this!' The most difficult part of this recipe is getting hold of the blood. However, I have found that some specialty butchers are able to order pig's blood in 2 litre bottles, so you just use what you need, then freeze the rest for the next time the urge to make this strikes you. My uncle, who owns a charcuterie in France, gave me this recipe, and I feel like I am paying tribute to all he taught me by passing it on to you.

SERVES 6–8

300 g pork back fat (see page 209), cut into 5 mm dice
1 onion, finely chopped
1 stick celery, finely chopped
300 ml pig's blood (order from your butcher)
pinch freshly grated nutmeg
3 tablespoons finely chopped curly parsley
sea salt and freshly ground black pepper
3 pink lady apples
150 g unsalted butter
50 g caster sugar

1. Place the pork back fat in a large heavy-based saucepan over medium heat, then cook for 20–30 minutes or until it is translucent and can be stirred in the pan. Add the onion and celery, then cook for another 10 minutes or until softened.

2. Remove the pan from the heat and add the blood, nutmeg and parsley and season to taste with salt and pepper. Return the pan to medium heat and cook, stirring constantly with a wooden spoon (like you would cook custard), for 10–12 minutes or until it reaches a porridge-like consistency.

3. Preheat the oven to 120°C.

4. Line a small terrine mould or loaf tin (mine is 26 cm × 10 cm) with heatproof plastic film or baking paper, leaving enough overhanging to help lift the black pudding from the mould. Add the blood mixture. Cover with foil and place in a deep roasting pan. Pour enough hot water in the roasting pan to come halfway up the sides of the mould.

5. Bake for 1–1½ hours or until a small knife inserted in the middle of the black pudding comes out clean. Remove the mould from the roasting pan and refrigerate the black pudding immediately for 2 hours or until firm.

6. Meanwhile, cut the apples into 8 wedges each, then remove and discard the cores. Melt 100 g of the butter in a large heavy-based frying pan over medium heat, then sprinkle in the caster sugar and add the apple. As the butter and sugar combine to form a caramel, toss the apple in the pan for 5–6 minutes or until golden brown. Set aside.

7. Lift the black pudding out of the terrine mould using the overhanging plastic film or baking paper, then place on a chopping board and cut into 8 slices. Heat the remaining butter in a large heavy-based frying pan over medium heat and pan-fry each slice of black pudding for 3–4 minutes or until crisp on each side.

8. Divide the pan-fried black pudding and caramelised apple among plates, then serve with the caramel sauce.

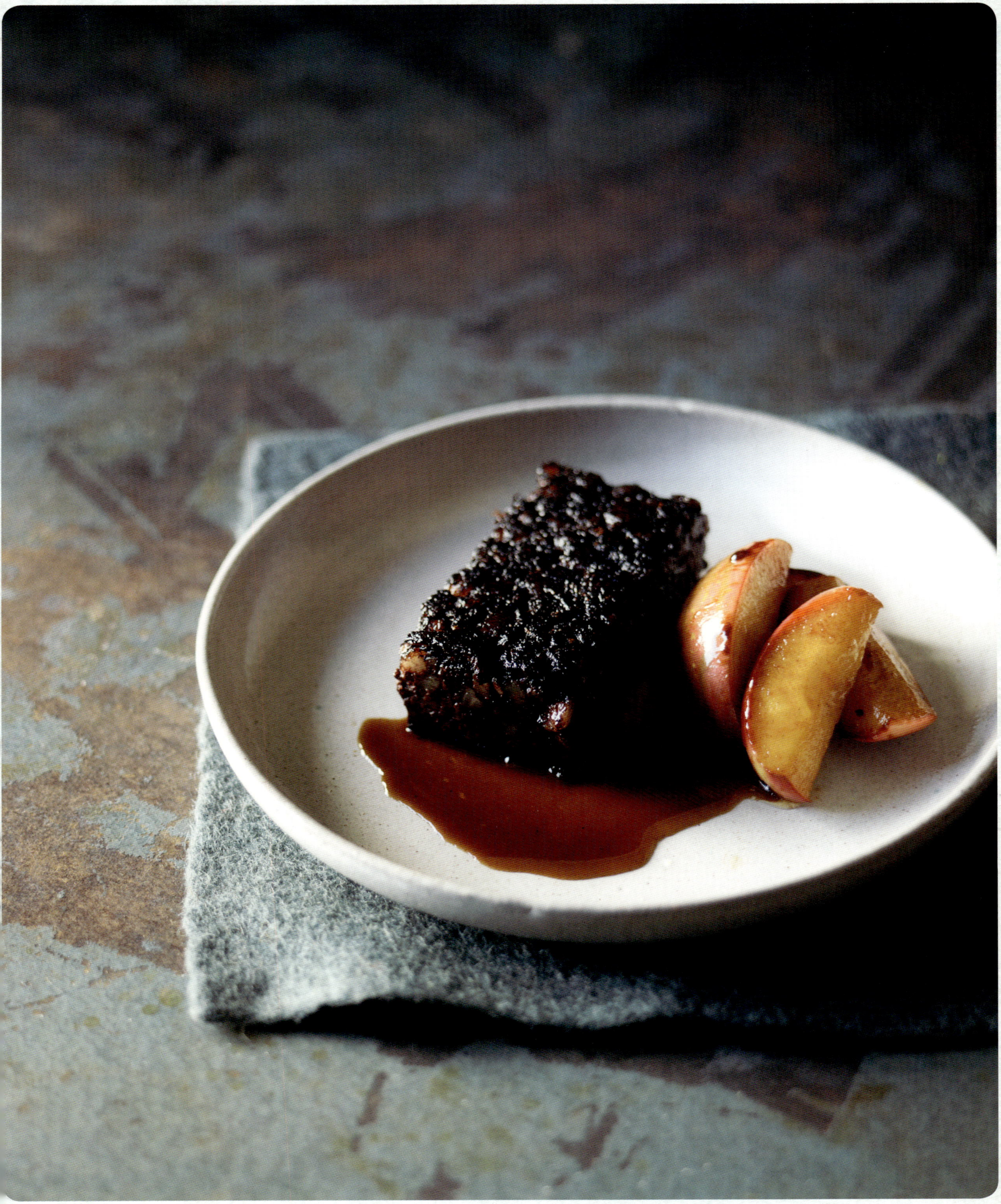

FILET MIGNON DE PORC AUX POMMES ET SAUGE
PORK STUFFED WITH APPLE & SAGE

People have been serving apple with pork for as long as they have been eating them — here I replace the more traditional apple sauce with a lovely apple stuffing. I love cooking with pork filet mignon, as it is not only the most succulent cut of pork, but also the quickest to cook. This is a simple and elegant meal for two for a special occasion; the recipe can easily be doubled to serve four.

SERVES 2

1 × 400 g piece pork filet mignon
olive oil, for cooking
1 granny smith apple, peeled, cored and cut into 6 wedges
sea salt and freshly ground black pepper
20 g unsalted butter
5 sage leaves
vegetable oil, for deep-frying
500 g Jerusalem artichokes, skin-on and thinly sliced
flat-leaf parsley or thyme leaves, to serve

1. Preheat the oven to 200°C.

2. Use a sharp knife to make a hole through the centre of the pork ready for the stuffing. Set aside.

3. Heat a little olive oil in an ovenproof frying pan over high heat. Add the apple and season well with salt and pepper. Cook for 2–3 minutes, turning until golden all over, then add the butter and sage. Fry for 1 minute or until the apple wedges are tender but firm and still hold their shape; take care not to overcook. Drain on paper towel to remove excess oil and butter. Remove the pan from the heat and wipe clean with paper towel. Roll the sage leaves around the apple and insert into the centre of the pork.

4. Heat a little more olive oil in the cleaned pan over high heat and cook the pork for 2–3 minutes on each side or until golden. Transfer to the oven and roast for 7 minutes. Set aside to rest.

5. Meanwhile, heat the vegetable oil for deep-frying in a large heavy-based saucepan over high heat until it registers 190°C on a sugar/deep-fry thermometer. Fry the artichoke slices for 1–2 minutes or until golden. Drain on paper towel and scatter with parsley or thyme.

6. Cut the pork on the diagonal into 2–3 cm thick slices, then spoon over any pan juices. Serve with the artichokes to the side.

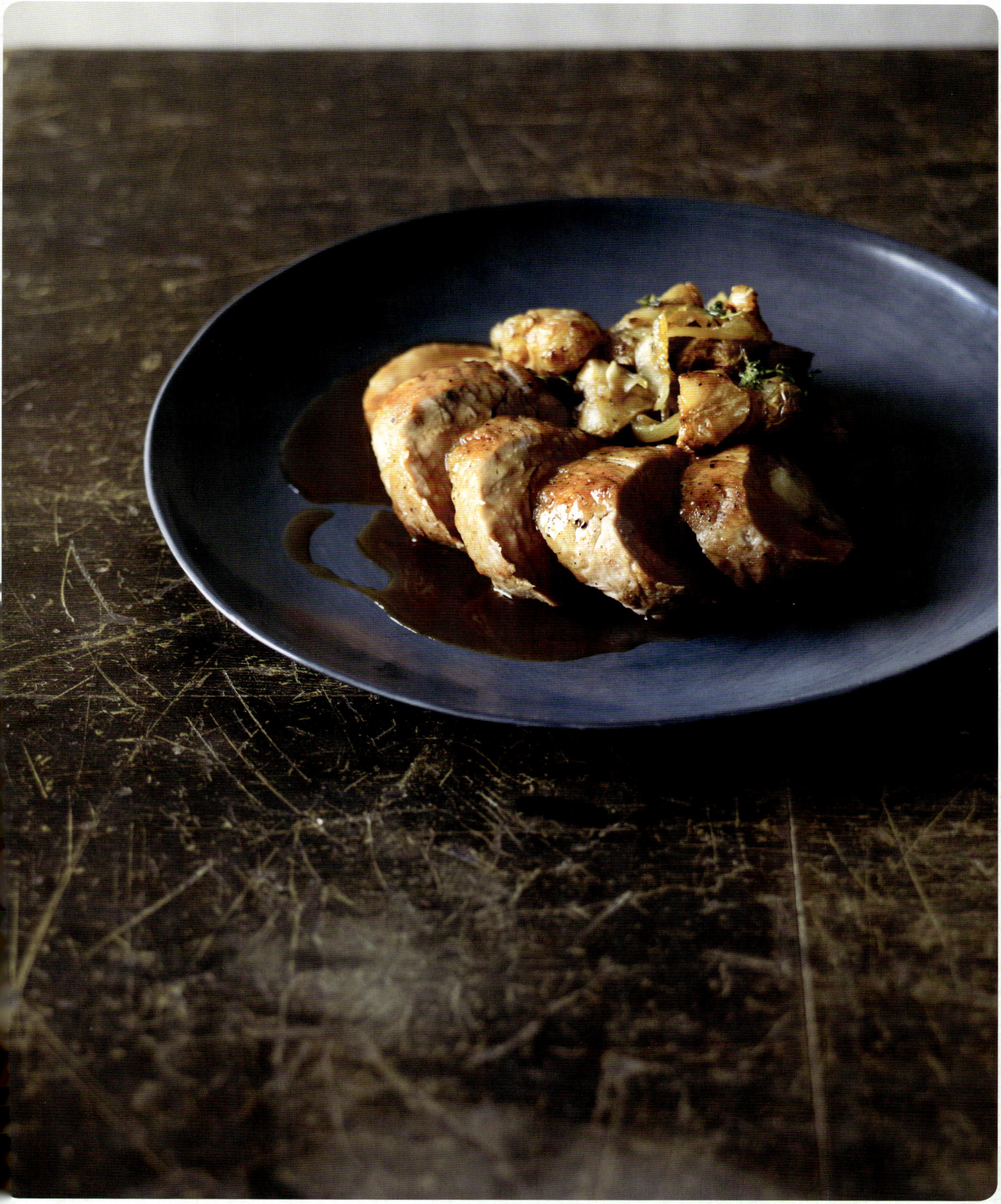

CONFIT DE PORC ET PURÉE DE POMMES
CONFIT PORK BELLY WITH APPLE PUREE

No French bistro cookbook worth its salt would be without a recipe for pork belly. Here is mine, using that perennial favourite pairing of pork with apple. I have served this with the chicken jus on page 206 and black pudding on page 126, but this is optional. Start this recipe two days in advance, and then savour every mouthful when it hits the table . . .

SERVES 4

3 star anise
1 tablespoon fennel seeds
5 cloves
1 teaspoon black peppercorns
1 tablespoon finely chopped thyme
150 ml olive oil
1 × 800 g piece pork belly, skin-on, bones removed
1 litre duck fat (see page 105)
2 tablespoons vegetable oil
Black Pudding (optional, see page 126) and wilted spinach leaves, to serve

APPLE PUREE

4 granny smith apples, peeled, cored and roughly chopped
2 teaspoons caster sugar
15 g unsalted butter
50 ml water
sea salt and freshly ground black pepper

1. Lightly crush the star anise, fennel seeds, cloves and black peppercorns with a mortar and pestle. Add the thyme and olive oil and mix well. Rub the pork belly flesh with the spice mixture; do not rub the skin. Place in a ceramic dish, cover with plastic film and refrigerate overnight.

2. Preheat the oven to 150°C.

3. Place the duck fat in a large roasting pan and place in the oven for 10 minutes or until melted. Add the pork belly and cook for 4 hours or until tender.

4. Remove the pork belly and place on a baking tray, then top with a heavy-based baking tray and wrap the whole thing tightly with plastic film. Refrigerate overnight to press (this creates a compact shape and width, making the belly easier to portion evenly). Cut the pork into four 200 g pieces.

5. Meanwhile, to make the apple puree, place the apple, sugar, butter and water in a saucepan, then cook over low heat for 10–12 minutes or until the apple is soft. Transfer to a food processor and process to form a smooth puree. Season to taste with salt and pepper. Return to the saucepan and keep warm.

6. Heat the vegetable oil in a large heavy-based frying pan over medium heat, then, working with two pieces of pork at a time, cook, skin-side down, for 8–10 minutes or until golden and crisp. The pork should be warmed through.

7. Divide the pork belly among plates and serve with the apple puree, black pudding (if using) and wilted spinach.

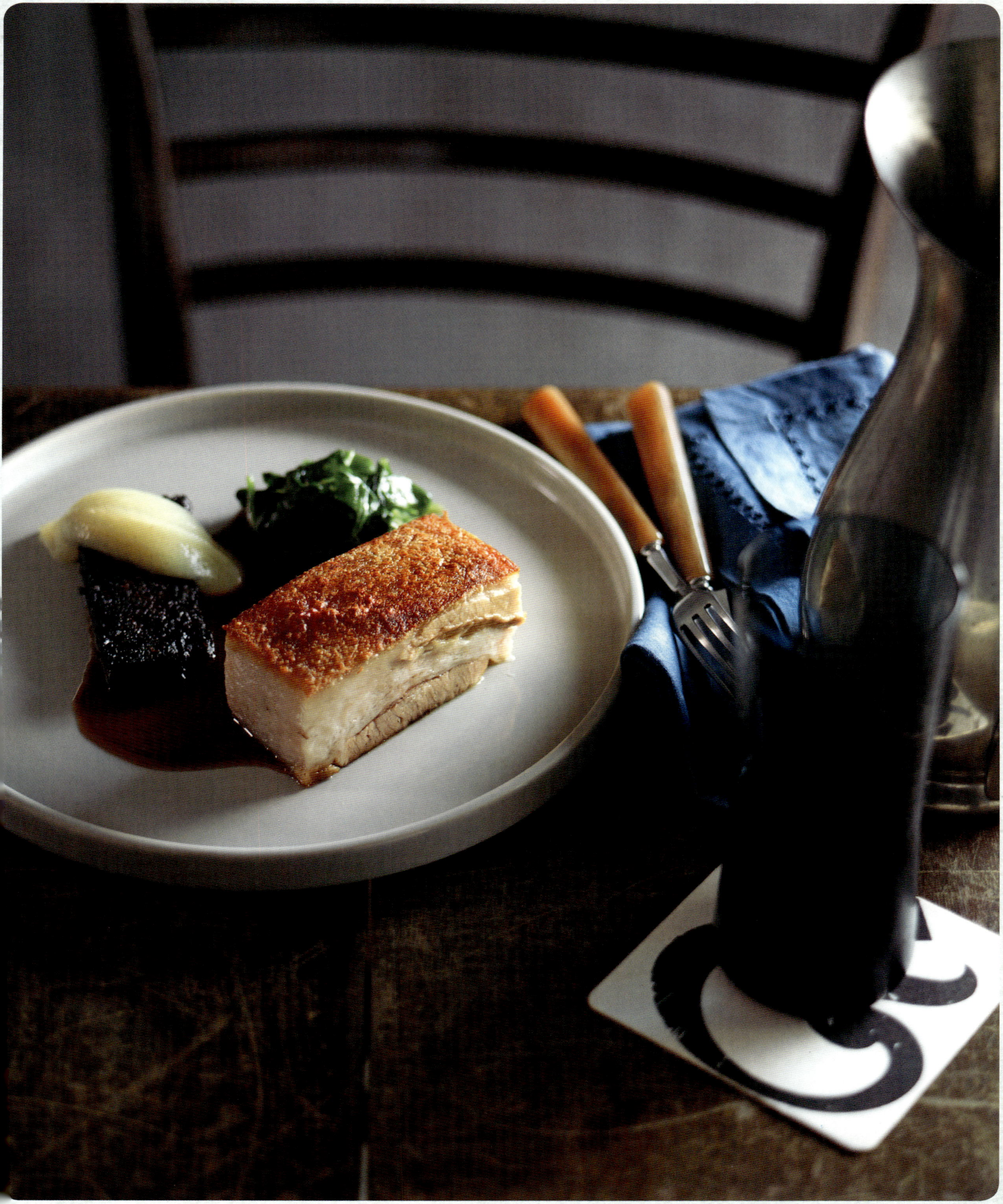

CÔTE DE BŒUF ET MOELLE, SAUCE BORDELAISE
RIB-EYE OF BEEF WITH BONE MARROW & BORDELAISE SAUCE

Bordelaise sauce is a gutsy red wine sauce that takes its name from the wine-producing Bordeaux region of France. It is one of the stars of the bistro kitchen, and requires time to reduce slowly so that it is as rich as possible. Adding orange zest is my innovation – it gives the sauce a lovely tanginess. You can omit the bone marrow from the sauce if you prefer.

SERVES 4

2 tablespoons vegetable oil
4 × 400 g beef rib-eye steaks, bone-in, brought to room temperature
sea salt and freshly ground black pepper
30 g unsalted butter
finely chopped flat-leaf parsley, to serve

BORDELAISE SAUCE

80 g unsalted butter, chopped
8 eschalots, coarsely chopped
400 g field mushrooms, trimmed and sliced
3 sprigs thyme
1 bay leaf
3 sprigs French tarragon (see page 208)
1 bouquet garni (see page 208)
freshly ground black pepper
1 star anise
3 juniper berries
3 cloves garlic
2 wide strips orange zest, white pith removed
1 tomato, coarsely chopped
500 ml red wine
50 ml port
30 ml balsamic vinegar
500 ml Brown Veal Stock (see page 205)
sea salt and freshly ground black pepper
200 g bone marrow, optional, cut into 1 cm thick rounds

1. To make the bordelaise sauce, melt 30 g of the butter in a large heavy-based saucepan over medium heat. When the butter starts to foam, add the eschalot and cook for 3–4 minutes or until softened. Add the mushrooms, thyme, bay leaf, tarragon, bouquet garni, pepper, star anise, juniper berries, garlic and orange zest and cook for 8–10 minutes or until well caramelised. Add the tomato and simmer gently for 5 minutes. Add the wine, port and vinegar, then bring to the boil and simmer over medium heat for 10 minutes or until reduced by one-third. Add the veal stock, then bring to the boil and simmer over medium heat for 25–30 minutes or until reduced by half.

2. Strain the sauce through a fine-mesh sieve into a clean saucepan, then discard the solids. Bring the sauce to the boil over medium heat. Gradually whisk in the remaining butter until well combined. Season to taste with salt and pepper. Add the bone marrow, if using, and simmer for 10–12 minutes. Keep warm.

3. Heat the oil in a heavy-based frying pan over high heat. Season the steaks well on both sides with salt and pepper. When the oil is hot, reduce the heat to low and add the butter. When the butter starts to foam, add the steaks and cook for 8 minutes on each side for medium–rare or until cooked to your liking. Remove the steaks from the pan and leave to rest for 5 minutes on a wire rack placed over a baking tray near the stove.

4. Place a steak on each plate, then spoon over the bordelaise sauce and scatter with chopped parsley.

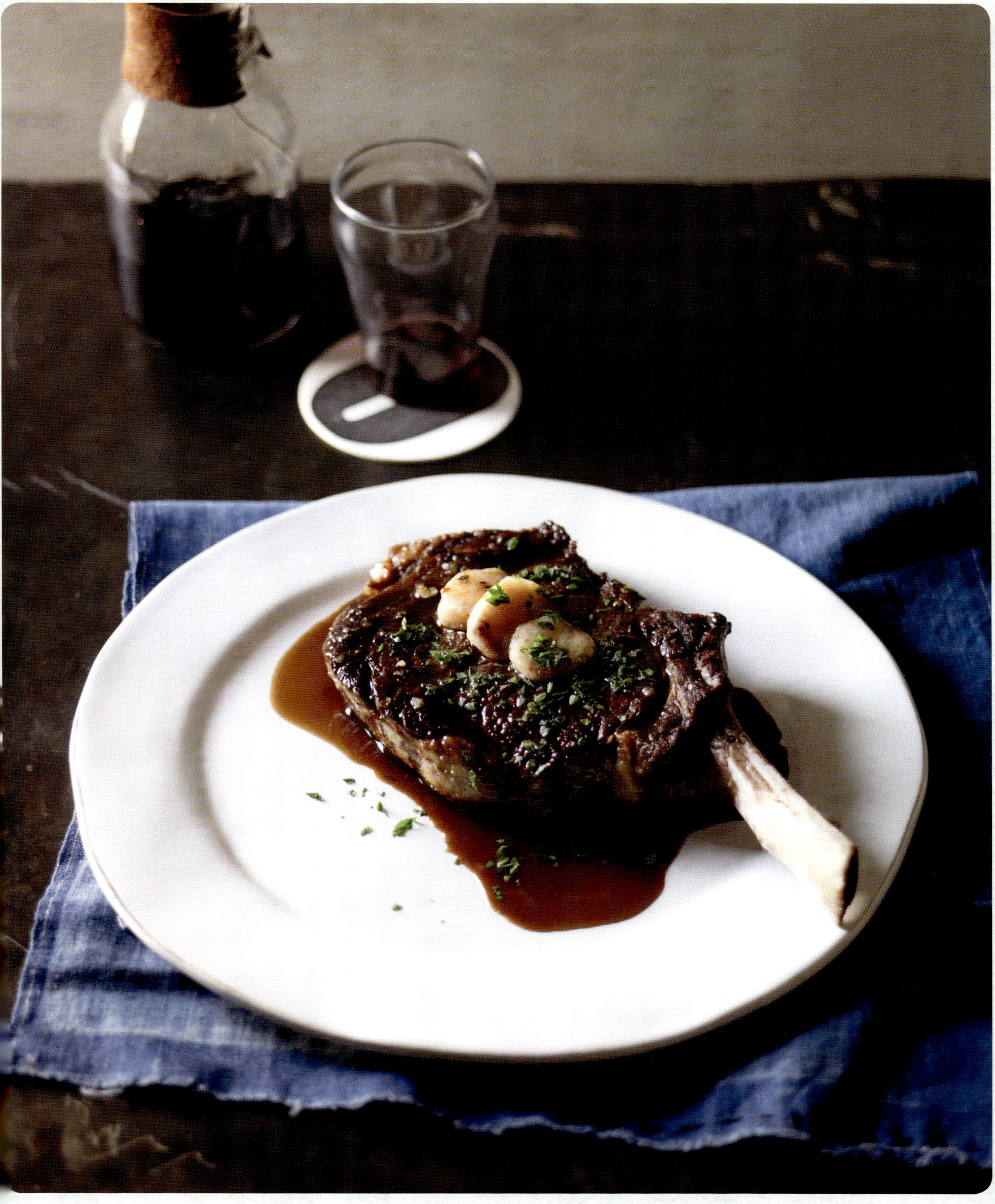

CÔTE DE BŒUF SAUCE BÉARNAISE
RIB-EYE OF BEEF WITH BEARNAISE SAUCE

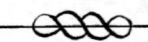

I have a real soft spot for bearnaise as it's my mother's favourite sauce. Every time I return to France, I make it for her. I have even been known to make up a batch of the wine reduction for her to keep in the fridge until my next visit! This iconic dish never disappoints.

SERVES 4

2 tablespoons vegetable oil
4 × 400 g beef rib-eye steaks, bone-in, brought to room temperature
sea salt and freshly ground black pepper
30 g unsalted butter

BEARNAISE SAUCE

250 g unsalted butter, chopped
3 eschalots, finely chopped
60 ml dry white wine
30 ml white wine vinegar
1 teaspoon dried tarragon
1 teaspoon black peppercorns, lightly crushed
4 egg yolks
sea salt
2 teaspoons finely chopped French tarragon (see page 208)
2 teaspoons finely chopped chervil
lemon juice, to to taste
freshly ground black pepper

1. To make the bearnaise sauce, melt the butter in a small saucepan over low heat, then simmer until the milk solids separate and fall to the bottom of the pan; be careful not to burn the butter. Strain off the clear butter, known as clarified butter, and discard the milk solids. Keep warm.

2. Meanwhile, place the eschalot, wine, vinegar, dried tarragon and peppercorns in a small saucepan and simmer over low heat for 4–5 minutes or until reduced to 30 ml. Strain through a fine-mesh sieve into a bowl, discard the solids, and set aside to cool.

3. Half-fill a saucepan with water and bring to a very gentle simmer over low heat. Combine the egg yolks, wine reduction and a pinch of salt in a large heatproof bowl that fits snugly over the saucepan – the bottom of the bowl should not touch the water. Whisk for 8–10 minutes or until the mixture leaves a trail and is thick and creamy; be careful not to overheat the egg mixture or it will scramble.

4. Pour the water out of the saucepan, then place the bowl back over the pan, off the heat (this helps stabilise the bowl while you whisk in the clarified butter). Whisk a thin stream of the warm clarified butter into the egg mixture until thick and emulsified, whisking continuously. Stir in the fresh tarragon and chervil and season to taste with lemon juice, salt and pepper. Keep warm.

5. Heat the oil in a heavy-based frying pan over high heat. Season the steaks well on both sides with salt and pepper. When the oil is hot, reduce the heat to low and add the butter. When the butter starts to foam, add the steaks and cook for 8 minutes on each side for medium–rare or until cooked to your liking. Remove the steaks from the pan and leave to rest for 5 minutes on a wire rack placed over a baking tray near the stove.

6. Place a steak on each plate, then serve with the bearnaise sauce.

STEAK À L'ÉCHALOTE
SIRLOIN STEAK WITH ESCHALOT SAUCE

You will find a sirloin steak dish of some description on the menu of any self-respecting French cafe or bistro. This recipe brings back happy memories for me, as my mother used to cook it as a special treat – steak was expensive – for weekend family lunches. I like to eat this with French fries. Often the simplest meals are the best.

SERVES 2

60 ml vegetable oil
80 g unsalted butter, chopped
2 × 300 g sirloin steaks, brought to room temperature
10 eschalots, thinly sliced
4 sprigs thyme, leaves picked
sea salt and freshly ground black pepper
100 ml white wine

1. Heat 30 ml of the oil and 40 g of the butter in a large heavy-based frying pan over high heat. When the butter starts to foam and turn brown, reduce the heat to medium. Add the steaks, then cook for 2–3 minutes on each side for medium–rare or until cooked to your liking. Remove the steaks from the pan and leave to rest in a warm place for 5 minutes.

2. Wipe the pan clean, then add the remaining oil and butter over medium heat. Add the eschalot and thyme, then season to taste with salt and pepper and cook over medium heat for 4–5 minutes or until the eschalot has browned. Add the wine, then increase the heat to high and cook for 2–3 minutes or until the sauce has thickened.

3. Serve the steaks with the eschalot sauce.

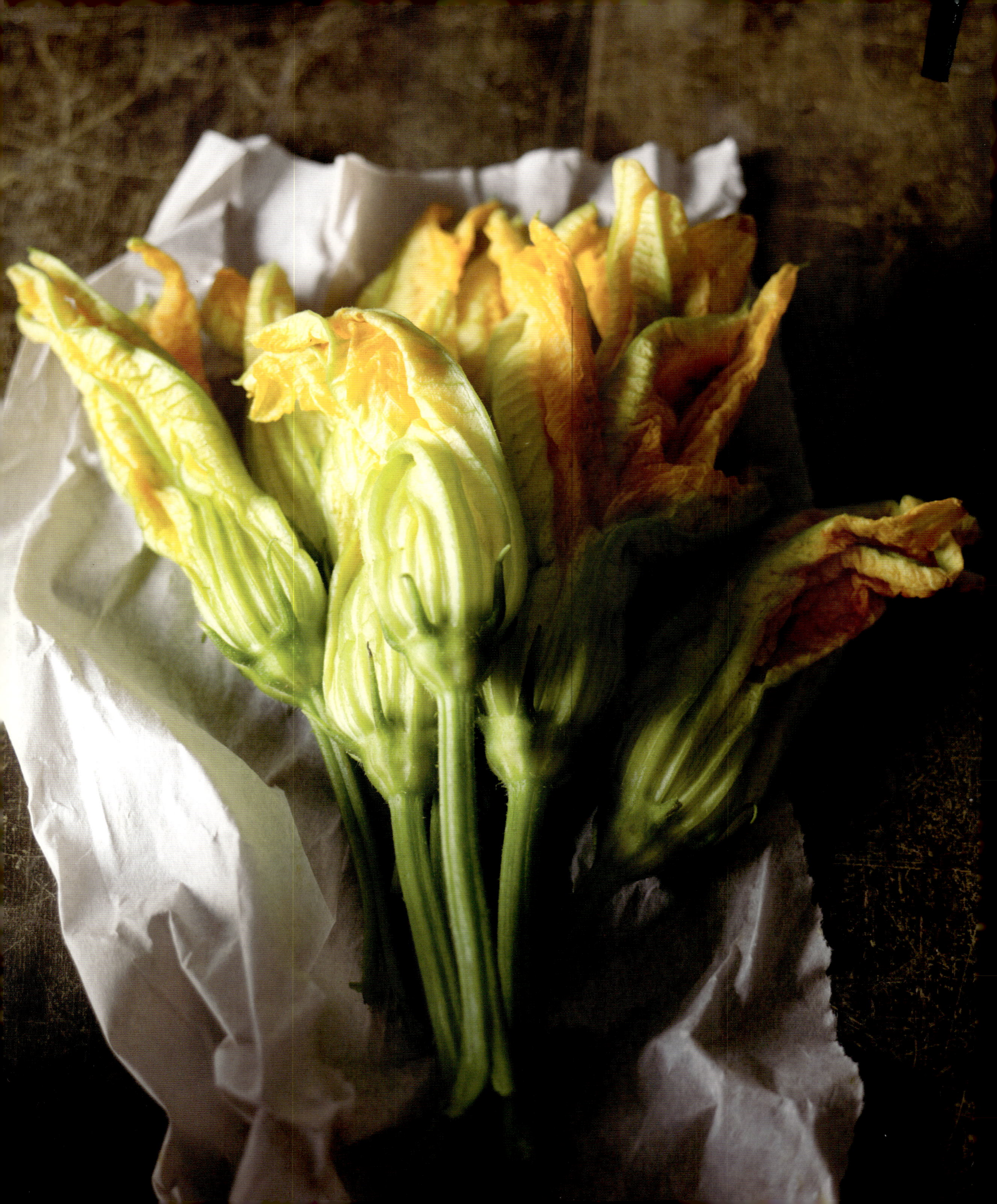

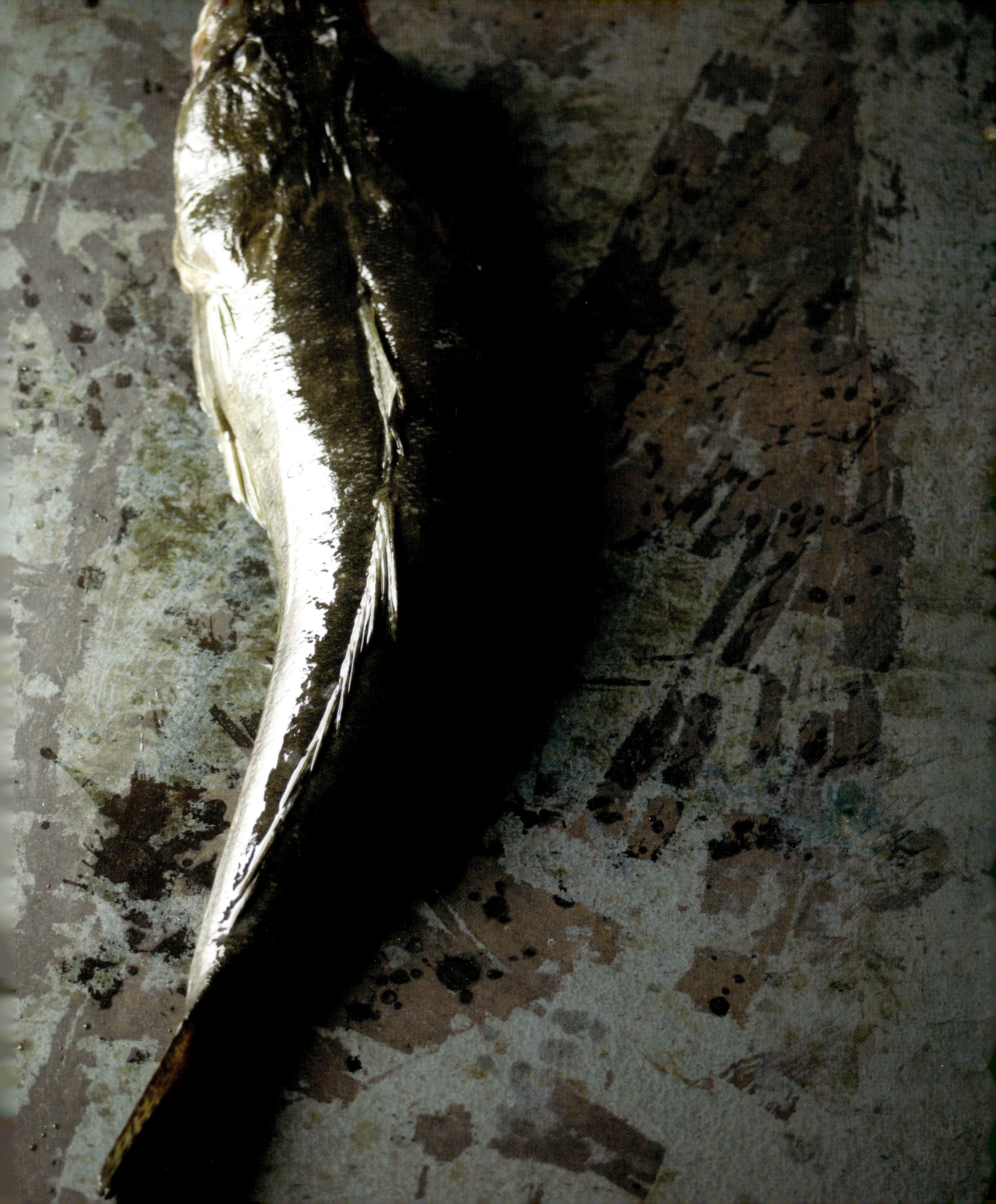

FAUX FILET DE BŒUF SAUCE MARCHAND DE VIN
SCOTCH FILLET BEEF WITH RICH RED WINE SAUCE

Literally meaning 'wine merchant's sauce', *marchand de vin* is an unctuous, rich red wine sauce. It is all you need to turn your favourite cut of steak into something special for either a weeknight treat or an elegant weekend dinner party. This serves two, but you could easily double the ingredients to serve four.

SERVES 2

60 ml vegetable oil
120 g unsalted butter
2 × 300 g scotch fillet, brought to room temperature
6 eschalots, thinly sliced
3 cloves garlic, lightly bruised
2 sprigs thyme, leaves picked
sea salt and freshly ground black pepper
150 ml White Chicken Stock (see page 204)
250 ml red wine (I use shiraz)
finely chopped chives, to serve

1. Heat a heavy-based frying pan over high heat, then add 30 ml of the oil and 40 g of the butter. When the butter starts to foam, reduce the heat to medium and add the steaks, then cook for 2–3 minutes on each side for medium–rare or until cooked to your liking. Remove the steaks from the pan and leave to rest in a warm place for 5 minutes.

2. Wipe the pan clean, then add the remaining oil and another 40 g of the butter and place over medium heat. When the butter starts to foam, add the eschalot, garlic and thyme and season with salt and pepper, then cook for 3–4 minutes or until the eschalot has caramelised. Add the chicken stock and wine, then increase the heat to high and bring to the boil. Reduce the heat to low and simmer for 4–5 minutes or until reduced by half. Bring the sauce to the boil again, then whisk in the remaining butter a piece at a time until the butter is incorporated and the sauce is glossy.

3. Place a steak on each serving plate. Pour the sauce over the beef, then garnish with chopped chives and serve.

PITHIVIER DE RIS DE VEAU
VEAL SWEETBREAD PIE

Sweetbreads are a delicacy in France, and veal sweetbreads are the most prized of all due to their lovely mild flavour and smooth texture. They are highly perishable, so prepare and consume them within 24 hours of purchase. While commonly available in France, in Australia you'll need to order them in advance from your butcher.

SERVES 4

150 g veal fillet, sinew and silver skin removed, finely chopped
1 egg white
ice cubes
2 tablespoons finely chopped chives
125 ml pouring cream
table salt
75 ml white wine vinegar
250 ml water
1 fresh bay leaf
2 sprigs thyme, leaves picked
3 cloves garlic, crushed
80 g veal sweetbreads (order from your butcher)
20 g unsalted butter
sea salt and freshly ground black pepper
2 sheets ready-rolled butter puff pastry, thawed
1 egg yolk, lightly beaten

MUSHROOM DUXELLES

180 ml olive oil
500 g button mushrooms, trimmed and thinly sliced
3 eschalots, finely chopped
2 tablespoons finely chopped thyme
4 cloves garlic, finely chopped
3 tablespoons finely chopped flat-leaf parsley
sea salt and freshly ground black pepper

1. Place the bowl, blade and lid of a food processor in the freezer for 20 minutes. Place the veal in the chilled bowl and process, gradually adding the egg white until combined. Spoon the mixture into a bowl set over a bowl of iced water and add the chives, cream and 1 teaspoon salt. Beat with a wooden spoon until the mixture becomes firm and silky, then cover with plastic film and refrigerate.

2. To make the mushroom duxelles, heat the olive oil in a large heavy-based saucepan over medium heat. Add the mushroom and eschalot and saute for 5 minutes. Add the thyme and garlic, then reduce the heat to low and cook for 2–3 minutes or until the moisture has evaporated. Stir in the parsley, then season to taste with salt and pepper and set aside.

3. Place the vinegar, water, bay leaf, thyme and garlic in a saucepan and bring to the boil. Add the sweetbreads, then reduce the heat to low and simmer for 5 minutes or until just cooked. Drain the sweetbreads, discarding the herbs and garlic, then place in iced water. Using a small sharp knife, gently peel the skin from the sweetbreads and cut each one into three pieces. Melt the butter in a frying pan over medium heat. When the butter starts to foam, add the sweetbreads and saute for 5–6 minutes or until well caramelised. Season with salt and pepper and set aside.

4. Cut out a 20 cm round from one sheet of the pastry and place on a baking tray lined with baking paper. Brush the edge with the beaten egg yolk. Spoon the chilled veal mixture over the base, leaving a 3 cm border. Top with the mushroom duxelles, followed by the veal sweetbreads. Cut a 23 cm round from the other sheet of pastry and place on top of the filling, pressing gently but firmly to remove any air pockets, then seal the edges well. Use a small sharp knife to cut a small hole in the top of the pastry to allow steam to escape. Brush the top with the egg yolk and refrigerate for 1 hour.

5. Preheat the oven to 180°C.

6. Using a small sharp knife, lightly decorate the top of the pastry in a spiral pattern, making sure not to cut all the way through. Bake for 30–35 minutes or until the pastry is puffed and golden. Serve.

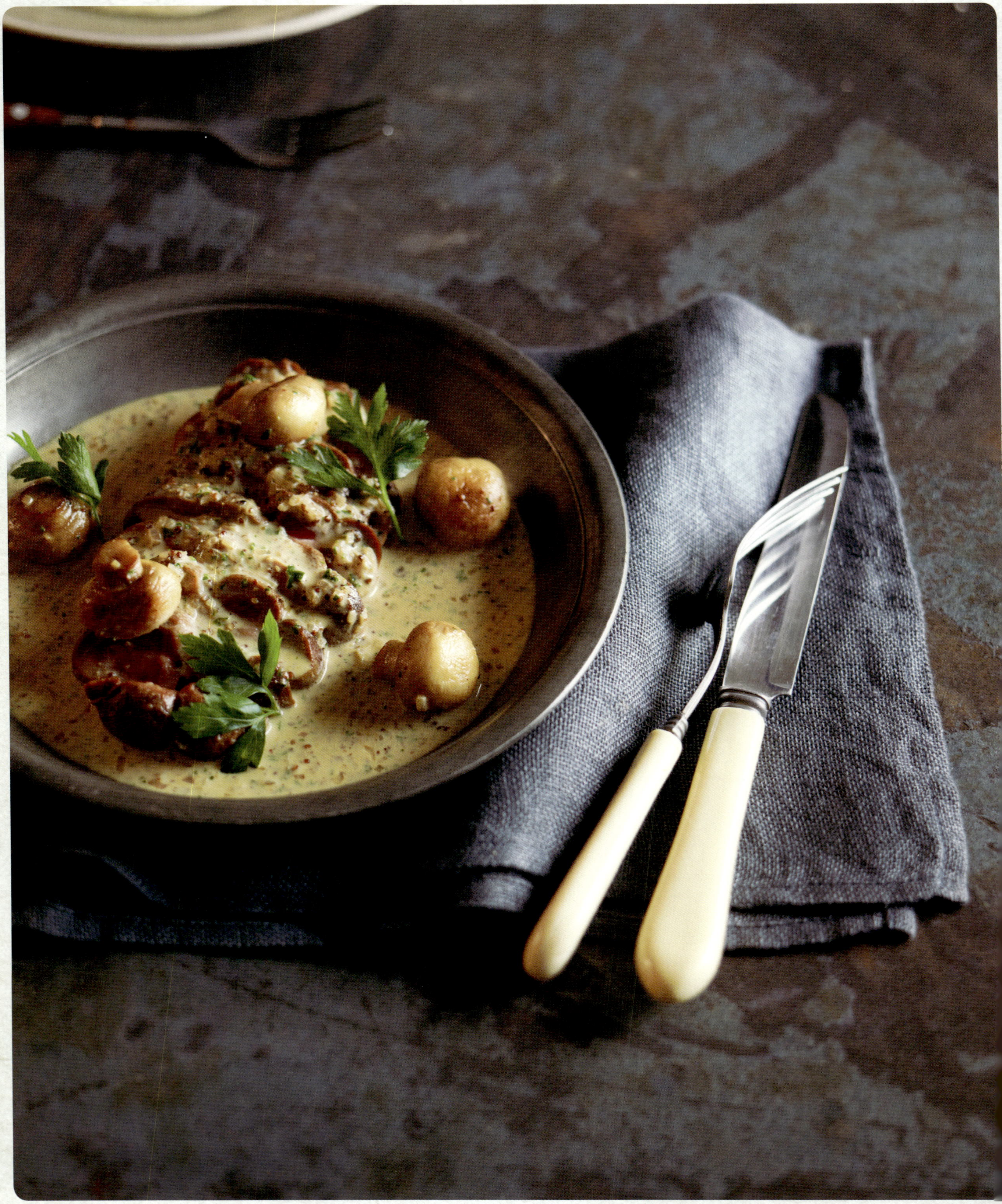

ROGNONS DE VEAU À LA MOUTARDE
VEAL KIDNEYS WITH MUSTARD SAUCE

As one of the first recipes I learnt as an apprentice chef, this dish holds a special place in my heart. The tanginess of the mustard sauce is a perfect counterpoint to the richness of the kidneys. You will need to peel off the outer membrane of the kidneys before you cook them (and be careful not to overcook them, as they dry out very quickly).

SERVES 4

2 tablespoons olive oil
60 g unsalted butter, chopped
2 veal kidneys, cleaned and cut into 4 cm dice
2 eschalots, finely chopped
50 ml brandy
60 g French Dijon mustard (see page 208)
40 g wholegrain Dijon mustard (see page 208)
100 ml dry white wine
200 ml Brown Veal Stock (see page 205)
100 ml pouring cream
250 g button mushrooms, trimmed
2 tablespoons finely chopped flat-leaf parsley
sea salt and freshly ground black pepper
Potato Puree (see page 152) and flat-leaf parsley leaves, to serve

1. Heat 1 tablespoon of the olive oil and 20 g of the butter in a large heavy-based frying pan over medium heat. When the butter starts to foam, add the kidney and cook for 2 minutes on each side or until golden brown. Immediately remove from the pan and set aside. Wipe the pan clean.

2. Melt another 20 g of the butter in the frying pan over medium heat, then add the eschalot and cook for 2–3 minutes or until golden. Add the brandy, then add both mustards and the white wine. Simmer for 2–3 minutes or until reduced by half.

3. Add the veal stock and simmer for 8–10 minutes or until reduced by half. Stir in the cream and continue to simmer for 3–4 minutes or until reduced to a sauce consistency. Set aside and keep warm.

4. Place a saucepan over medium heat and add the remaining oil and butter. When the butter starts to foam, add the mushrooms and saute for 4–5 minutes or until golden brown. Remove the mushrooms with a slotted spoon and drain on paper towel.

5. Stir the kidneys and mushrooms into the sauce and simmer over medium heat for 3–5 minutes or until just cooked. Stir in the chopped parsley and season to taste if necessary. Scatter with parsley leaves and serve with potato puree alongside.

JOUES DE BŒUF BRAISÉS ET PURÉE DE CAROTTE
BRAISED BEEF CHEEKS WITH CARROT PUREE

This carrot puree is based on a French dish called 'Vichy carrots', named after the French town of Vichy. This town was famous for its carbonated water, which was traditionally used in this dish to soften the carrots and accentuate their flavour. For best results, marinate the beef cheeks overnight so that they really take on all the flavours.

SERVES 4

10 juniper berries
6 cloves
1.5 kg beef cheeks, trimmed and halved
1 onion, coarsely chopped
1 carrot, coarsely chopped
1 stick celery, coarsely chopped
3 bay leaves
6 sprigs thyme
2 wide strips orange zest, pith removed
red wine
80 ml olive oil
90 g unsalted butter, chopped
sea salt
750 ml Brown Veal Stock (see page 205)
8 pearl onions, peeled, root ends intact
large pinch caster sugar
freshly ground black pepper
100 g speck (see page 209) or bacon, cut into bite-sized pieces
400 g button mushrooms, trimmed
micro herbs (optional), to serve

CARROT PUREE

2 carrots, thinly sliced
50 g unsalted butter
1 star anise
500 ml water or soda water
pinch sea salt

1. Finely crush the juniper and cloves with a mortar and pestle. Transfer to a large bowl, then add the beef, onion, carrot, celery, bay leaves, thyme and orange zest. Pour over the red wine and stir to combine well. Cover with plastic film and refrigerate overnight.

2. Remove the beef from the marinade and pat dry with paper towel. Strain the marinade through a fine-mesh sieve into a large bowl and set aside. Reserve the vegetables and herbs.

3. Preheat the oven to 180°C.

4. Heat 30 ml of the olive oil and 60 g of the butter in a large enamelled cast-iron casserole over medium–high heat. When the butter starts to foam, cook the meat in batches, seasoning with salt as you go, for 8–10 minutes or until golden all over. Remove from the pan, reduce the heat to low, then add the reserved vegetables and herbs and stir for 6 minutes or until golden. Return the beef to the pan, increase the heat to high, then add the reserved marinade and the stock, scraping the base of the pan to remove any cooked-on bits, and bring to the boil. Transfer to the oven and cook, covered, for 3 hours or until the beef is tender, regularly skimming the surface of any impurities.

5. Place the onions, sugar, remaining butter and a pinch of salt and pepper in a small saucepan. Add water to partially cover the onions, then cover with a lid and cook over medium heat for 10 minutes. Remove the lid and cook for another 5 minutes or until the water has evaporated and the onions are tender and lightly coloured. Set aside. Cook the speck in a large frying pan over medium heat for 6–7 minutes until golden. Set aside. Heat the remaining olive oil in the pan over medium heat, then add the mushrooms and season to taste. Toss for 5–6 minutes or until golden.

6. To make the carrot puree, place all the ingredients in a saucepan and bring to the boil. Simmer for 15 minutes or until the carrot is tender. Discard the star anise, then, using a slotted spoon, transfer the carrot to a blender and blend with enough of the water to form a smooth puree.

7. Serve the beef cheeks, onions, speck and mushrooms with carrot puree, topped with micro herbs, if desired.

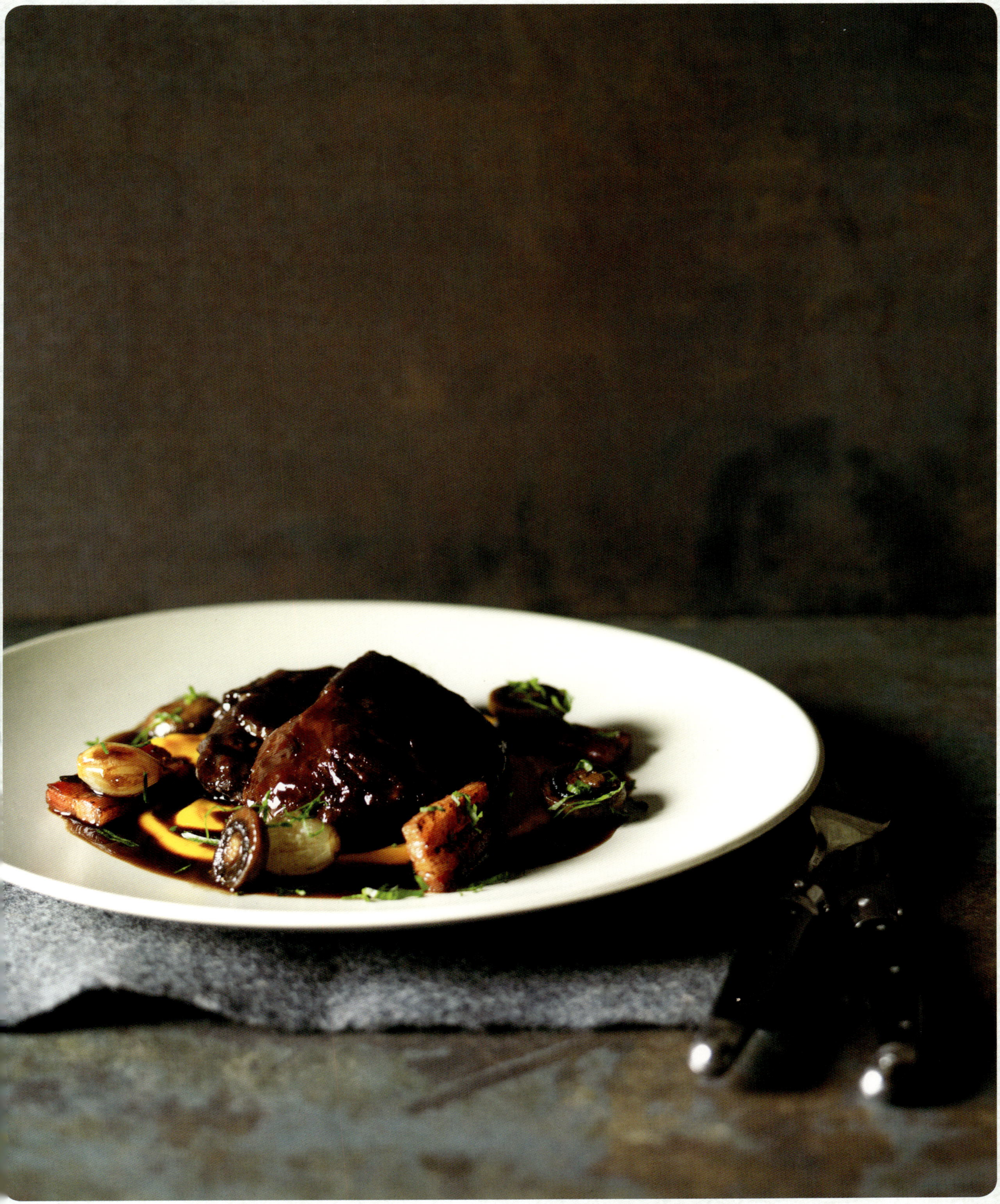

TOURNEDOS DE CHEVREUIL SAUCE AU POIVRE
FILLET OF VENISON WITH PEPPER SAUCE

Inspired by that perennial bistro favourite, pepper steak, here I've used venison and juniper berries – a classic French combination. Venison is a very lean and tender meat that is becoming more popular in Australia, so you should be able to order it from your butcher. You only need to cook it for a short time as the lack of fat means that it dries out when cooked for too long.

SERVES 4

2 tablespoons black peppercorns, crushed
1 teaspoon juniper berries, crushed
2 × 200 g venison fillets
30 ml vegetable oil
30 g unsalted butter
5 eschalots, finely chopped
1 clove garlic, finely chopped
splash of brandy
50 ml red wine
150 ml Brown Veal Stock (see page 205)
150 ml pouring cream
sea salt
roasted carrots (optional) and chervil or small flat-leaf parsley sprigs (optional), to serve

PUMPKIN PUREE

½ butternut pumpkin (about 1 kg), seeded
1 tablespoon olive oil
3 sprigs thyme
1 clove garlic, crushed
sea salt and freshly ground black pepper
125 ml White Chicken Stock (see page 204)
125 ml pouring cream
100 g unsalted butter, chopped

1. Preheat the oven to 160°C.

2. To make the pumpkin puree, place the pumpkin on a baking tray, then drizzle with olive oil, scatter with thyme and garlic and season with salt and pepper. Roast for 45–50 minutes or until the pumpkin is tender. Set aside until cool enough to handle, then scoop out the flesh into the bowl of a food processor and blend until smooth. Place the stock, cream and butter in a small saucepan and bring to the boil. Remove from the heat. With the motor running, slowly add the cream mixture to the puree and process until combined. Season to taste with salt and pepper. Keep warm.

3. Mix together the pepper and juniper on a plate. Roll the venison in the pepper mix until well coated.

4. Place the oil and butter in a large heavy-based frying pan over high heat. When the butter starts to foam, add the venison and cook for 1–2 minutes on each side or until the pepper crust is golden. Remove the venison from the pan and cover loosely with foil to keep warm.

5. Add the eschalot and garlic to the pan and cook gently over low heat for 5–6 minutes or until golden brown. Add the brandy and wine and bring to the boil. Add the stock and simmer for 5–6 minutes or until reduced by half. Stir in the cream and simmer for 5 minutes or until it reaches a sauce consistency. Season to taste with salt.

6. Add the venison to the sauce and gently warm through. Cut the venison into 2 cm thick slices on the diagonal, then serve with the sauce, pumpkin puree and roasted carrots topped with chervil or parsley, if desired.

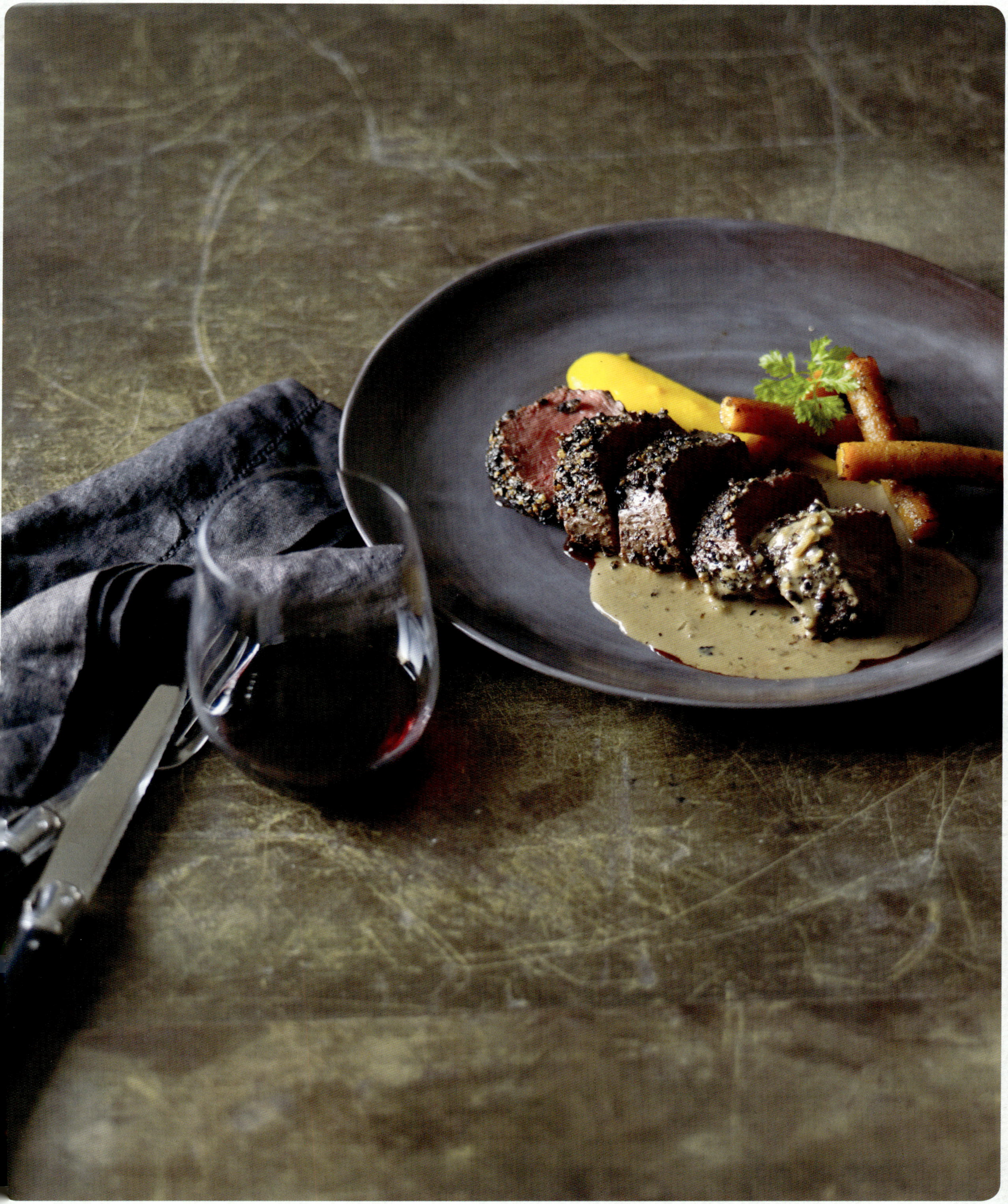

CASSOULET
CASSOULET

~~~~~

Cassoulet takes its name from the *cassole*, the deep round earthenware pot it is cooked in. The dish is said to date back to the siege of Castelnaudry in south-western France during the Hundred Years' War, when it was made to fortify the city's soldiers. Cassoulet has become such an institution in France that it even has an academy, the *Académie Universelle du Cassoulet* (Universal Cassoulet Academy), dedicated to it. For the confit duck legs, use the recipe for confit chicken legs on page 105, adjusting it slightly as suggested in the recipe introduction. I recommend you eat cassoulet the day after you make it so the flavours have time to develop. This is perfect in winter with a good bottle of red.

SERVES 4

2 tablespoons duck fat (see page 105)
1 × 200 g piece speck (see page 209) or bacon, finely chopped, rind reserved for the bouquet garni
1 onion, coarsely chopped
3 cloves garlic, crushed
1 tablespoon tomato paste
2 small tomatoes, coarsely chopped
250 g dried cannellini beans, soaked overnight in cold water, drained
1 bouquet garni (2 sprigs thyme, 1 fresh bay leaf and 1 stick celery, wrapped in the reserved speck rind and tied with kitchen twine)
500 ml White Chicken Stock (see page 204)
1 tablespoon vegetable oil
2 Toulouse sausages
2 confit duck legs
200 g Confit Pork Belly (optional, see page 130)
125 g fresh breadcrumbs
2 tablespoons coarsely chopped thyme

1. Heat the duck fat in a large saucepan over medium heat. Add the speck and onion and cook, stirring, for 5 minutes or until the onion is just translucent. Add the garlic, tomato paste and tomato and cook for a further 5 minutes. Add the drained beans, then stir to mix well. Add the bouquet garni and chicken stock and bring to the boil, skimming the surface of any impurities. Reduce the heat to low and simmer for 45–50 minutes or until the beans are tender.

2. Preheat the oven to 200°C.

3. Meanwhile, heat the oil in a frying pan over high heat, then cook the sausages, turning occasionally, for 6 minutes or until golden brown all over. Remove from the pan and cut in half widthways. Add the sausages, chicken and pork to the beans and cook for a further 10 minutes. Transfer to a 2.5 litre capacity baking dish.

4. Mix the breadcrumbs and thyme in a small bowl and sprinkle over the cassoulet, then transfer to the oven and bake for 10 minutes or until the breadcrumbs are golden brown. Serve.

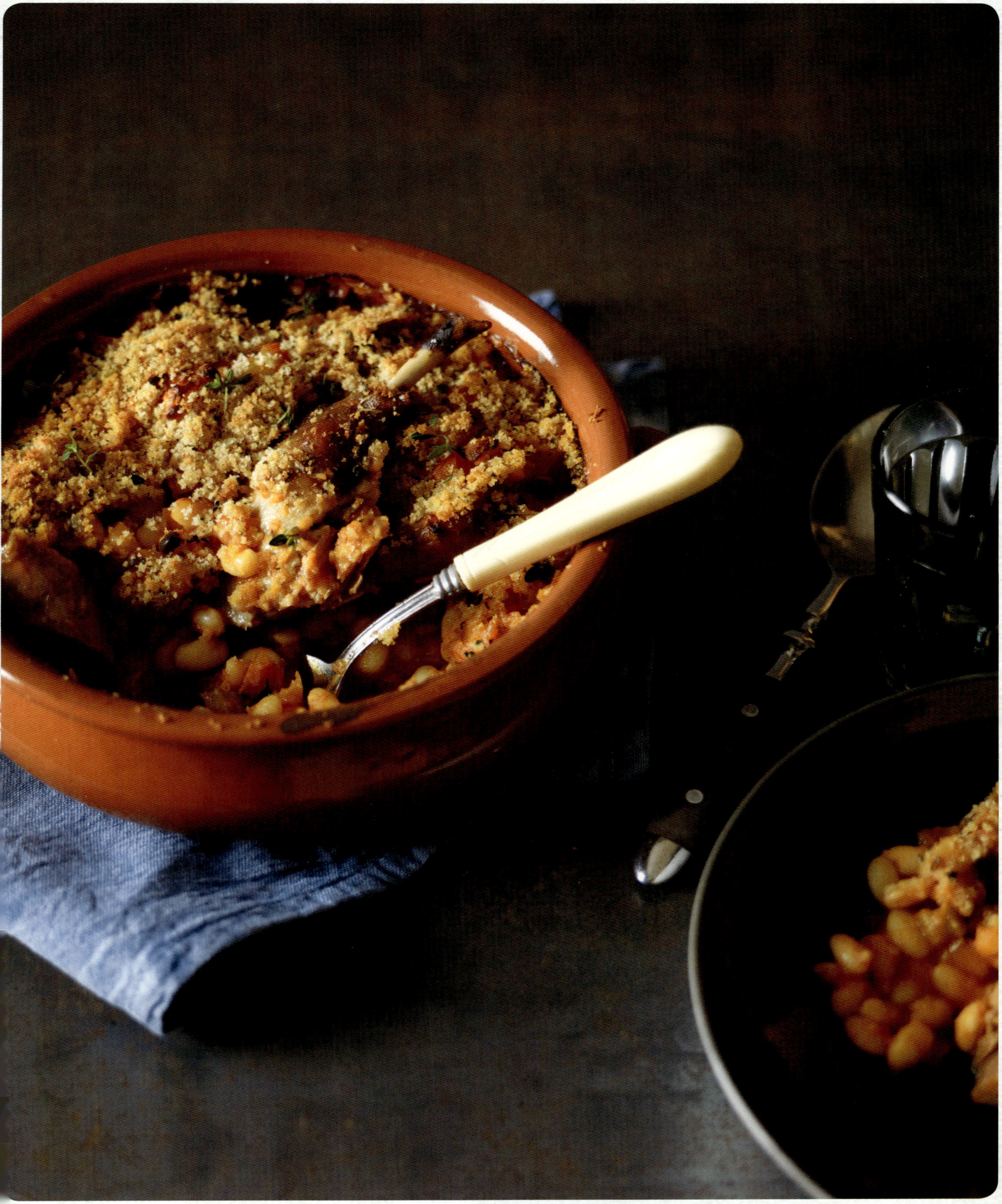

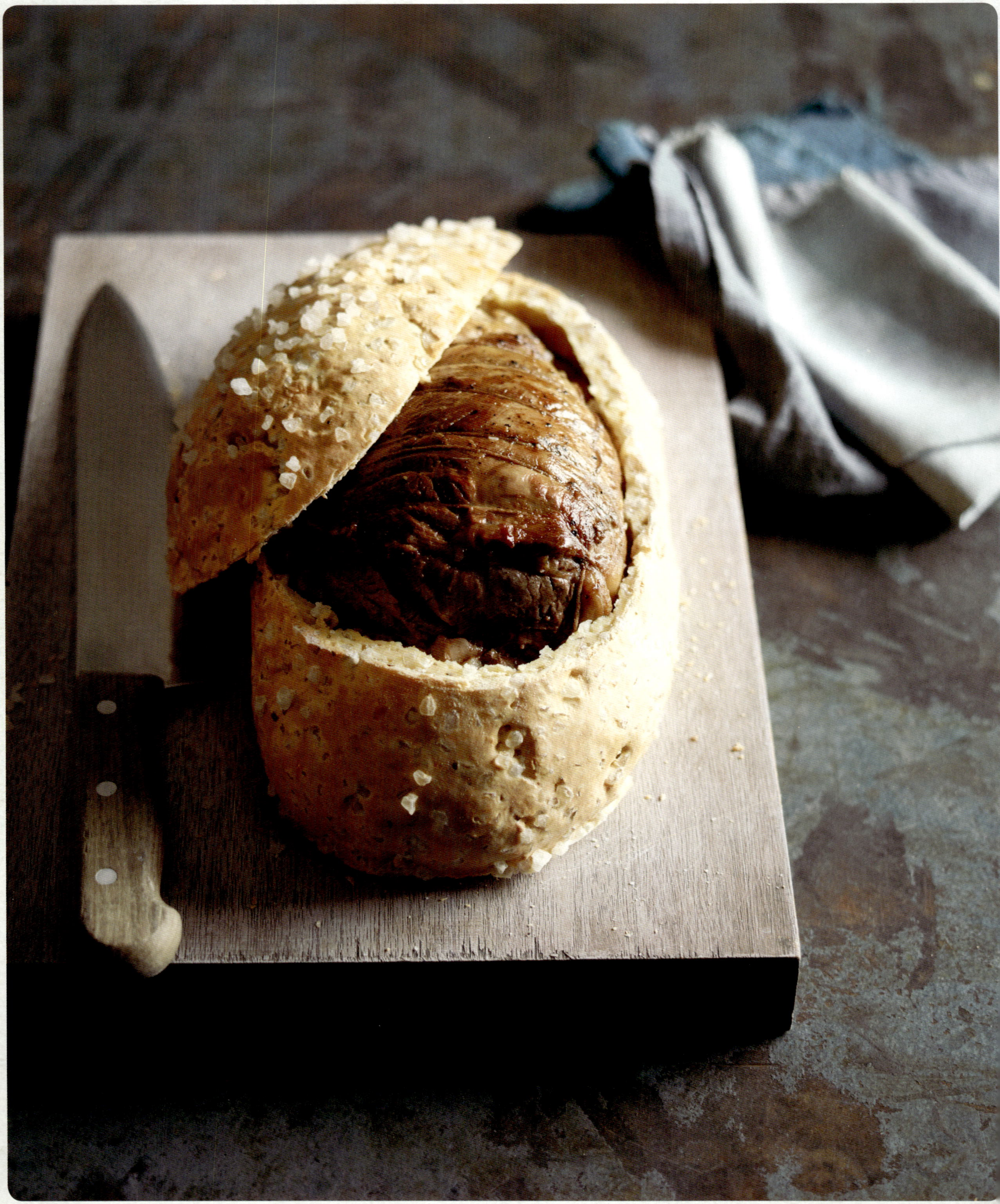

RÔTI D'AGNEAU EN CROÛTE DE SEL
ROAST LAMB SHOULDER IN SALT CRUST

I learnt how to make this dish from my friend Jean-Francois Salet, owner of the fantastic Le Pelican restaurant in Sydney. Cooking in a salt crust is a simple technique that works beautifully with lamb. The salt crust keeps the meat moist and adds flavour. You need to prepare the salt crust the night before, then discard it after cooking.

SERVES 4

1 × 1.2 kg rolled boneless lamb shoulder, tied with kitchen twine (ask your butcher to do this)
freshly ground black pepper
olive oil, for cooking

SALT CRUST
600 g plain flour
400 g rock salt, plus extra to sprinkle
1 teaspoon finely chopped rosemary
350 ml water
1 egg, lightly beaten

1. To make the salt crust, in a large bowl, mix the flour, salt, rosemary and water. Knead the mixture until it forms a dough. Shape the dough into a ball, then wrap in plastic film and set aside at room temperature until needed.

2. Season the lamb with pepper. Heat a splash of olive oil in a large heavy-based frying pan over medium heat. Add the lamb and cook for 3–4 minutes on each side or until golden brown. Set aside to cool.

3. Preheat the oven to 220°C.

4. Place a large piece of baking paper on a work surface, then roll out the dough until 5 mm thick. Place the lamb in the centre of the dough, then fold the sides of the dough over to completely enclose the lamb. Brush well with the beaten egg and sprinkle with extra salt.

5. Roast the lamb for 45–50 minutes, then switch off the oven, open the door and leave the lamb to rest in the oven for 15 minutes; the lamb will be medium–rare. (Or continue to roast until cooked to your liking.)

6. To serve, cut the top off the crust (like removing the lid from a chest), then remove the lamb from the salt crust. Discard the salt crust, then slice the lamb and serve immediately.

SELLE D'AGNEAU RÔTIE ET PANISSE
LAMB SADDLE WITH CHICKPEA PANISSE

This terrific spring dish looks very elegant on the plate. Lamb saddle is not used much in Australia, which is a shame as it is very good. This cooking method rewards you with succulent, flavourful meat.

SERVES 4

1 × 1.5 kg lamb saddle, bone removed (ask your butcher to do this)
sea salt and freshly ground black pepper
12 sage leaves (optional)
80 ml olive oil, plus extra for drizzling
4 cloves garlic, bruised
1 bay leaf
6 sprigs thyme, plus extra (optional), to serve
1 small red capsicum (pepper), seeded and cut into 1 cm dice
1 small yellow capsicum (pepper), seeded and cut into 1 cm dice
1 small eggplant (aubergine), cut into 1 cm dice
1 zucchini (courgette), cut into 1 cm dice

CHICKPEA PANISSE

300 ml water
150 ml olive oil
1 teaspoon finely chopped thyme
sea salt and freshly ground black pepper
100 g chickpea flour (available from health food stores and specialty food stores)

1. To make the chickpea panisse, place 200 ml of the water in a wide saucepan with 50 ml of the olive oil, the thyme and salt and pepper to taste. Bring to the boil over high heat. Remove from the heat. Meanwhile, place the remaining water and chickpea flour in a bowl and whisk until a smooth paste forms. Gradually whisk the hot water mixture into the chickpea paste, then return to the saucepan. Cook over low heat, stirring continuously, for 3 minutes or until the mixture has thickened. Line a 20 cm square cake tin with baking paper, then transfer the chickpea batter to the tin. Cover with baking paper and refrigerate for 1 hour or until the chickpea batter has set.

2. Preheat the oven to 180°C.

3. Place the lamb saddle on a chopping board and cut the meat along the centre, leaving the fat flap intact so that you have two lamb loins on either side, with the flap remaining in the middle. Remove and discard excess fat. Sprinkle the meat with salt and pepper and top with sage leaves (if using). Roll the saddle to enclose, then use ten 8 cm lengths of kitchen twine to tie the lamb at even 5 cm intervals to keep the roll intact. Season all over with salt and pepper.

4. Heat 2 tablespoons of the olive oil in a large heavy-based roasting pan over high heat, then add the lamb and cook for 4 minutes each side until golden all over. Add the garlic, bay leaf and thyme and drizzle generously with olive oil.

5. Roast the lamb for 35–40 minutes for medium–rare or until cooked to your liking. Cover loosely with foil, then leave to rest in a warm place for 10 minutes.

6. Heat another 2 tablespoons of the olive oil in a frying pan over medium heat. Add the capsicum, eggplant and zucchini and cook for 5–6 minutes or until tender, then season well with salt and pepper. Keep warm.

7. Cut the chickpea panisse into eight 10 cm × 5 cm rectangles. Heat the remaining 100 ml olive oil in a heavy-based saucepan over medium heat, then, working in batches, deep-fry the panisse for 3 minutes on each side or until golden. Drain on paper towel. (Leftover panisse can be stored in an airtight container in the fridge for up to 3 days.)

8. Slice the lamb, then divide among plates. Add the chickpea panisse and top with a generous spoonful of the capsicum mixture, then scatter with thyme sprigs (if using) and drizzle with pan juices. Serve.

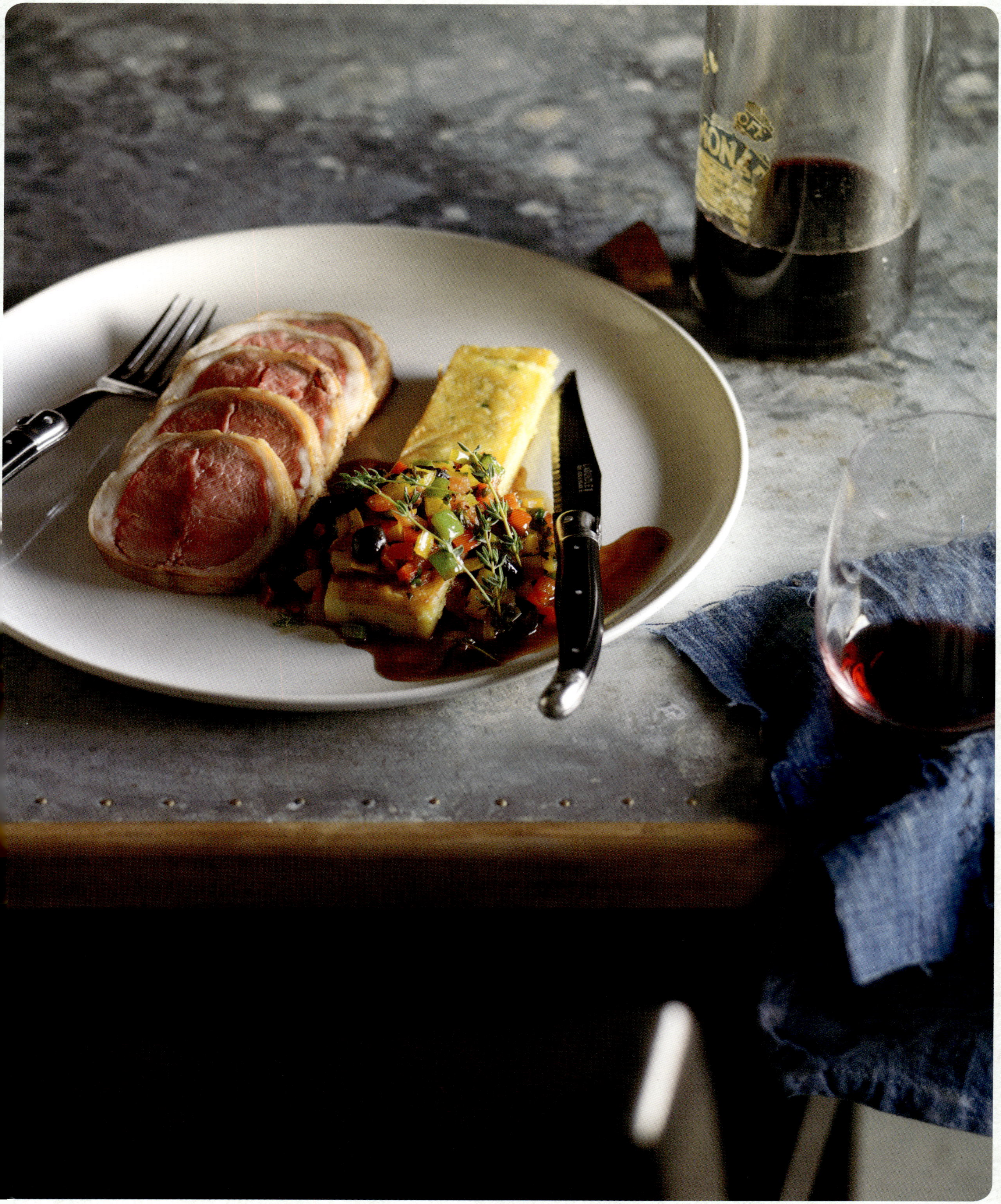

ÉPAULE D'AGNEAU BRAISÉE, PURÉE DE POMMES DE TERRE
BRAISED LAMB SHOULDER WITH POTATO PUREE

When I serve this signature braised lamb dish at L'étoile, I accompany it with a special potato puree made with smoked butter (see page 207). The butter adds an addictive smoky quality to the puree. This recipe needs to be started a day in advance and is perfect for anyone seeking a culinary challenge. The braised lamb is shredded and rolled into small sausage-shapes before being fried and served warm. If you prefer, you can simply serve the lamb after braising, with the potato puree and roasted cherry tomatoes alongside.

SERVES 4

1 tablespoon finely chopped thyme
3 cloves garlic, crushed
5 black peppercorns
½ bay leaf
2 tablespoons olive oil
1 kg lamb shoulder, bone removed (ask your butcher to do this)
500 ml dry white wine
sea salt and freshly ground black pepper
20 g unsalted butter

POTATO PUREE
4 desiree potatoes, peeled, cut in half
250 ml pouring cream
50 g unsalted butter, chopped
sea salt and freshly ground black pepper

1. Preheat the oven to 100°C.

2. Pound the thyme, garlic, peppercorns and bay leaf with 1 tablespoon of the olive oil, in a mortar and pestle, then rub this paste over the inside of the shoulder.

3. Place the lamb in a roasting pan, then add the wine and cover tightly with foil. Roast the lamb for 6 hours or until falling apart. (The lamb can be served now with potato puree, if desired.)

4. Leave the lamb at room temperature until cool enough to handle. Shred the meat with your fingers, then place in a bowl and moisten it with a little of the braising juices. Taste and adjust the seasoning.

5. Lay eight 20 cm sheets of plastic film on a work surface, then place about 180 g of meat in the centre of each piece of plastic film, shaping the meat into a sausage-shape. Roll the plastic film over to enclose the meat well. Tie both ends tightly. Refrigerate the lamb overnight to set.

6. Meanwhile, to make the potato puree, place the potato in a saucepan of lightly salted water and bring to the boil over high heat, then reduce the heat to low and simmer for 25–30 minutes or until tender. Drain well, then return to the pan and shake over low heat to allow any excess moisture to evaporate. Push the potato through a ricer or fine-mesh sieve into a bowl. Bring the cream just to the boil in a small saucepan, then add to the potato along with the butter and season to taste with salt and pepper. Stir to combine well.

7. Preheat the oven to 180°C.

8. Heat the remaining olive oil and the butter in a heavy-based ovenproof frying pan over medium heat. Carefully remove the lamb rolls from the plastic film and fry for 2 minutes on each side or until browned all over. Transfer to the oven for 5–7 minutes or until heated through.

9. Serve the lamb with the potato puree.

ROMSTECK D'AGNEAU AUX FLAGEOLETS
LAMB RUMP WITH SPICED FLAGEOLET BEANS

This dish epitomises the very best of produce that spring has to offer – lamb, broad beans and baby vegetables. Flageolet beans are small green kidney-shaped beans traditionally served with lamb. In fact, lamb and flageolet beans in France is a bit like steak and chips in Australia.

SERVES 4

4 × 400 g lamb rumps, cleaned and trimmed of sinew and excess fat
100 ml olive oil
3 cloves garlic, crushed
5 sprigs thyme
1 bay leaf
sea salt and freshly ground black pepper
500 ml Brown Veal Stock (see page 205)
8 baby (Dutch) carrots, trimmed and peeled
8 baby turnips, peeled
250 g podded broad beans (about 500 g in pods)

SPICED FLAGEOLET BEANS

2 tablespoons olive oil
2 eschalots, finely chopped
½ teaspoon ground cumin
1 × 400 g tin flageolet beans (available from specialty food stores) or cannellini beans, drained and rinsed
sea salt and freshly ground black pepper

1. Place the lamb in a large bowl, then add the olive oil, garlic, thyme and bay leaf and season to taste with salt and pepper. Cover with plastic film and marinate in the fridge for at least 2 hours, or 24 hours if time permits.

2. To make the spiced flageolet beans, heat the olive oil in a large heavy-based saucepan over medium heat. Cook the eschalot for 3–4 minutes or until translucent, then add the cumin and cook for another minute or until fragrant. Add the beans and stir to coat in the eschalot mixture, then cook for 4–5 minutes or until just heated through.

3. Preheat the oven to 180°C.

4. Heat a large heavy-based ovenproof frying pan over high heat. Cook the lamb, skin-side down, for 5–6 minutes or until golden brown. Turn the lamb over, then transfer the pan to the oven and roast the lamb for 10–12 minutes for medium–rare or until cooked to your liking. Transfer to a wire rack over a baking dish and set aside to rest.

5. Place the stock in a saucepan over high heat and bring to the boil. Add the carrots and turnips and cook for 10–12 minutes or until tender. Remove with a slotted spoon to a bowl, then cover and keep warm. Add the broad beans to the pan and cook for 3–4 minutes, then remove with a slotted spoon. Double-peel the broad beans and add to the carrots and turnips. Increase the heat to high and simmer the veal stock for 5–6 minutes or until thickened slightly.

6. Thickly slice the lamb, then serve with the warm vegetables and spiced flageolet beans. Season to taste with salt, then finish with a spoonful of the reduced veal stock.

AUTUMN

MENU

ENTREES

Salade de chèvre chaud
Goat's cheese salad 33

Terrine de canard et confiture de pruneaux
Duck terrine with prune jam 60

Tartes d'aubergine et d'echalote, crème de cêpes
Eggplant tarts with cep cream 28

'Chowder' de Saint-Pierre
John Dory chowder 8

Boudin blanc de volaille aux morilles
Chicken & morel mushroom sausages 59

MAINS

Risotto d'orge perlé aux champignons sauvages
Pearl barley risotto with wild mushrooms 118

Filet de 'kingfish', purée de panais, petits oignons au vinaigre et speck
Kingfish with parsnip puree, pickled onions & speck 82

Thon façon Rossini
Tuna Rossini 84

Côte de bœuf et moelle, sauce bordelaise
Rib-eye of beef with bone marrow & bordelaise sauce 132

Filet mignon de porc aux pommes et sauge
Pork stuffed with apple & sage 128

DESSERTS

Pain perdu et sorbet au yaourt
French toast with yoghurt sorbet 192

Poires rôties au miel, madeleines tièdes
Honey-roasted pears with warm honey madeleines 166

Soufflés au chocolat
Chocolate souffles 165

Fromage au four
Oven-baked white mould cheese 194

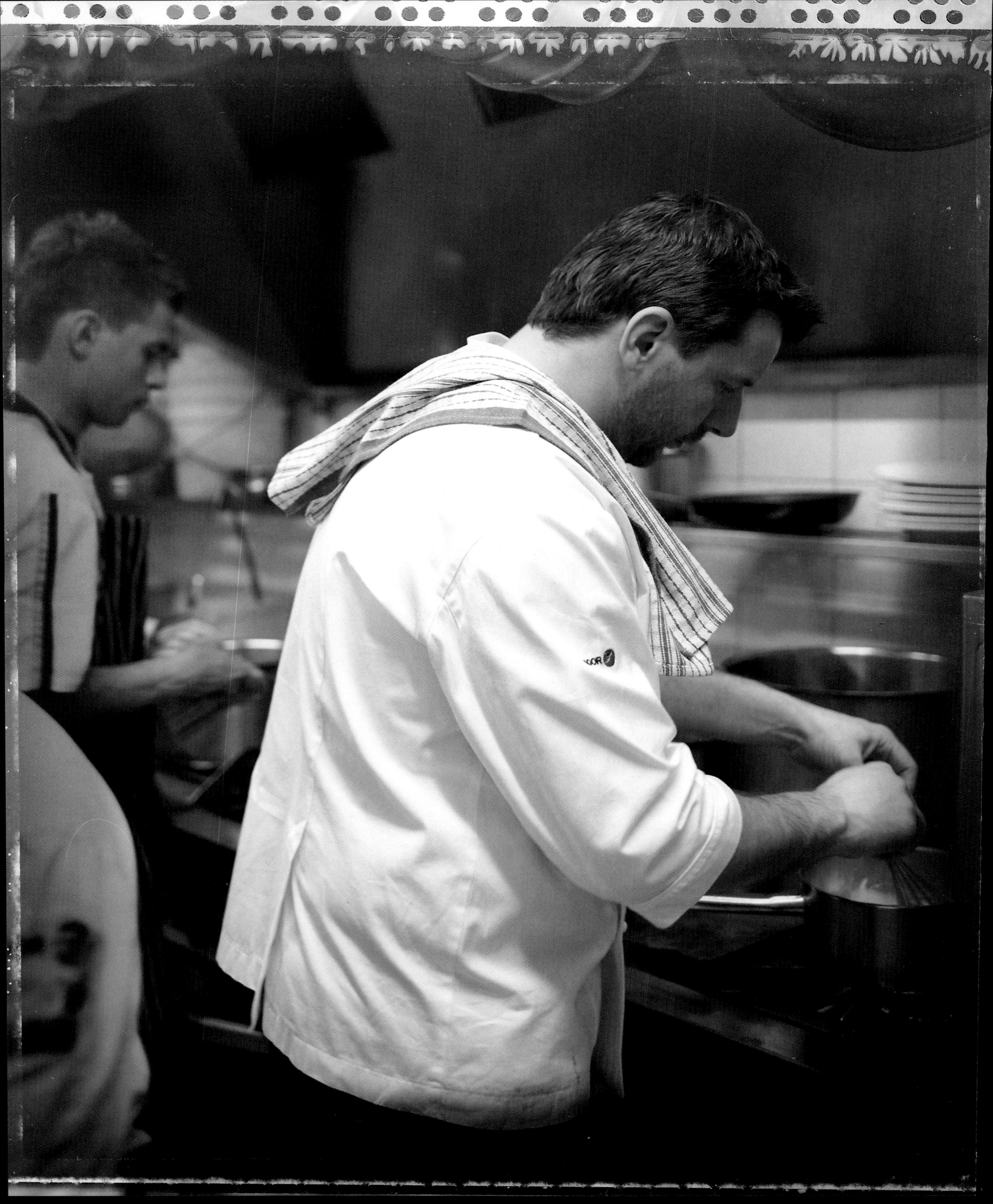

CHEWY WALNUT & CARAMEL TART

HONEY-ROASTED PEARS WITH WARM HONEY MADELEINES

CHILLED NOUGAT SOUFFLES

DESSERTS

PAIN PERDU ET SORBET AU YAOURT

LEMON-CURD CREPE SUZETTE MILLEFEUILLE

APPLE & ALMOND FRANGIPANE TARTS

SOUFFLÉS AU ROQUEFORT

BOMBE ALASKA

PERFECT CHOCOLATE TART

RICE PUDDING WITH LEMON RICOTTA CAKE

TARTE AU CHOCOLAT PARFAITE
PERFECT CHOCOLATE TART

This fabulous tart could not be simpler. Make sure you buy the best-quality chocolate you can afford, and the result will be a melt-in-the-mouth tart with a smooth, silky texture and a lovely shiny top. Perfect as is, or with vanilla ice cream – it's up to you.

SERVES 8

1 quantity Sweet Shortcrust Pastry (see page 207)
500 g dark couverture chocolate (70 % cocoa solids, see page 208), finely chopped
200 ml milk
300 ml pouring cream
3 eggs
vanilla ice cream, to serve

1. Roll out the pastry on a lightly floured work surface until 4 mm thick, then use to line a 23 cm tart tin with a removable base. Use a small sharp knife to trim off excess pastry. Refrigerate for 30 minutes.

2. Preheat the oven to 180°C.

3. Line the pastry shell with baking paper, then fill with pastry weights, dried beans or rice and bake for 15 minutes. Remove the weights and paper and cook for another 5 minutes or until the tart shell is dry.

4. Increase the oven temperature to 250°C.

5. Melt the chocolate in a heatproof bowl over a saucepan of just simmering water, stirring occasionally; take care that the base of the bowl does not touch the water. Place the milk and cream in a small saucepan and bring just to the boil.

6. Break the eggs into a bowl and lightly beat. Pour the milk mixture over the beaten egg, then strain through a fine-mesh sieve into the bowl of melted chocolate. Gently stir the mixture with a wooden spoon until it is smooth and silky.

7. Pour the chocolate mixture into the tart shell and turn the oven off. Place the tart tin in the turned-off oven for 30 minutes or until the filling has cooked enough to set like custard.

8. Serve slices of the tart with vanilla ice cream.

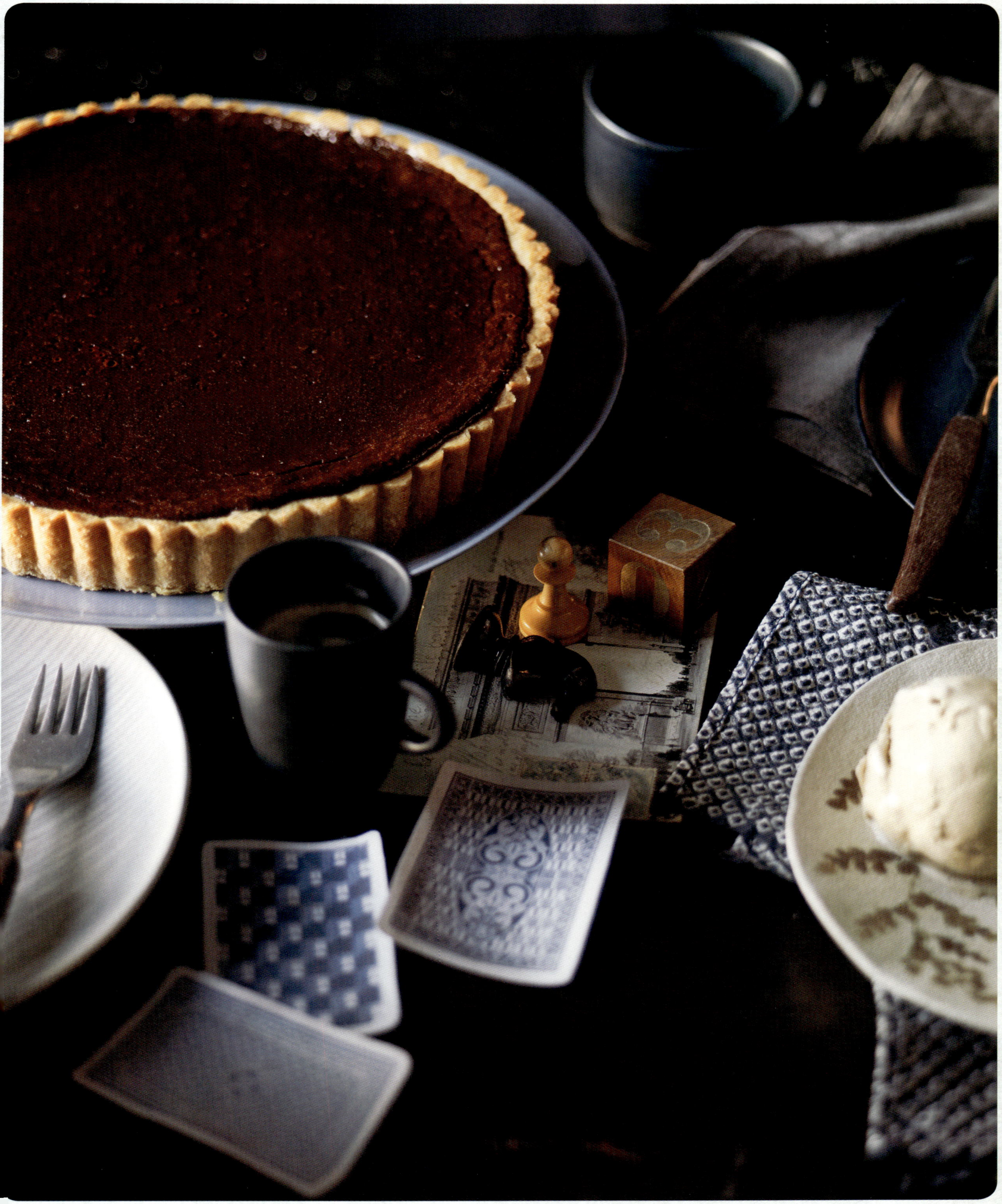

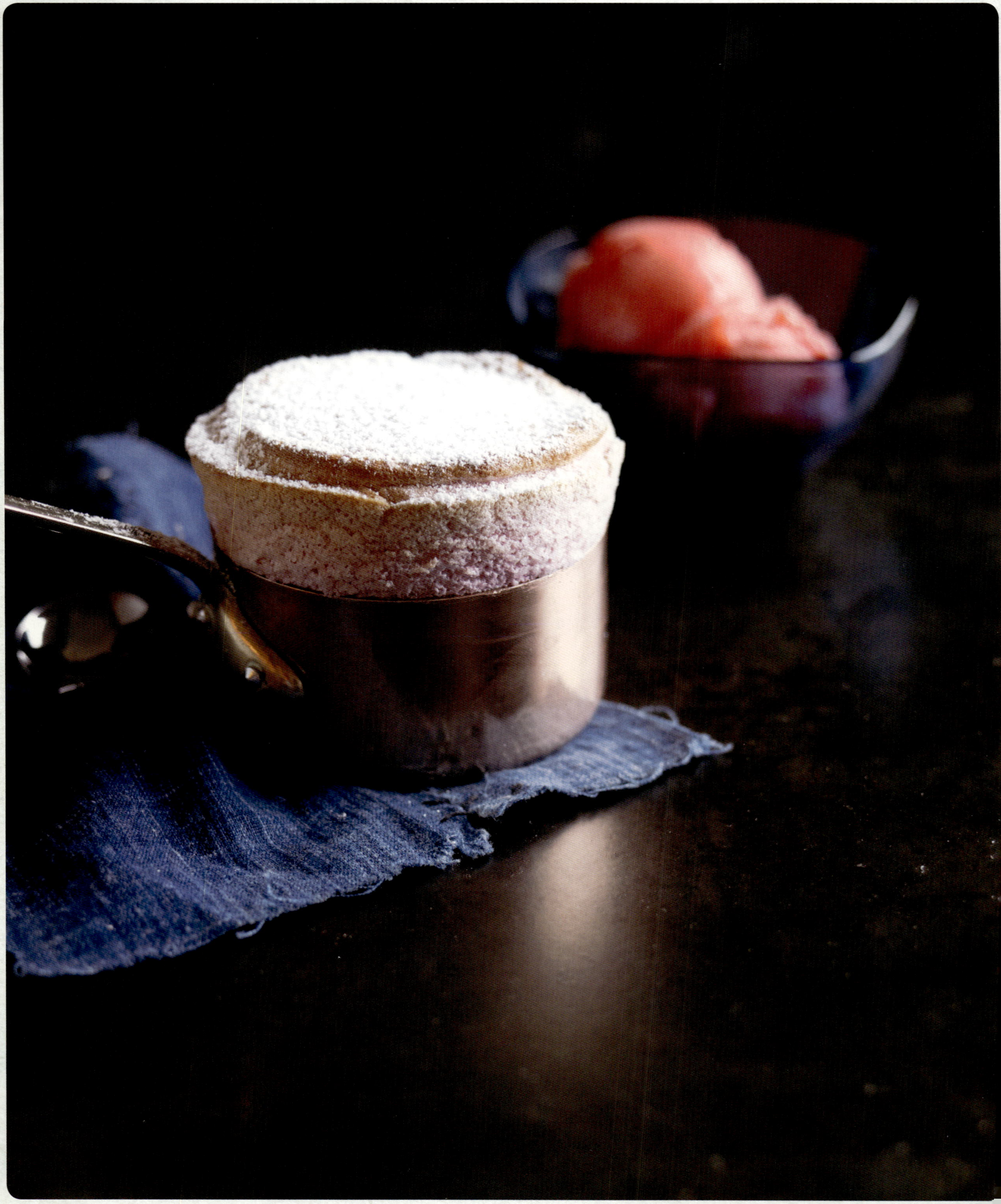

SOUFFLÉS À LA FRAMBOISE
RASPBERRY SOUFFLES

I know that some people are a little apprehensive at the thought of making a souffle, but please give this a try – I promise this recipe is 100 per cent foolproof! Just follow each step carefully and you will be rewarded with perfect, light-as-a-feather souffles, and great acclaim from your guests. You will need a sugar thermometer for this recipe.

SERVES 4

25 g unsalted butter, softened
105 g caster sugar, plus extra for sprinkling
150 g fresh or frozen raspberries
100 ml water
1½ teaspoons cornflour
3 egg whites
icing sugar, for dusting
raspberry sorbet (optional), to serve

1. Brush four 250 ml capacity ramekins (or copper saucepans) with the softened butter, working from the base to the rim and using upward strokes. Sprinkle a little extra caster sugar into each ramekin, tilting and rolling the ramekins to cover evenly with sugar (this helps the souffles to rise).

2. Blend the raspberries in a blender to form a puree, strain through a fine-mesh sieve into a small saucepan and set aside.

3. Place 30 g of the caster sugar and 30 ml of the water in a small saucepan, then bring to the boil and simmer, stirring to dissolve the sugar, until the sugar syrup reaches 118°C on a sugar thermometer.

4. Pour the sugar syrup into the raspberry puree. Combine the cornflour and remaining water in a small bowl, then whisk it into the raspberry mixture. Bring to the boil over medium heat, then simmer for 10 minutes. Set aside to cool.

5. Preheat the oven to 180°C.

6. Place the egg whites in the bowl of an electric mixer, then whisk to form soft peaks. With the motor running, gradually add the remaining caster sugar, whisking well after each addition. Continue to whisk until the mixture is thick and glossy.

7. Fold one-third of the egg white mixture into the raspberry mixture until well combined. Gently fold in the remaining egg white mixture, taking care not to over-mix, as you will knock out the air.

8. Divide the mixture among the ramekins, then level the surface with a palette knife. Pinch the rim of each ramekin between your thumb and index finger, running them around the rim to create a clean edge; the clean rim helps to achieve a perfect rise.

9. Bake the souffles for 12–15 minutes or until they are well risen and slightly wobbly in the centre. Dust with icing sugar and serve immediately with raspberry sorbet, if desired.

TARTE AUX NOIX ET AU CARAMEL MOU
CHEWY WALNUT & CARAMEL TART

This tart was created by my head chef at L'étoile, Troy Spencer. Troy and I have worked together for some time now. We have a really great connection, as we both share the same passion for good food. I have to confess that I don't really have a sweet tooth, but even I find this tart irresistible.

SERVES 8

1 quantity Sweet Shortcrust Pastry (see page 207)
350 g caster sugar
2 tablespoons water
100 ml milk
100 ml double cream
165 g unsalted butter, chopped
4 eggs, lightly whisked
250 g walnuts, coarsely chopped
icing sugar, for dusting
vanilla or rum-and-raisin ice cream, to serve

1. Roll out the pastry on a lightly floured work surface to 4 mm thick, then use to line a 24 cm tart tin with a removable base. Use a small sharp knife to trim off excess pastry. Prick the pastry shell all over with a fork, then refrigerate for 30 minutes.

2. Preheat the oven to 180°C.

3. Place a piece of baking paper over the pastry, then fill with pastry weights, dried beans or rice. Place the tart tin on a baking tray and bake for 10–15 minutes or until the pastry is light golden.

4. Remove the weights and the paper and bake the pastry for another 10 minutes or until the base is dry. Remove from the oven and set aside to cool.

5. Meanwhile, place a heavy-based saucepan over medium heat, add the sugar and water and stir until the sugar has dissolved. Continue to cook for 15–20 minutes or until the sugar is golden; do not stir. Immediately remove the caramel from the heat and set aside.

6. Place the milk and cream in a small saucepan and bring to the boil over high heat. Whisk into the caramel until well combined. Leave to cool for 5 minutes. Gradually add the butter, stirring after adding each piece, until well combined. Whisk in the egg until well combined. Add the walnuts and stir until well combined.

7. Pour the caramel and walnut mixture into the cooled tart shell and bake for 35–40 minutes or until the filling has just set. Remove from the oven and set aside to cool for 20 minutes.

8. Dust the tart heavily with icing sugar, then serve with ice cream to the side.

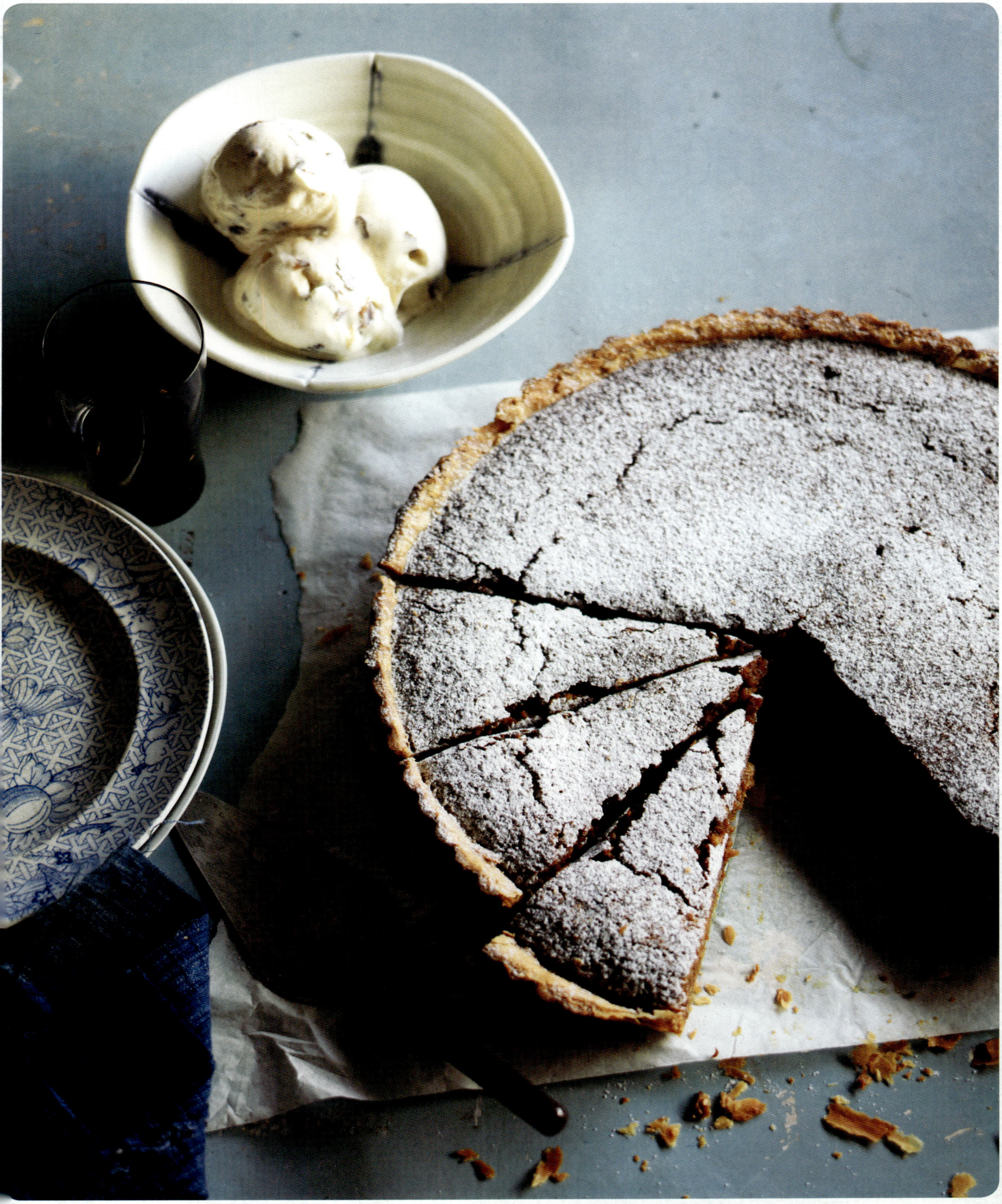

CRÈME BRÛLÉE AU CHOCOLAT
CHOCOLATE CREME BRULEE

On the one hand, it is difficult to improve upon a classic creme brulee. On the other hand, it does taste pretty amazing with an injection of chocolate. But then again, what doesn't? You can easily double this to serve eight if you are cooking for a crowd.

SERVES 4

500 ml pouring cream
80 ml milk
1 × 4 g sheet (or 2 × 2 g sheets) titanium-strength gelatine (see page 208)
5 egg yolks
125 g caster sugar, plus 2 tablespoons extra for sprinkling
75 g dark couverture chocolate (70 % cocoa solids, see page 208), finely chopped

1. Bring the cream and milk to the boil in a heavy-based saucepan over medium heat. Set aside.

2. Place the gelatine in a shallow dish and cover with cold water, then leave for 5 minutes. Drain well, squeezing to remove excess moisture. Set aside.

3. Place the egg yolks and caster sugar in a bowl and whisk until well combined. Gradually whisk in the cream mixture. Transfer to a clean saucepan and cook over medium heat for 3–5 minutes or until the sauce thickens. Stir in the gelatine and chocolate and mix until well combined.

4. Divide the mixture among four 250 ml capacity ovenproof dishes. Cover with plastic film and refrigerate for at least 2–3 hours or until set.

5. Just before serving, sprinkle the surface of each brulee with 2 teaspoons extra sugar, using the back of a teaspoon to spread it evenly. Using a kitchen blowtorch (see page 208) or hot oven grill, melt and caramelise the sugar. The sugar should be dark golden but not burnt. Serve immediately.

SOUFFLÉS AU CHOCOLAT
CHOCOLATE SOUFFLES

This is a little more involved than the recipe for raspberry souffles on page 161, but for a special occasion, you just can't beat it. When you dig your spoon into the finished product, the warm chocolate filling oozes out like molten lava – sublime!

SERVES 4

25 g unsalted butter, softened
Dutch-process cocoa (available from specialty food stores), for dusting
1½ teaspoons cornflour
100 ml milk
100 g dark couverture chocolate (70% cocoa solids, see page 208), finely chopped
1 egg yolk
3 egg whites
75 g caster sugar
chocolate sorbet (optional), to serve

1. Preheat the oven to 180°C.

2. Brush four 125 ml capacity ramekins (mine are 8 cm × 4.5 cm) with the butter in upward strokes, from the base to the rim, then sprinkle a little cocoa into each one. Tilt and roll the ramekins around to line them with an even layer of cocoa (this step is very important for a perfect rise of the souffle). Place on a baking tray.

3. Mix the cornflour with 2 tablespoons of the milk in a bowl, then gradually whisk in the remaining milk until you have a smooth mixture. Transfer to a small saucepan, then slowly bring to the boil over medium heat, stirring continuously. Boil for 30 seconds and remove from the heat. Add the chocolate and whisk until smooth. Add the egg yolk and beat with a wooden spoon until smooth. Transfer to a bowl to cool.

4. Place the egg whites in the bowl of an electric mixer, then whisk until soft peaks form. Gradually add the caster sugar, whisking well after each addition. Once all of the sugar has been added, continue to whisk until thick and glossy.

5. Fold one-third of the egg white mixture into the chocolate mixture and mix well. Gently fold in the remaining egg white mixture; do not over-mix as it will become too hard and stiff.

6. Divide the mixture among the ramekins, then level the surface with a palette knife. Pinch the rim of each ramekin between your thumb and index finger, running them around the rim to create a clean edge; the clean rim helps to achieve a perfect rise.

7. Bake the souffles for 12 minutes or until they are well risen with a slightly wobbly centre. Remove from the oven and dust with extra cocoa.

8. Serve immediately with a scoop of chocolate sorbet alongside, if desired.

POIRES RÔTIES AU MIEL, MADELEINES TIÈDES
HONEY-ROASTED PEARS WITH WARM HONEY MADELEINES

Serve this dessert in winter, when pears are at their juicy best. The honey-scented madeleines are an old favourite. They are apparently named after a peasant girl from the Lorraine region in north-eastern France who first made them sometime in the eighteenth century. While relatively simple to master, there are a few tricks to getting them perfect – rest the batter before you bake them, and only fill the moulds two-thirds full. This recipe makes 25 madeleines.

SERVES 4

250 g caster sugar
750 ml water
1 vanilla pod, seeds scraped
small pinch saffron threads
zest of ½ orange, cut into wide strips, white pith removed
2 corella or honey pears, peeled and cored
200 g honey
vanilla ice cream, to serve

HONEY MADELEINES

2 teaspoons honey
35 g unsalted butter
25 g caster sugar
1 egg
2 vanilla pods, seeds scraped
½ teaspoon orange blossom water
100 g plain flour, sifted, plus extra for dusting
1 teaspoon baking powder, sifted
icing sugar, for dusting

1. To make the madeleines, place the honey and butter in a small saucepan over medium heat for 3–4 minutes or until the butter has melted and combined with the honey. Set aside to cool.

2. Place the sugar, egg, vanilla seeds and orange blossom water in a food processor and process until a smooth paste forms, then add the flour and baking powder and process for 1 minute or until a smooth batter forms. Add the cooled honey mixture and process for another minute. Transfer to a bowl, then cover and leave to rest for 1 hour at room temperature.

3. Lightly grease the moulds of a 25-hole madeleine tray, then lightly dust with extra flour, tapping out any excess. Place 1 teaspoon of the batter in each mould, then refrigerate for 10–15 minutes.

4. Preheat the oven to 180°C.

5. Bake the madeleines for 10 minutes or until light golden. Remove from the oven and leave in the tray for a couple of minutes. Turn onto a wire rack to cool slightly, then dust with icing sugar.

6. Meanwhile, place the sugar, water, vanilla seeds, saffron and orange zest in a saucepan and bring slowly to the boil over low heat, stirring to dissolve the sugar. Add the pears, then cover closely with a round of baking paper (called a cartouche, see page 208) and simmer for 10–12 minutes or until the pears are tender and the tip of a sharp knife can be inserted without resistance. Using a slotted spoon, remove the pears from the syrup and set aside to cool. Cut the pears in half lengthways, removing any remaining core and seeds.

7. Place the honey in a heavy-based frying pan and bring to the boil over medium heat. Working in batches, place two pear halves at a time, cut-side down, in the pan, then reduce the heat to low and cook for 5–6 minutes or until the pears are evenly caramelised. Remove from the heat and place one pear half on each plate.

8. Add as many madeleines to each plate as you like, then place a scoop of ice cream alongside. Serve.

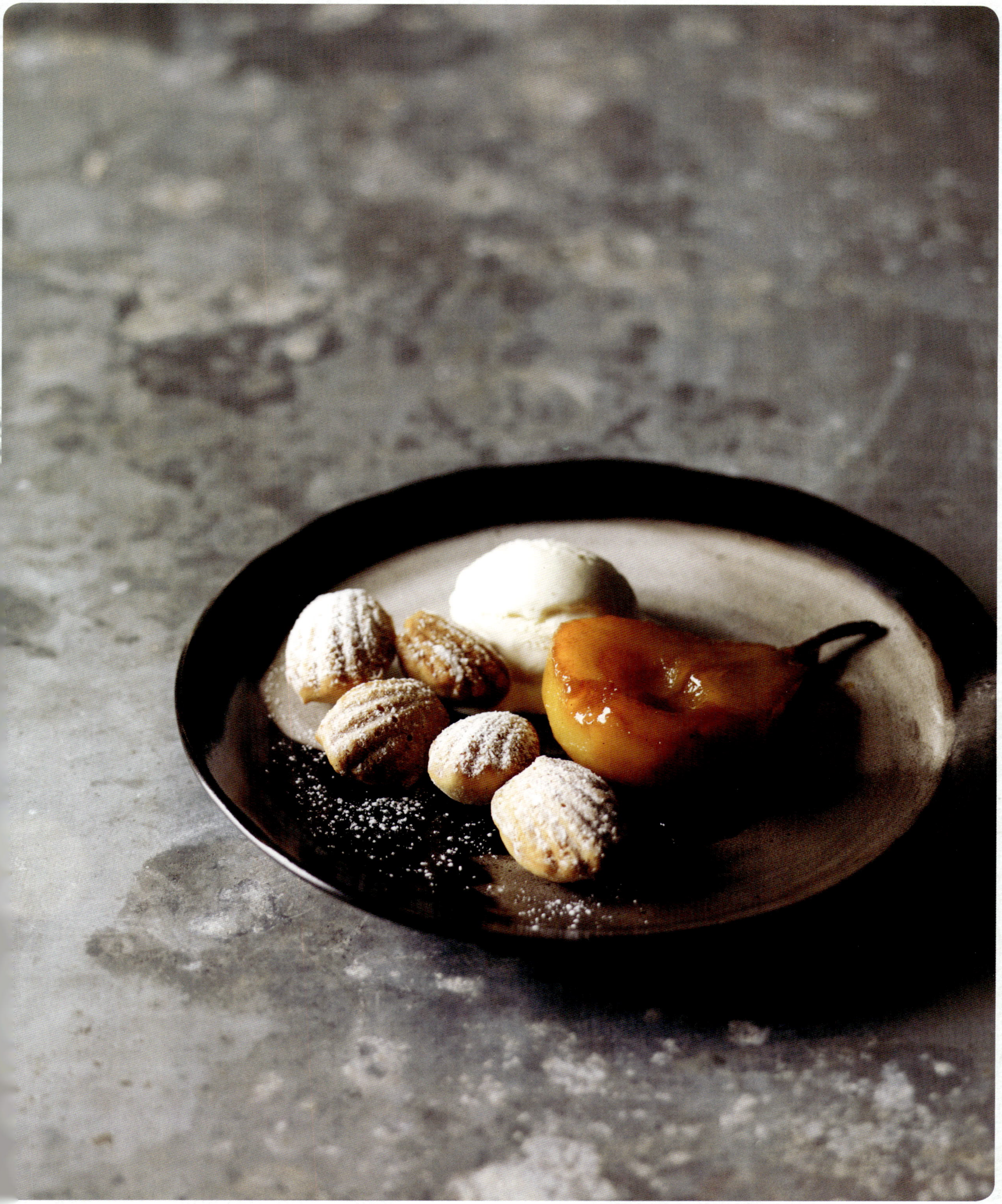

BEIGNETS Á LA CONFITURE DE FRAMBOISE
NAT'S RASPBERRY JAM DONUTS

I'll bet you're asking how a recipe for jam donuts found its way into a French bistro cookbook. The answer is simple — I was given the recipe by a special friend who once turned up at L'étoile demanding I make jam donuts. I didn't have a recipe for them at the time — I do now.

MAKES ABOUT 30

2 teaspoons dry yeast
75 ml water, lukewarm
125 ml milk, lukewarm
75 g caster sugar
50 g unsalted butter
2 eggs, lightly whisked
500 g plain flour, sifted, plus extra for dusting
vegetable oil, for deep-frying
300 g raspberry jam
icing sugar, for dusting

1. Place the yeast, water, milk and ½ teaspoon of the sugar in a large bowl, then leave to stand for 10 minutes or until the mixture becomes foamy. (If it doesn't foam then the yeast is 'dead' and you will need to start with a new batch of yeast.)

2. Melt the butter in a small saucepan over low heat, cool slightly, then add it to the yeast mixture. Add the egg, sifted flour and remaining sugar and stir with a flexible spatula until a sticky dough forms. Turn the dough out onto a lightly floured work surface and knead for 5 minutes or until smooth. Transfer the dough to a lightly greased large bowl, cover with a clean tea towel and set aside in a warm place for 45 minutes or until the dough has doubled in volume.

3. Knead the dough on a lightly floured work surface for a further 5 minutes or until smooth and elastic. Using a rolling pin, roll out the dough until 1 cm thick. Use a 4 cm round cutter to cut out about 30 rounds. Place the rounds at 5 cm intervals on a baking tray lined with baking paper, then cover with a tea towel and stand for 30 minutes or until the dough has doubled in volume.

4. Heat enough oil for deep-frying in a heavy-based saucepan (or deep-fryer) over medium heat until it registers 180°C on a sugar/deep-fry thermometer. Working in batches of about 5 at a time, deep-fry the donuts, turning occasionally, for 2 minutes or until golden brown. Drain on paper towel. Set aside until cool enough to handle.

5. Fill a piping bag fitted with a plain nozzle with the jam, then pipe approximately 1 teaspoon jam into each cooled donut.

6. Dust the donuts generously with icing sugar. Serve. (Store any leftover donuts in an airtight container for up to 3 days.)

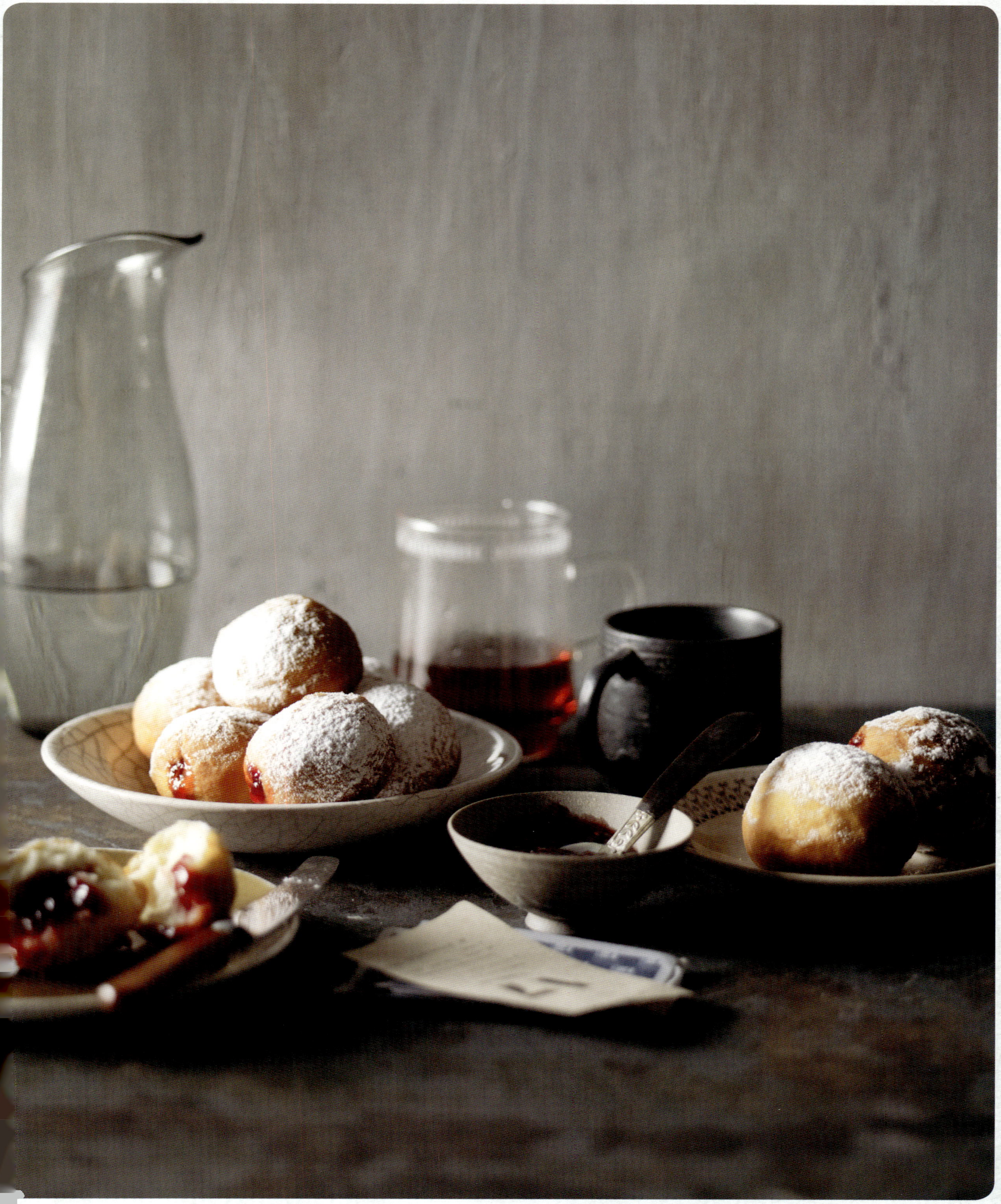

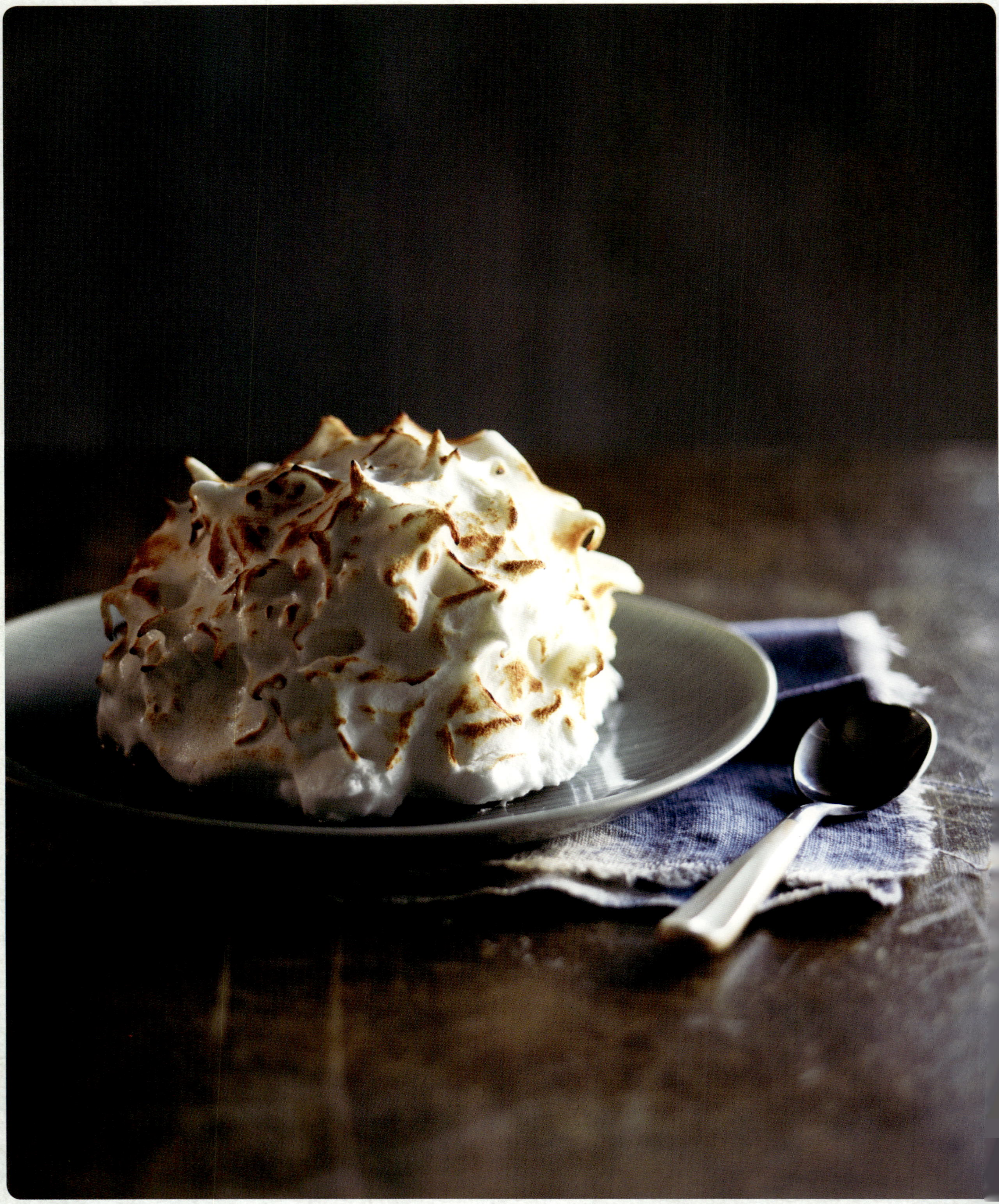

OMELETTE NORVÈGIENNE
BOMBE ALASKA

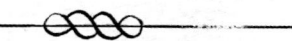

While this culinary triumph had its heyday in the 60s and 70s, it seems to be making a bit of a comeback. I learnt how to cook this as an apprentice, and sometimes make it in the shape of a battleship for extra effect. The air in the sponge and meringue insulates the ice cream to prevent it from melting. This can be whipped up very easily, using bought ice cream and cake, to make a great celebratory dessert for Bastille Day (or any other occasion). Just add candles and sparklers, and set the bombe alight with your favourite alcohol.

SERVES 4

4 egg whites
150 g caster sugar
4 × 8 cm rounds store-bought sponge cake
4 scoops vanilla ice cream
125 ml brandy

1. Preheat the oven to 200°C.

2. Place the egg whites in the bowl of an electric mixer, then whisk to form soft peaks. With the motor running, gradually add the caster sugar and whisk until firm peaks form. Transfer the meringue to a piping bag fitted with a star nozzle and set aside.

3. Place the sponge cake rounds on a baking tray lined with baking paper, then top each one with a scoop of ice cream. Pipe the meringue over the sponge and ice cream, starting from the base of the ice cream and working all the way to the top to cover the ice cream completely. (Alternatively, if you don't have a piping bag, spoon one-quarter of the meringue over each sponge cake round and ice cream scoop.)

4. Bake the bombe Alaskas for 3–5 minutes or until the peaks of the meringue are golden brown. Alternatively, if you have a kitchen blowtorch (see page 208), use this to brown the meringue.

5. Heat a small frying pan over high heat, then add the brandy and bring it to the boil. Carefully pour an even amount of alcohol over each bombe Alaska. Serve immediately.

BLANC-MANGER AUX AMANDES ET SALADE DE FRUIT ROUGE
ALMOND BLANCMANGE WITH BERRY SALAD

Some say blancmange has its origins in medieval Europe, when it was made with chicken, sugar, rice and ground almonds. Others say it comes from the Middle East, where the use of chicken in sweet dishes was quite common. By the seventeenth century, the chicken had been replaced with cream, eggs and gelatine, and it had evolved into the delicious mousse-like dessert we know today. Served here with fresh berries, it's a stunning summer dessert. You will need to make the blancmange a few hours in advance to allow time for it to chill and set.

SERVES 8

2 × 4 g sheets (or 4 × 2 g sheets) titanium-strength gelatine (see page 208)
350 ml pouring cream
70 g caster sugar
100 g natural Greek-style yoghurt
100 g ground almonds
½ teaspoon almond extract
3 egg whites
edible flowers (optional), to serve

BERRY SALAD

375 g raspberries
1 tablespoon caster sugar
1 tablespoon water
2 teaspoons lemon juice
125 g blueberries
125 g strawberries, hulled and halved or quartered, if large

1. Place the gelatine in a shallow bowl, then cover with cold water. Set aside for 5 minutes. Drain well and squeeze out excess liquid.

2. Place 100 ml of the cream, 30 g of the caster sugar, the yoghurt and ground almonds in a bowl and whisk until well combined. Whisk in the gelatine until well combined.

3. Place the remaining cream and the almond extract in a bowl and whisk until soft peaks form. Gradually fold this into the yoghurt mixture until well combined. Using hand-held electric beaters, whisk the egg whites and remaining 40 g caster sugar until soft peaks form. Gradually fold into the yoghurt mixture until well combined.

4. Divide the mixture among eight 250 ml capacity glasses and refrigerate for 2–3 hours or until set.

5. Meanwhile, to make the berry salad, blend 250 g of the raspberries with the caster sugar, water and lemon juice in a blender until a puree forms. Press through a fine-mesh sieve into a bowl. Add the blueberries, strawberries and remaining raspberries and fold until well coated in coulis.

6. Spoon the berry mixture on top of the blancmange, then top with edible flowers, if desired. Serve.

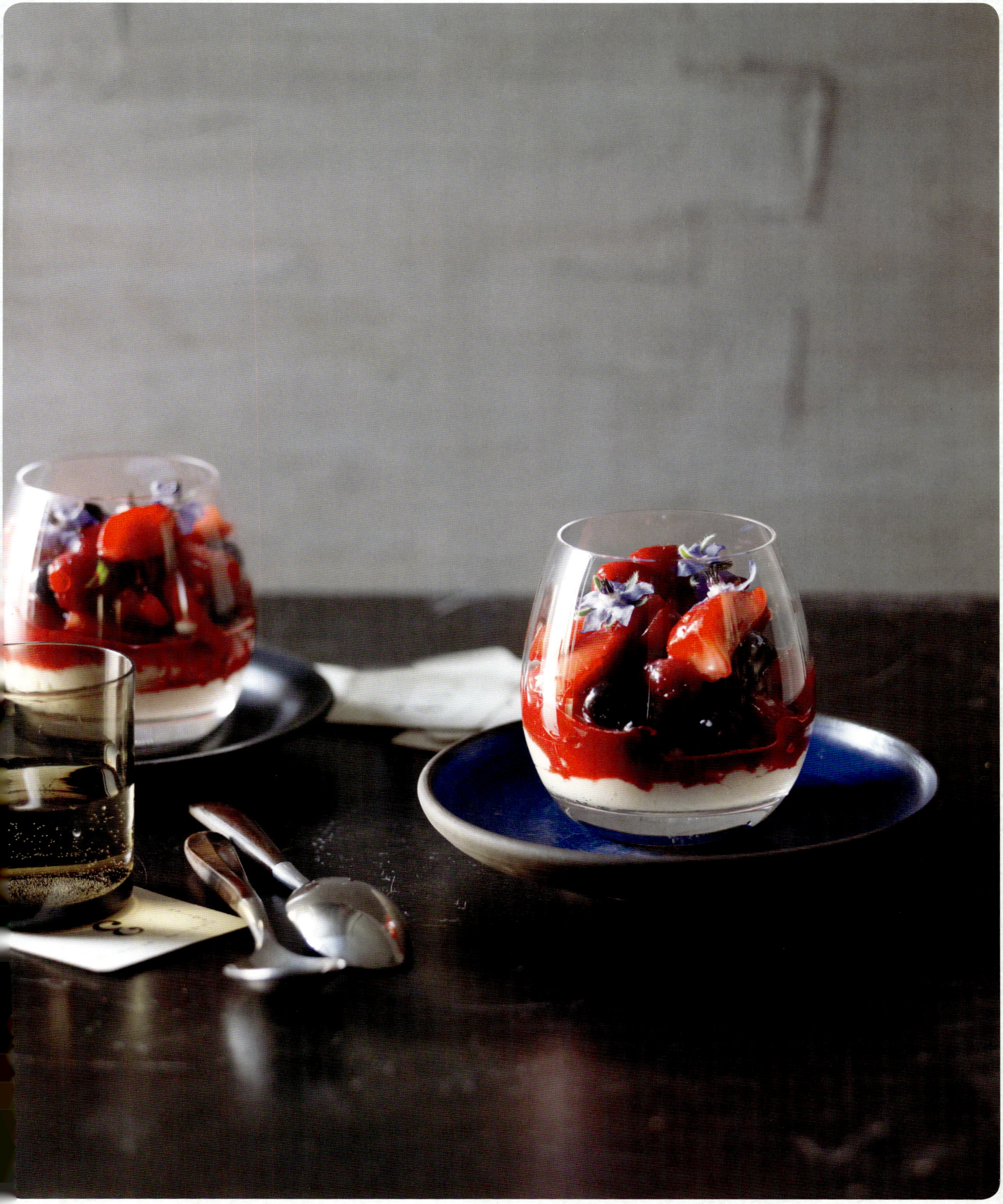

MOUSSE DE FROMAGE BLANC ET COMPOTE DE FRUITS ROUGE
FROMAGE BLANC MOUSSE WITH BERRY COMPOTE

We serve this a lot in summer at my restaurant, often with little biscuits we make called *oreilletes*, but you could use purchased *specuulas* (Dutch windmill biscuits) instead. It's great with a glass of dessert wine. You will need a sugar thermometer for this recipe.

SERVES 6

250 g quark (a fresh white cheese, available from specialty food stores)
1 tablespoon honey
1 tablespoon Muscat
80 g caster sugar
30 ml water
3 eggs, separated
300 ml pouring cream
1 × 4 g sheet (or 2 × 2 g sheets) titanium-strength gelatine (see page 208)
ice cubes

BERRY COMPOTE

50 ml water
80 g caster sugar
150 g fresh or frozen raspberries
80 ml port
100 ml Muscat
30 ml red wine
finely grated zest of ½ orange
½ stick cinnamon
100 g mixed berries, including blueberries, blackberries and strawberries

1. To make the berry compote, place the water and sugar in a saucepan over medium heat and stir until the sugar has dissolved. Increase the heat to high and simmer for 5 minutes or until thickened. Add the raspberries, port, Muscat, red wine, orange zest and cinnamon and bring to the boil, then cook for a further 5 minutes or until thickened slightly. Remove from the heat, then leave to cool to room temperature. Stir through the mixed berries and set aside.

2. Place the quark, honey and Muscat in a food processor and process until smooth. Transfer to a large bowl and set aside.

3. Place the caster sugar and water in a small saucepan and bring to a simmer over medium heat. Simmer until the mixture registers 121°C on a sugar thermometer.

4. Place the egg yolks in the bowl of an electric mixer and whisk until doubled in volume, then, with the motor running, drizzle the sugar syrup into the yolks and continue to mix for 6–8 minutes or until the mixture is fluffy and cool.

5. Whip the cream with hand-held electric beaters until soft peaks form.

6. Soak the gelatine in iced water for 1–2 minutes or until soft. Remove and squeeze out any excess water, then add to the quark mixture, whisking gently to incorporate. Gently fold the egg yolk mixture into the quark mixture until well combined, then gently fold in the whipped cream.

7. Using a clean and dry electric mixer, whisk the egg whites until stiff peaks form, then gently fold into the quark mixture. Divide the mousse among six 500 ml capacity glasses, then refrigerate for 2 hours or until set.

8. Top the mousse with spoonfuls of compote. Serve.

TARTE FINE AUX POMMES
APPLE & ALMOND FRANGIPANE TARTS

You can hold your head high whenever you serve these iconic little tarts. Frangipane is a sweet almond-based filling used in fruit tarts. The name is said to have come from an Italian gentleman called Frangipani who invented an almond scent for gloves. Here I've paired frangipane with apples for a beautiful autumn or winter dessert. The smell of these tarts baking is almost as good as their taste.

SERVES 4

2 sheets ready-rolled butter puff pastry, thawed
plain flour, for dusting
4 granny smith apples, peeled and cored
50 g unsalted butter, melted
vanilla ice cream, to serve

ALMOND FRANGIPANE

85 g caster sugar
110 g ground almonds
110 g unsalted butter, chopped and softened
1 egg, lightly whisked
1/2 teaspoon almond extract (optional)
1 tablespoon plain flour

1. To make the frangipane, place the sugar and almonds in a food processor and process for 2 minutes or until very finely ground. Add the butter and process until combined. Add the egg and almond extract (if using) and process for 1 minute or until smooth. Add the flour and process until combined.

2. Preheat the oven to 180°C.

3. Place the puff pastry on a floured chopping board, then use a 10 cm pastry ring to cut out four pastry rounds. Place the pastry rounds on two baking trays lined with baking paper, then prick all over with a fork.

4. Spoon 2 tablespoons of the frangipane onto each pastry round, then spread it to form an even layer, leaving a 1 cm border. Thinly slice the apples and place on the frangipane in a circular pattern, slightly overlapping, then brush the apple with melted butter.

5. Bake the tarts for 25–30 minutes or until the pastry is golden and the apple starts to caramelise around the edge.

6. Serve the warm tarts with scoops of vanilla ice cream.

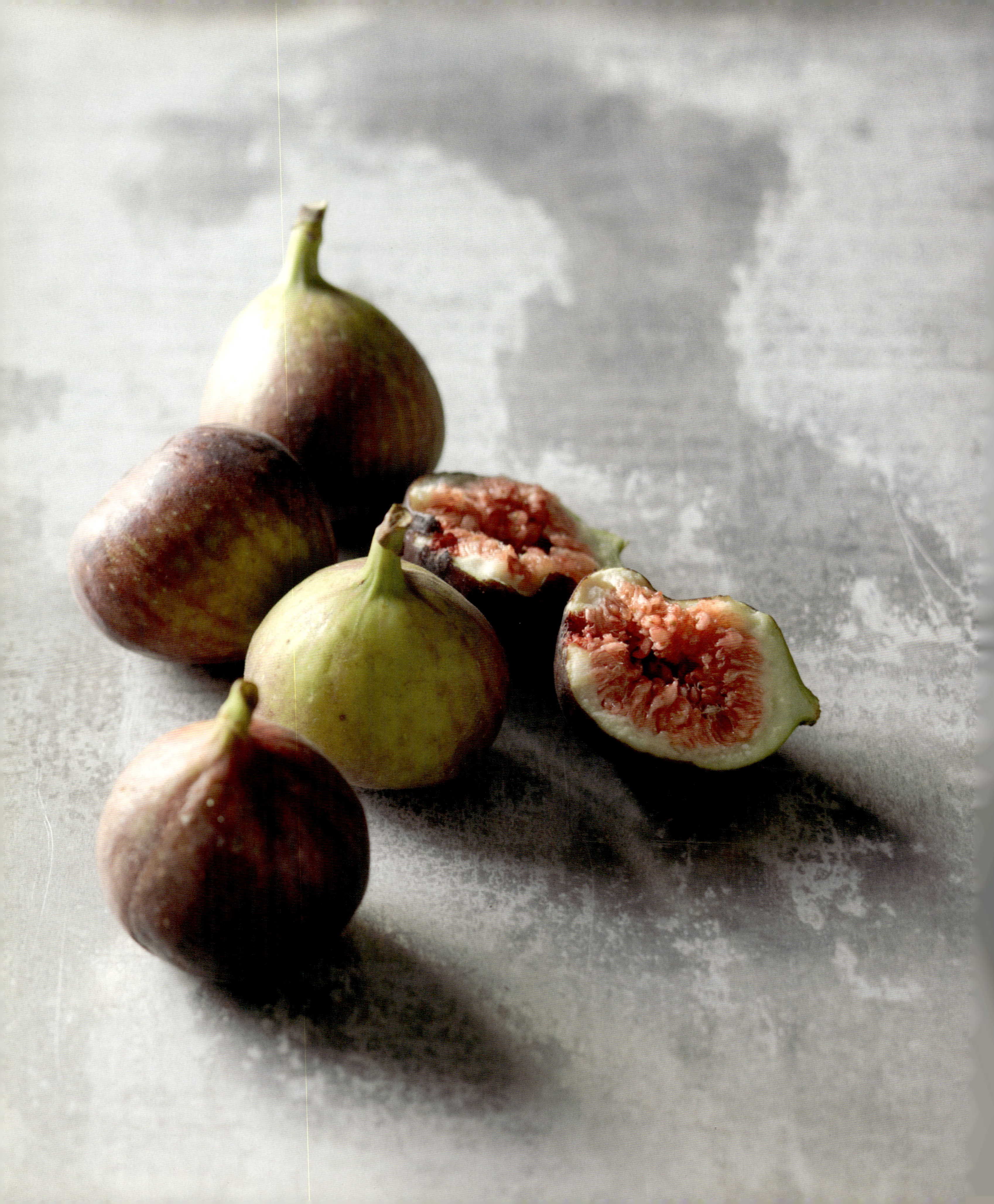

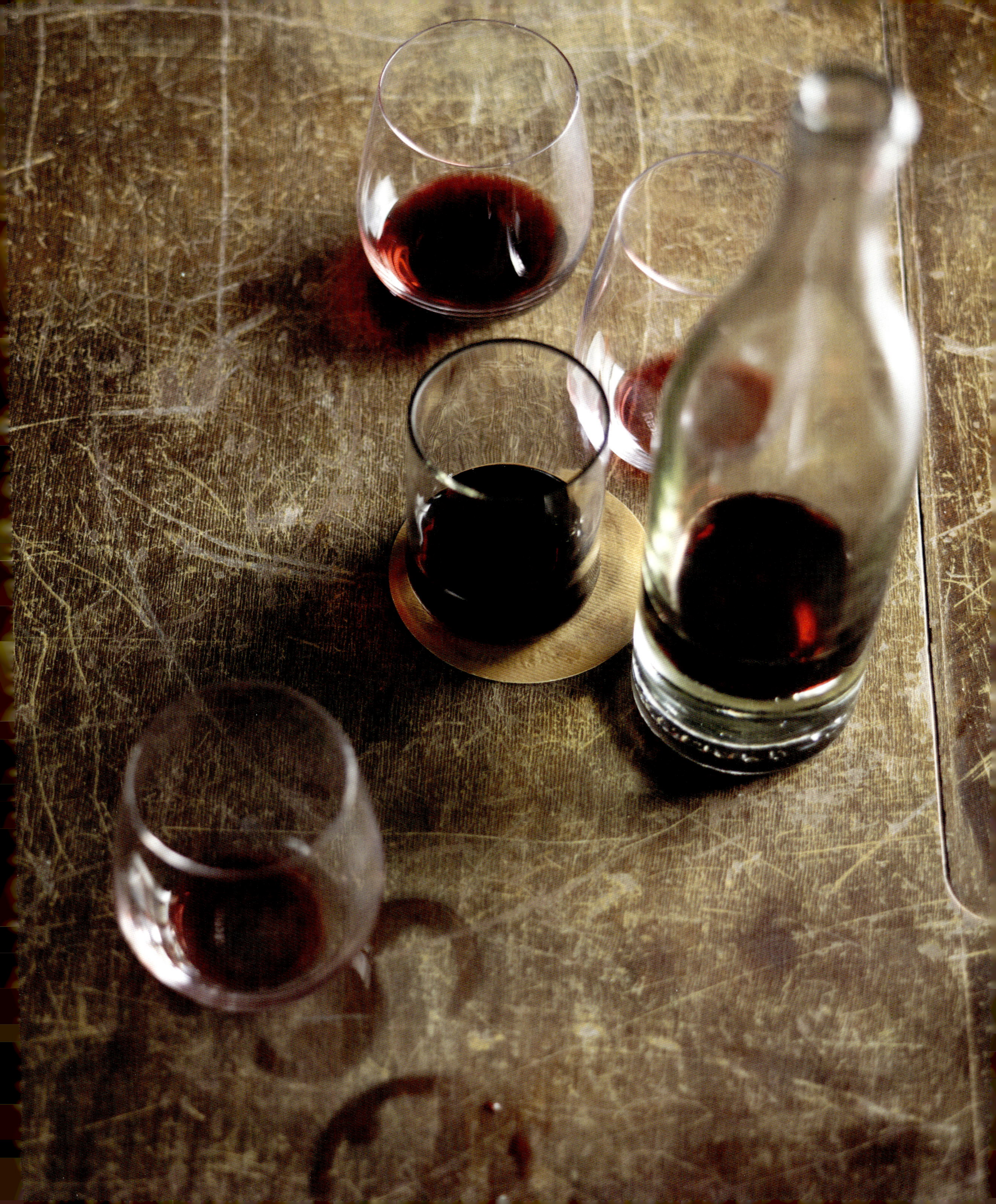

RIZ AU LAIT ET SON GÂTEAU À LA RICOTTA CITRONNÉ
RICE PUDDINGS WITH LEMON RICOTTA CAKE

While you need to invest a little time into making this, it is great for entertaining as it can be made well in advance. *Riz au lait* is the French version of rice pudding, often made with a hint of spice. I have reinvented it by serving it with a dense and moist ricotta and lemon cake.

SERVES 6

150 g arborio rice
850 ml milk
1 vanilla pod, seeds scraped
1 wide strip lemon zest, white pith removed
pinch ground cinnamon
table salt
60 g caster sugar
1 egg yolk
30 g unsalted butter
30 ml Cointreau
vanilla ice cream, to serve

LEMON RICOTTA CAKE
750 g firm fresh ricotta, drained
650 g caster sugar
10 eggs
2 teaspoons baking powder
finely grated zest of 4 lemons
1 teaspoon rosewater

1. Place the rice, milk, vanilla seeds and pod, lemon zest, cinnamon and a pinch of salt in a large saucepan and bring to the boil over medium heat. Cook for 15–20 minutes or until the rice is almost tender. Add the caster sugar, stirring to dissolve, then continue to cook for 10 minutes. Remove from the heat, then add the egg yolk, butter and Cointreau. Divide the rice among six 500 ml capacity serving glasses, then cover with plastic film. Refrigerate for 1 hour or until chilled.

2. Preheat the oven to 180°C. Line a 30 cm × 20 cm baking tin with baking paper.

3. Meanwhile, to make the cake, place the ricotta and caster sugar in the bowl of an electric mixer and beat until well combined. Add the eggs and baking powder and continue to beat until well combined, then add the lemon zest and rosewater and mix to combine. Transfer the batter to the prepared tin and bake for 40 minutes or until set. Leave in the tin to cool to room temperature, then cover with plastic film and refrigerate.

4. Cut the cake into slices, then serve with the rice puddings and a scoop of ice cream to the side.

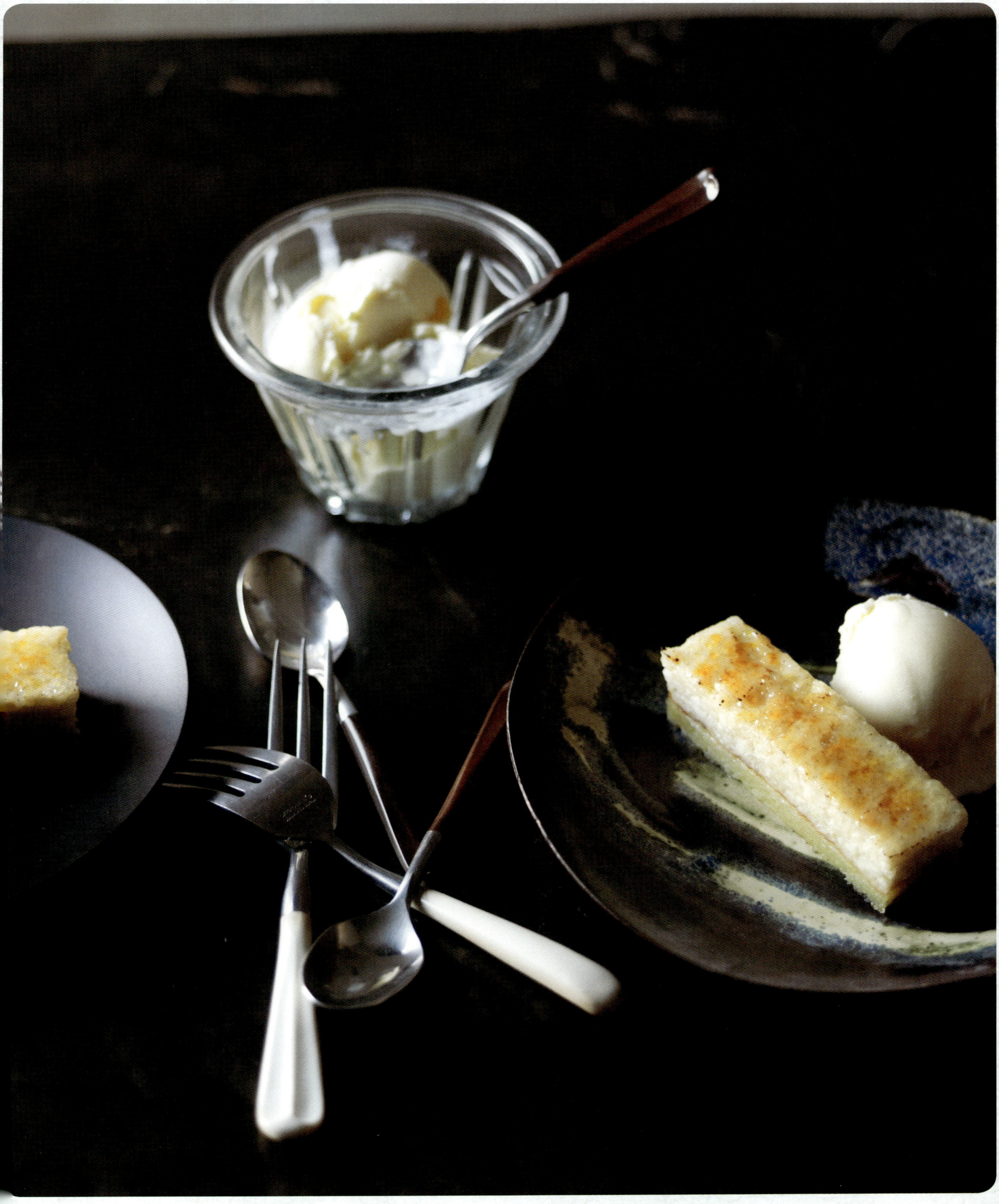

TARTE AU CITRON EN VERRINE
VERRINE OF LEMON 'TART'

Over the past few years it has become very fashionable in France to serve desserts *verrine*-style, meaning layered in a glass. Here is my version of a deconstructed lemon tart. As refreshing as it is delicious, it couldn't be simpler, yet looks special – the perfect summer dessert.

SERVES 4

2 egg whites
table salt
110 g caster sugar

ALMOND SHORTCRUST PASTRY

125 g unsalted butter, chopped and softened
1 egg
90 g icing sugar
30 g ground almonds
250 g plain flour, plus extra for dusting

LEMON CURD

1 × 4 g sheet (or 2 × 2 g sheets) titanium-strength gelatine (see page 208)
250 ml lemon juice, strained
5 eggs
1 egg yolk
375 g caster sugar
50 g custard powder, sifted
150 g unsalted butter, chopped

1. Preheat the oven to 120°C.

2. Line a baking tray with baking paper. Place the egg whites and a pinch of salt in the bowl of an electric mixer and whisk until soft peaks form. Gradually add the caster sugar, whisking until thick and glossy. Spread the meringue evenly over the prepared baking paper-lined baking tray.

3. Reduce the oven temperature to 90°C. Bake the meringue for 1½ hours or until crisp. Turn the oven off and leave the meringue to cool completely in the oven. Break the cooled meringue into small pieces. (Any leftover meringue can be stored in an airtight container for up to 4 days.)

4. Preheat the oven to 180°C.

5. To make the pastry, place the butter, egg, icing sugar and ground almonds in the bowl of an electric mixer and beat until smooth and well combined. Add the flour and continue to beat until the dough just comes together. Place the dough on a lightly floured work surface and roll out to form a 40 cm × 30 cm rectangle. Carefully transfer to a large baking tray lined with baking paper and bake for 15–20 minutes or until golden. Leave to cool completely, then break into large pieces. Set aside.

6. To make the lemon curd, place the gelatine in a small bowl of cold water and leave for 5 minutes or until softened. Place the lemon juice in a small saucepan and bring just to the boil. Place the eggs, egg yolk, sugar and custard powder in a large heatproof bowl, then stir in the lemon juice. Transfer the lemon mixture back to the saucepan, then cook over medium heat for 6–8 minutes or until thickened. Remove from the heat.

7. Drain the gelatine and squeeze out any excess water, then whisk into the lemon mixture until well combined. Leave to cool for 15 minutes or until cooled to room temperature. Stir in the butter and mix until well combined. (Makes 500 ml. Leftovers can be stored in an airtight container in the fridge for up to 3 days.)

8. Half-fill four 250 ml capacity serving glasses with lemon curd, then scatter with meringue and pastry. Serve.

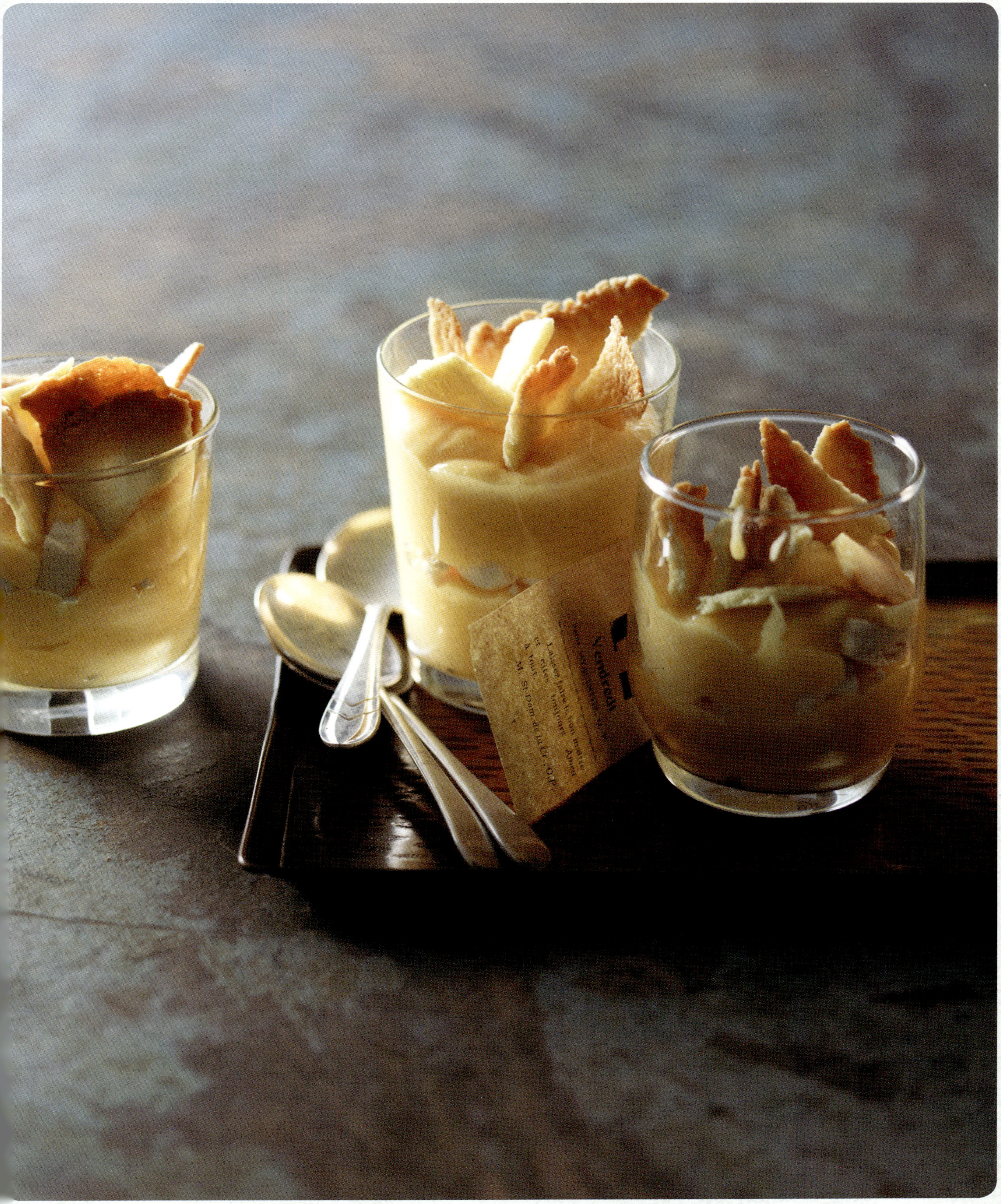
Vendredi

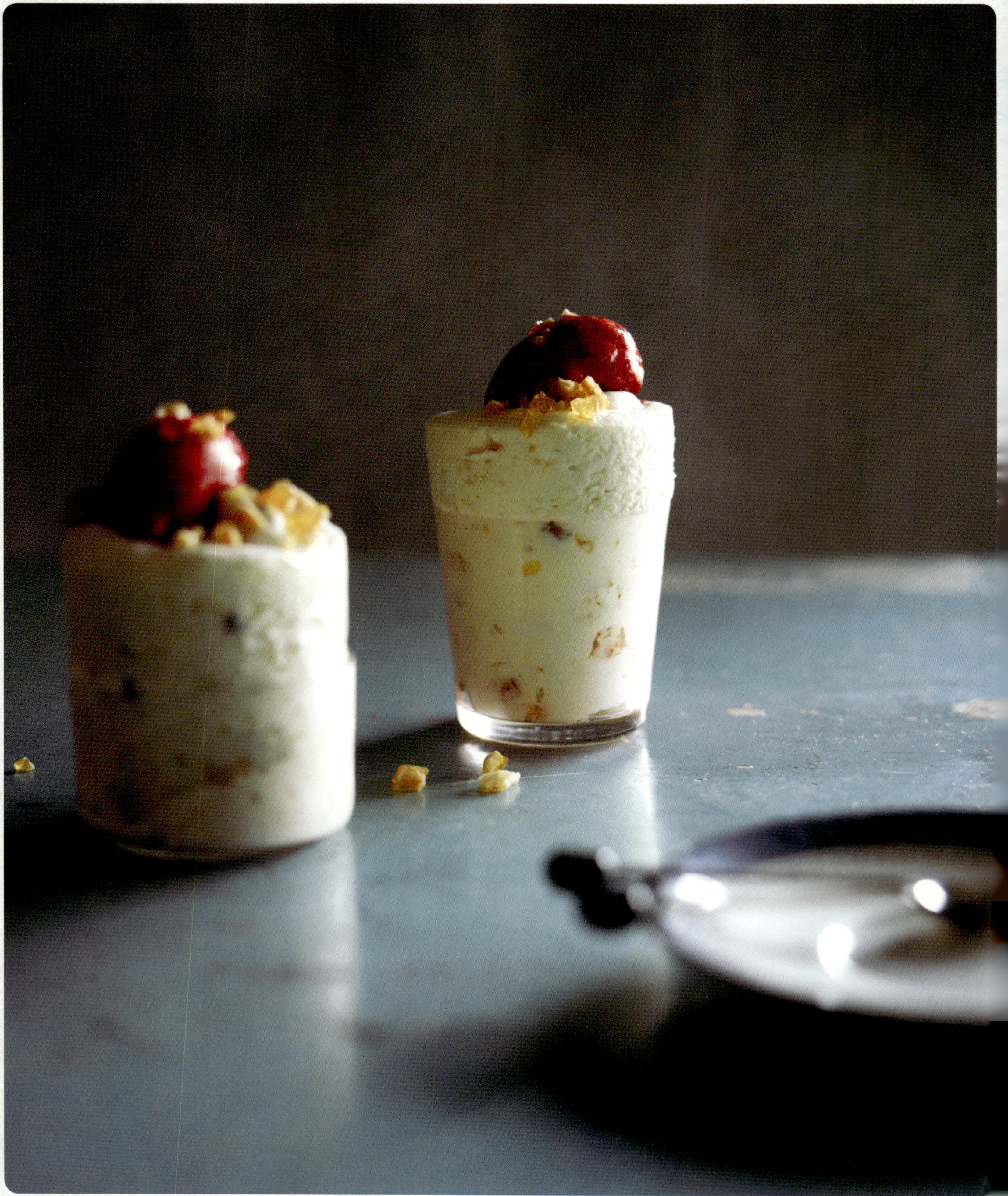

SOUFFLÉS AU NOUGAT GLACÉS
CHILLED NOUGAT SOUFFLES

This fabulous dessert ticks all the boxes. It is dead-easy to make, looks elegant and tastes wonderful. Make these the day before to allow time for them to freeze overnight. At the restaurant, I serve these topped with scoops of cherry sorbet, but you could use your favourite sorbet or plump, ripe cherries, if they are in season, instead.

SERVES 6

30 g unsalted pistachios, chopped
30 g dried apricots, finely chopped
30 g dried cherries, finely chopped
30 g dried mango, finely chopped
375 ml pouring cream
5 egg whites
100 g caster sugar
cherry or raspberry sorbet (optional), to serve

ALMOND PRALINE

125 g caster sugar
2 tablespoons water
75 g slivered almonds

1. Place a strip of baking paper inside six 125 ml capacity ramekins or glasses, ensuring the paper sits 5 cm above the top of the ramekins or glasses.

2. To make the praline, place the caster sugar and water in a saucepan over medium heat and cook, stirring, for 5 minutes or until the sugar has dissolved. Increase the heat to high and bring to the boil, then continue to cook for 5–7 minutes or until golden. Remove from the heat and stir in the almonds. Pour onto a baking tray lined with baking paper and leave to cool and set.

3. Break the praline into large chunks and place in the bowl of a food processor and process until roughly chopped. Transfer three-quarters of the praline to a bowl with the pistachios, apricots, cherries and mango. Set the remaining praline aside.

4. Place the cream in a large bowl and, using hand-held electric beaters, whisk until soft peaks form.

5. Using an electric mixer, whisk the egg whites, gradually adding the caster sugar and continuing to whisk until soft peaks form. Gently fold the cream into the egg whites until well combined. Gently fold in the praline and fruit mixture. Spoon the mixture evenly into the ramekins or glasses to reach the top of the baking paper. Place on a baking tray and freeze for 2–3 hours or until set (overnight is best, if time permits).

6. Carefully remove the baking paper. Serve the chilled souffles with your favourite sorbet, scattered with the reserved praline.

CRÊPE SUZETTE CITRONNÉE EN MILLEFEUILLE
LEMON-CURD CREPE SUZETTE MILLEFEUILLE

Millefeuille is French for 'a thousand leaves' and usually refers to a dessert made with layers of puff pastry. Here I have simply layered crepes with a luscious lemon curd to create an impressive dessert that is much easier than making your own puff pastry. Interestingly, when I tried to create this as a twist on crepe Suzette by using orange curd instead of lemon, it wasn't nearly as good – there is something about the tartness of the lemon paired with the sweetness of the crepes that really works. I added a couple of confit orange slices to the side when this was photographed as a nod to the traditional use of orange; however, this is optional.

SERVES 6

2 eggs
30 g caster sugar
360 ml milk
250 g plain flour
80 g unsalted butter
table salt
1 quantity Lemon Curd (see page 180)

1. Whisk the eggs and sugar together in a large bowl, then add the milk. Sift the flour into the egg mixture, whisking continuously until the batter is the consistency of thick cream.

2. Melt the butter in a small saucepan, then add 1 tablespoon to the crepe batter, along with a pinch of salt.

3. Heat a 20 cm non-stick frying pan over medium heat, then add 1 teaspoon of the melted butter to coat the base of the pan. Add a ladleful (about 50 ml) of crepe batter, turning the pan to coat the base completely. Cook the batter for 1 minute or until you see the edge of the crepe beginning to crisp and loosen from the side, and the base of the crepe is golden. Turn over and cook for another 15–20 seconds. Transfer to a plate and keep warm. Repeat with the remaining melted butter and crepe batter, stacking the crepes on top of each other as you go. (Makes 12 crepes.)

4. Place 1 crepe on a serving platter. Spoon 2 tablespoons of the lemon curd onto the crepe and spread over the crepe, leaving a 1 cm border at the edge. Top with another crepe and repeat with another 2 tablespoons of the lemon curd. Repeat with the remaining crepes and lemon curd, finishing with a crepe.

5. Cut the crepe stack into slices and serve.

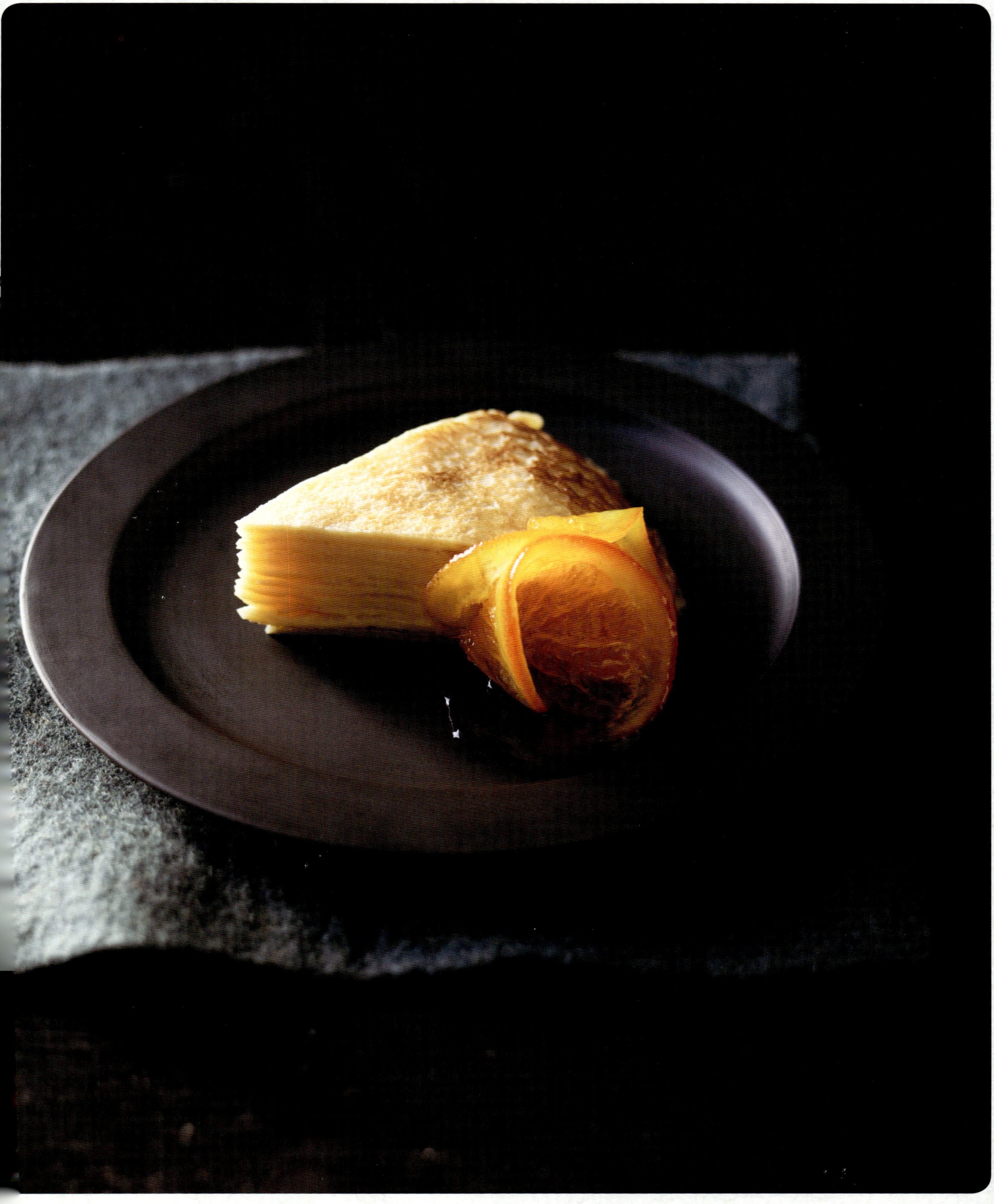

MOUSSE AU CHOCOLAT BLANC ET TUILE DE CHOCOLAT AMER
WHITE CHOCOLATE MOUSSE WITH DARK CHOCOLATE TUILES

If you love white chocolate, then this mousse is for you. It is one of my favourite summer desserts. Technically, white chocolate is not chocolate at all, as it doesn't contain cocoa solids. Make sure you buy the best-quality white chocolate, one that contains cocoa butter not vegetable fat. You need to make the mousse at least a couple of hours in advance to allow it time to set (even better to start it the day before, if you have time). If you decide to make the tuiles, you will require a sugar thermometer.

SERVES 6

1 × 4 g sheet (or 2 × 2 g sheets) titanium-strength gelatine (see page 208)
400 ml pouring cream
1 vanilla pod, seeds scraped
150 g white chocolate, finely chopped

DARK CHOCOLATE TUILES (OPTIONAL)
100 g caster sugar
100 g liquid glucose (see page 208)
75 ml water
110 g dark couverture chocolate (70% cocoa solids, see page 208), finely chopped

1. Place the gelatine in a shallow bowl and cover with cold water. Set aside for 5 minutes. Drain and squeeze out excess liquid.

2. Place the cream and vanilla seeds in a small saucepan and bring just to the boil. Add the gelatine and whisk until well combined.

3. Place the white chocolate in a heatproof bowl. Strain the cream mixture into the bowl of chocolate and whisk until smooth. Cover with plastic film and refrigerate for at least 2–3 hours.

4. Meanwhile, if making the chocolate tuiles, place the caster sugar, glucose and water in a saucepan and simmer until it reaches 160°C on a sugar thermometer, stirring to dissolve the sugar. Remove from the heat, then whisk in the chocolate until smooth. Leave to cool completely.

5. Preheat the oven to 180°C.

6. Coarsely chop the chocolate mixture and place in a food processor, then process until finely chopped. Line 2 baking trays with baking paper and sprinkle with the chopped chocolate. Bake for 8 minutes or until melted. Set aside to cool, then break into desired shapes.

7. Just before serving, using hand-held electric beaters, whisk the white chocolate mousse until light and fluffy. Place a large spoonful (or quenelle, see page 209) on each plate, then top with a tuile, if desired, and serve.

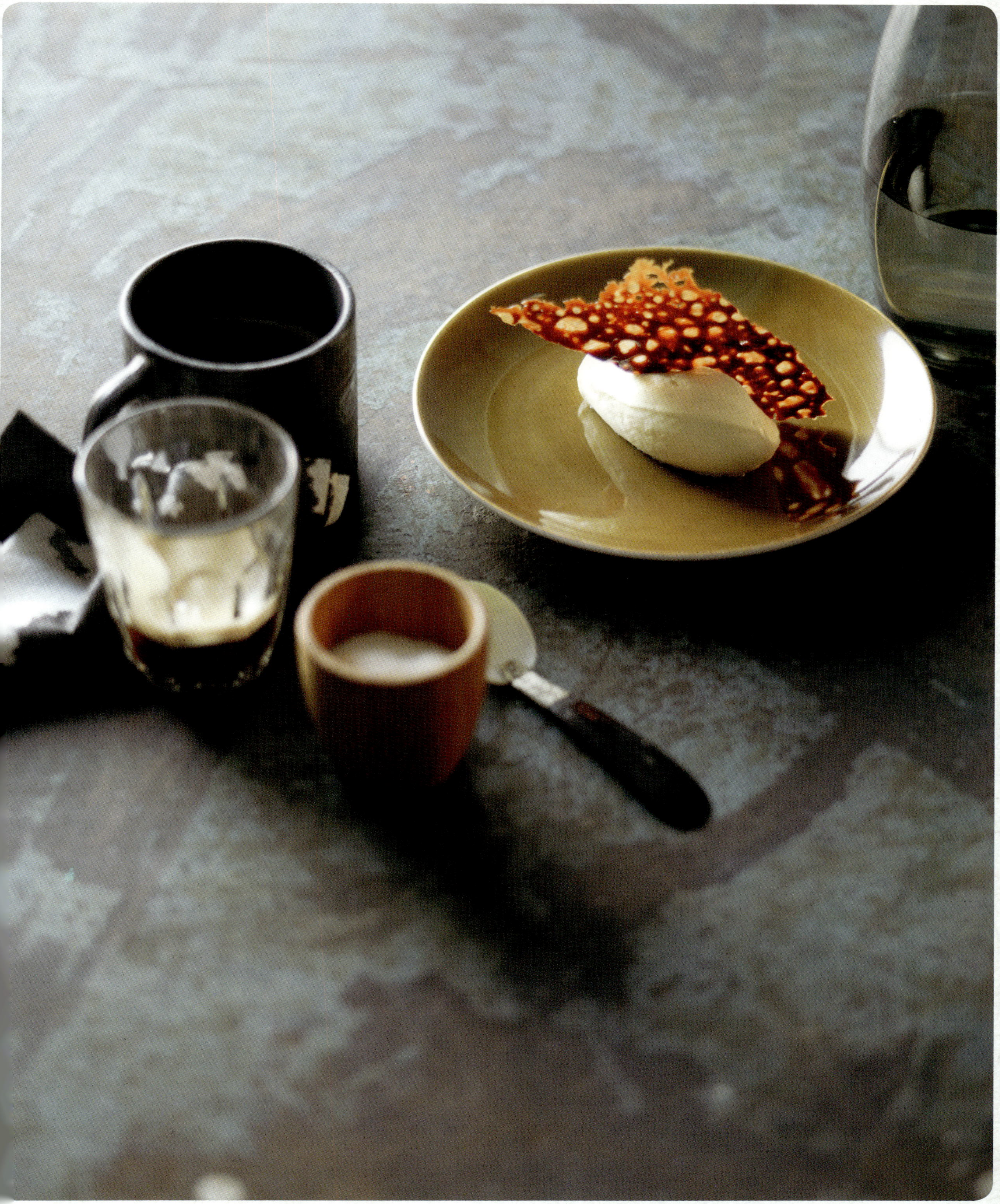

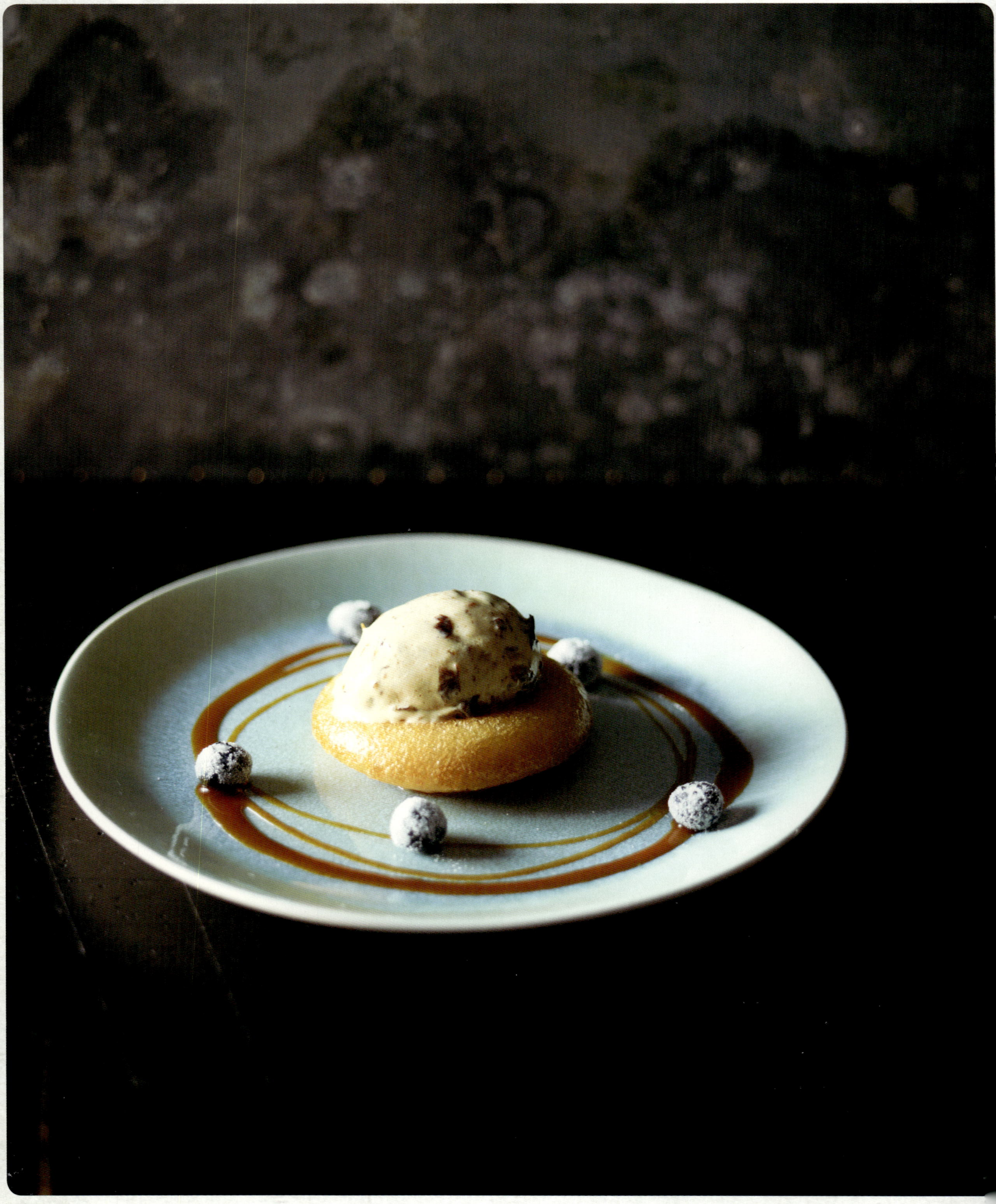

BABA AU RHUM
RUM BABA

Babas are a yeast-based dessert that originated in western Russia and Poland, making their way to the Alsace-Lorraine region of France by the mid-eighteenth century. They are cooked in cylindrical moulds called savarin moulds, which are available from specialty kitchenware stores. Their light, spongy texture means they soak up the rum syrup beautifully. They are the perfect dinner party dessert, as they taste great and can be made in advance. Serve them with rum-and-raisin ice cream to go with the rum-spiked syrup and see what you think.

SERVES 6

250 g plain flour
table salt
7 g fresh yeast
2 teaspoons caster sugar
125 ml milk, warmed
3 eggs
75 g unsalted butter, chopped and softened
rum-and-raisin or vanilla ice cream, to serve

CARAMEL SAUCE

125 g caster sugar
150 ml pouring cream
30 g unsalted butter, chopped

SUGAR-COATED BLUEBERRIES (OPTIONAL)

150 g blueberries
55 g caster sugar

RUM SYRUP

250 g caster sugar
100 ml water
1 vanilla pod, seeds scraped
2 tablespoons white rum

1. Combine the flour, pinch of salt, yeast, sugar and 60 ml of the warm milk in the bowl of an electric mixer and whisk for 5 minutes or until the dough is smooth and elastic. Change the whisk to the paddle attachment, then gradually add the eggs, beating well after adding each one. Gradually add the butter and beat until well combined. Slowly add the remaining milk and beat for 5 minutes or until the mixture is smooth and silky. Remove the bowl from the mixer, cover with plastic film and set aside in a warm place for 1 hour or until the dough has doubled in volume.

2. Transfer the dough to a piping bag, then use to fill six 80 ml capacity savarin moulds up to two-thirds. Set the dough aside to prove again for 30 minutes or until it has risen to the top of the moulds.

3. Preheat the oven to 200°C.

4. Bake the babas for 15–20 minutes or until golden. Turn out onto a wire rack and leave to cool.

5. Meanwhile, to make the caramel sauce, place the sugar, pouring cream and butter in a saucepan over medium heat, then cook for 3 minutes or until the mixture comes to a boil, stirring to dissolve the sugar. Reduce the heat to low and simmer for 2 minutes. Set aside to cool to room temperature.

6. To prepare the blueberries (if using), place the berries and sugar in a small bowl and toss until well coated.

7. To make the rum syrup, place the sugar, water, vanilla seeds and rum in a heavy-based saucepan over high heat. Bring to the boil, then reduce the heat to low and simmer for 20 minutes. Remove from the heat and, working in batches, soak the cooled babas in the syrup for 1–2 minutes, turning until well coated.

8. Using a slotted spoon, remove the babas from the syrup and discard the remaining syrup. Place a baba on each plate, then top with a scoop of ice cream. Drizzle some caramel sauce around the edge of each plate, then add the sugar-coated blueberries, if desired. Serve.

CRÉMEUX AU CHOCOLAT ET À LA NOISETTE
CHOCOLATE & HAZELNUT MOUSSE

These make for a wickedly decadent dessert. The chocolate layer is basically a combination of chocolate ganache and custard, topped off with a hazelnut cream. You could serve these in summer or winter, but I would precede them with a fairly light main course. You'll need to chill this dessert for at least three hours before serving, or overnight, if you have time.

SERVES 8

250 g dark couverture chocolate (70% cocoa solids, see page 208), finely chopped, plus extra for grating
250 ml pouring cream
3 egg yolks
50 g caster sugar
250 ml milk

HAZELNUT CREAM
250 ml pouring cream
75 g hazelnut praline paste (available from specialty food stores)

1. Place the chocolate in a heatproof bowl. Bring the cream to the boil in a small saucepan, then pour it over the chocolate and whisk until the chocolate has melted and the mixture is smooth.

2. Place the egg yolks and sugar in the bowl of an electric mixer and whisk until pale and fluffy. Place the milk in a small saucepan over medium heat and bring just to the boil. Gradually whisk the hot milk into the egg mixture until well combined. Transfer to a clean saucepan and cook over medium heat for 2–3 minutes or until the sauce thickens.

3. Fold the chocolate mixture into the egg yolk mixture until well combined. Divide among six 180 ml capacity serving glasses. Refrigerate for 3 hours or until set.

4. Meanwhile, to make the hazelnut cream, bring the cream to the boil in a small saucepan over high heat. Reduce to heat to low and whisk in the hazelnut paste until dissolved. Strain through a fine-mesh sieve placed over a bowl, then cover with plastic film and refrigerate for 2–3 hours or until set.

5. To serve, using hand-held electric beaters, whisk the hazelnut cream until light and fluffy, then pipe or spoon it over the chocolate mousse and top with grated chocolate.

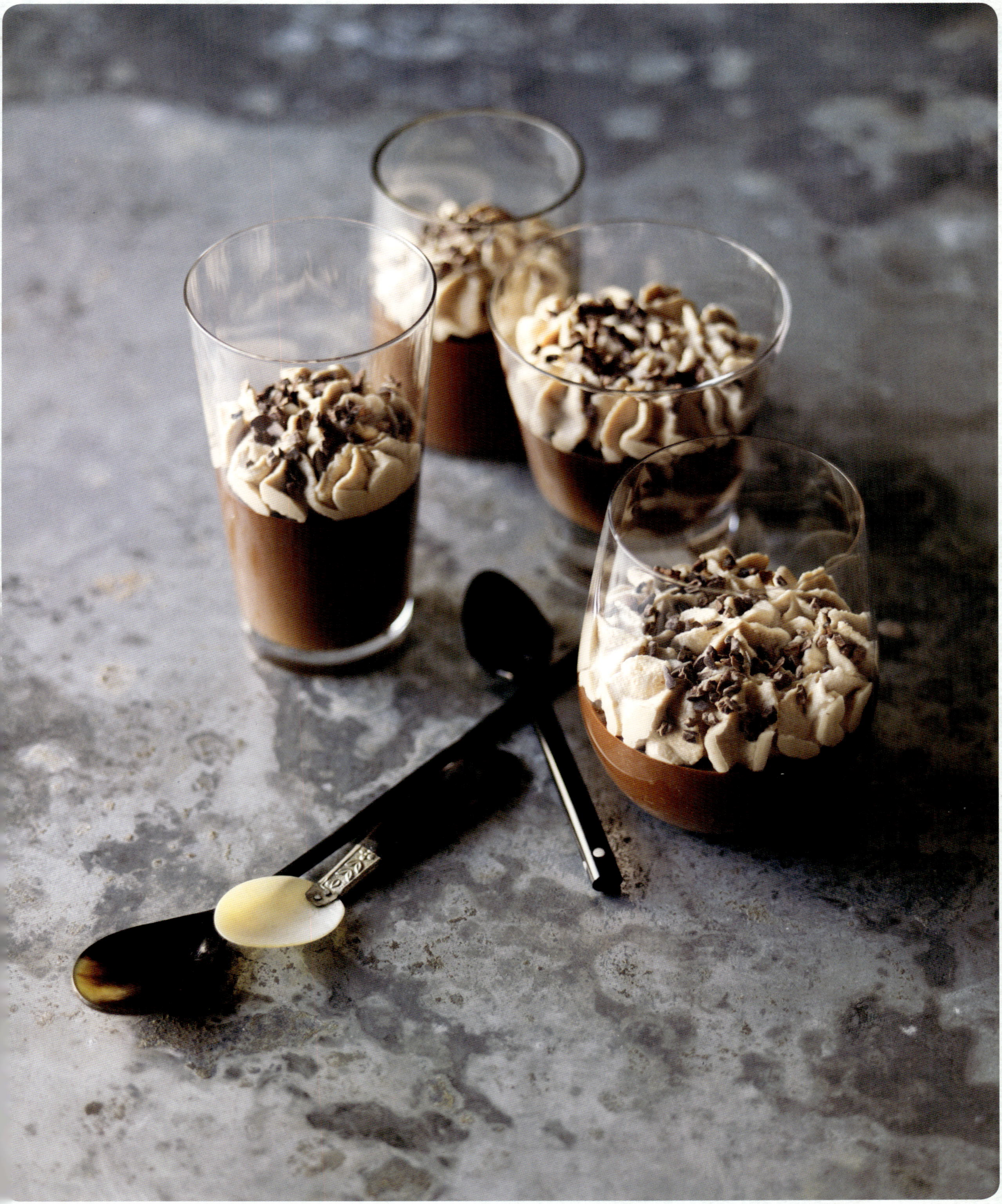

PAIN PERDU ET SORBET AU YAOURT
FRENCH TOAST WITH YOGHURT SORBET

This dessert is a cross between French toast and that old-fashioned English favourite, bread and butter pudding. It brings back happy childhood memories for me, as Mum used to make us French toast for dessert as a treat. A lovely autumn dish, especially when accompanied by the tanginess of the yoghurt sorbet. You'll need an ice-cream machine to make the sorbet.

SERVES 6

150 g unsalted butter, chopped
1 × 450 g brioche, crusts removed and discarded, cut into 2 cm cubes
250 ml milk
3 eggs
110 g caster sugar, plus 1 tablespoon extra for sprinkling
1 vanilla pod, seeds scraped
Caramel Sauce (optional, see page 189), to serve

YOGHURT SORBET

150 g caster sugar
150 g liquid glucose (see page 208)
300 ml water
750 g natural Greek-style yoghurt

1. To make the yoghurt sorbet, place the sugar, glucose and water in a small heavy-based saucepan and bring to the boil over medium heat, stirring often until the sugar dissolves and the mixture is smooth. Remove the syrup from the heat and leave to stand until cool, then refrigerate until cold.

2. Place the yoghurt in a large bowl, whisk in the cooled sugar syrup, then churn the mixture in an ice-cream machine according to the manufacturer's instructions. (Makes about 1 litre. Sorbet will keep in the freezer for up to 6 weeks.)

3. Preheat the oven to 160°C.

4. Melt 100 g of the butter in a large heavy-based frying pan over medium heat and cook the brioche, in batches, for 2–3 minutes or until golden.

5. Place the milk, eggs, 75 g of the caster sugar and the vanilla seeds in a wide flat baking dish and whisk until well combined. Line a 1 litre capacity loaf tin with baking paper, then add the brioche and pour the egg mixture over. Set aside for 10 minutes to soak up the liquid.

6. Bake the brioche mixture for 15 minutes, then sprinkle with the extra caster sugar and bake for another 10 minutes or until the top is golden. Remove from the oven and refrigerate for 2 hours or until cold. Cut the French toast into six equal slices.

7. Melt the remaining butter in a large non-stick frying pan over medium heat, then add the remaining 35 g caster sugar. Cook the French toast slices for 1–2 minutes on each side or until golden.

8. To serve, smear a little of the caramel sauce on each plate (if using). Add a slice of French toast, then top with a large spoonful (or quenelle, see page 209) of yoghurt sorbet.

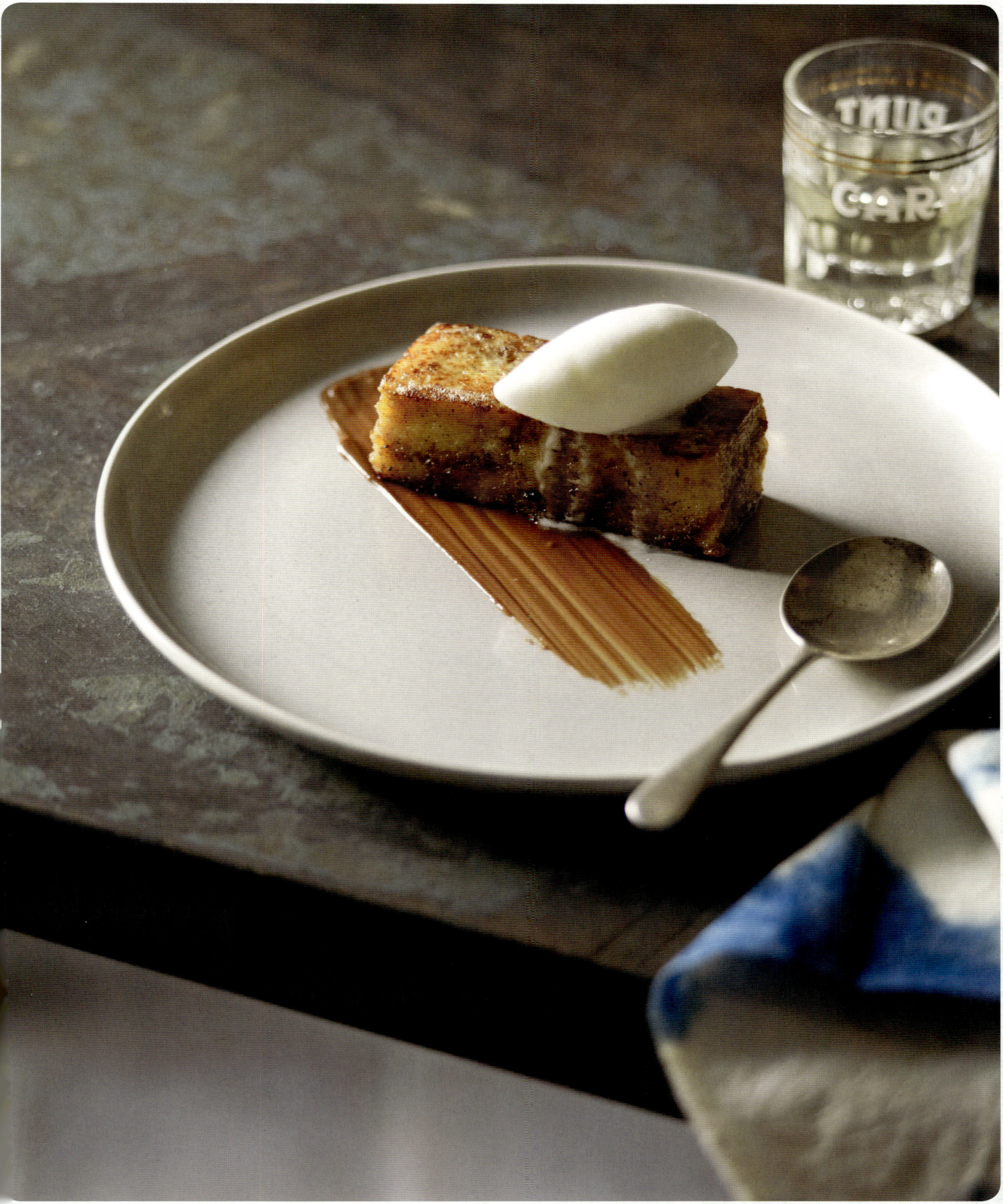

FROMAGE AU FOUR
OVEN-BAKED WHITE MOULD CHEESE

This is a great cheese course to serve instead of dessert for people who, like me, do not have a sweet tooth. The only problem is that it is impossible to stop eating it, because you'll find you'll need more bread to finish the cheese, then you'll need more cheese to finish the wine, and more wine to finish the bread . . . you get the picture!

SERVES 4

1 × 250 g Clarine des Perrins cheese (or other white mould cheese, such as Camembert, Brie or Coulommiers), in its wooden box
2 cloves garlic, sliced
5 sprigs thyme, cut into 1 cm lengths
100 ml red wine
fresh figs and crusty bread, to serve

1. Preheat the oven to 200°C.

2. Remove the lid from the cheese, then wrap the bottom of the box with foil and place on a baking tray. Stud the cheese with the garlic slices and thyme sprigs, then pour over the wine. Bake the cheese for 20 minutes or until melted.

3. Serve at once with figs and bread.

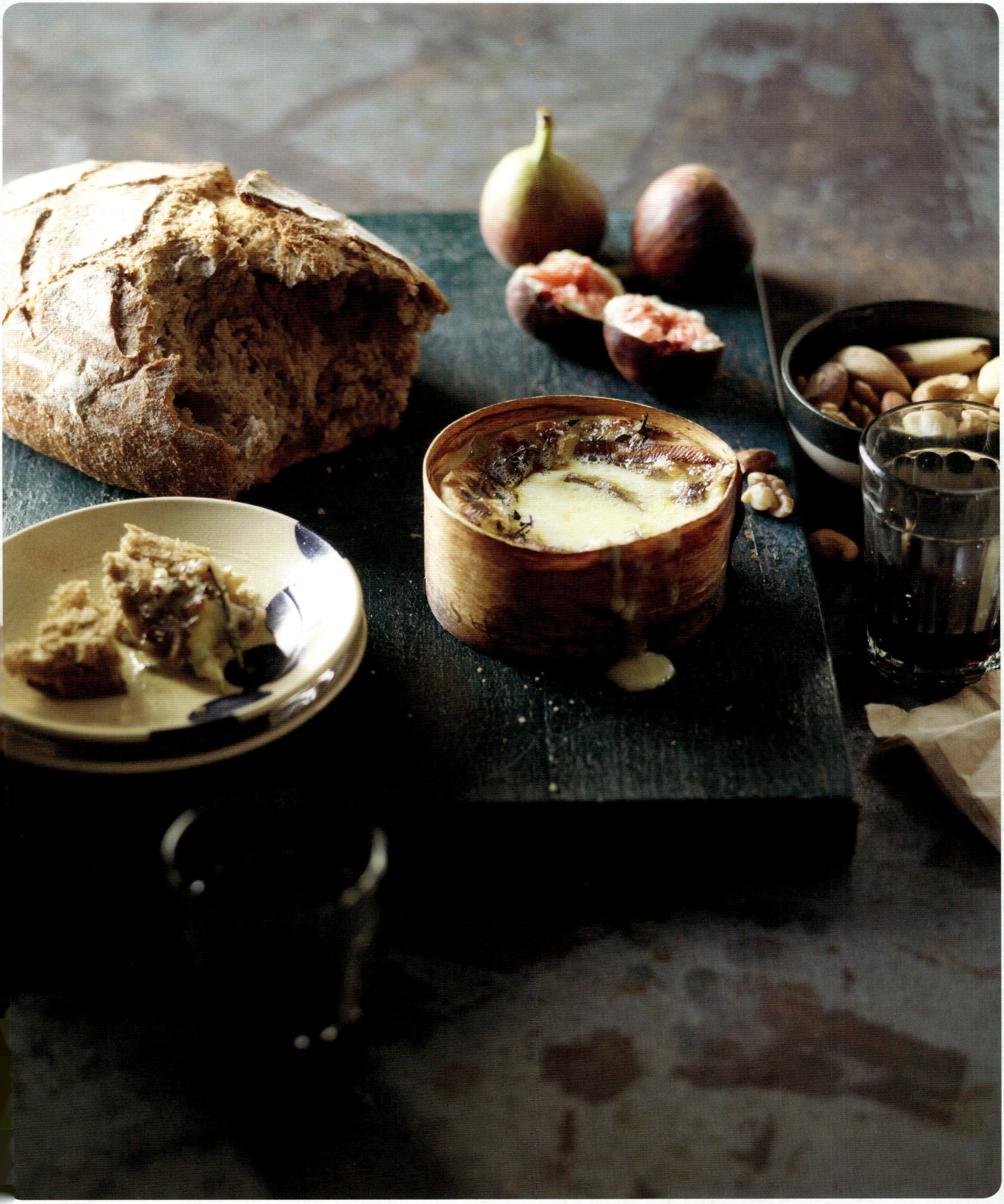

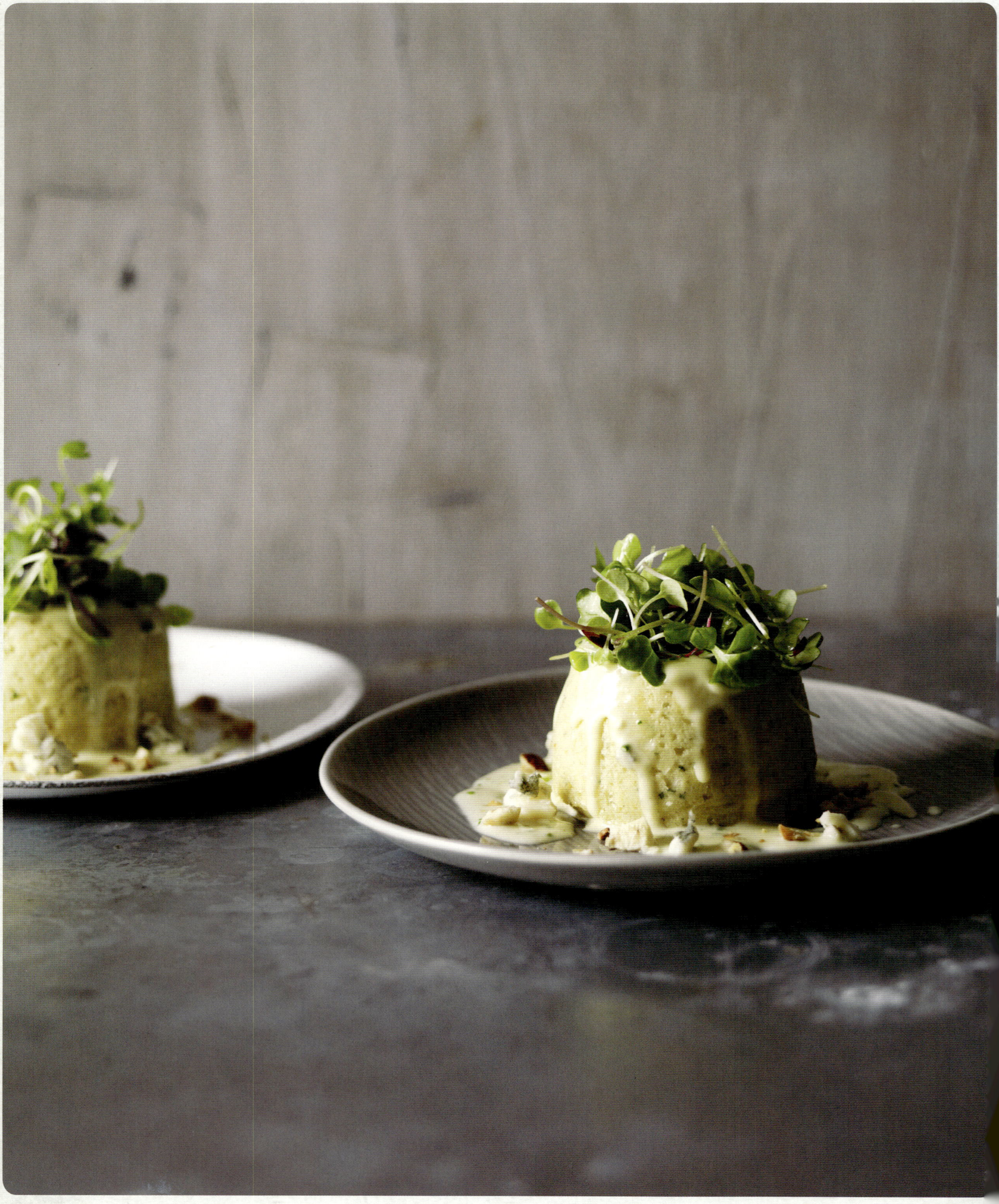

SOUFFLÉS AU ROQUEFORT
ROQUEFORT CHEESE SOUFFLES

A final dish for those people, like me, who prefer to finish their meal with cheese rather than something sweet. Roquefort, one of the world's most legendary blue cheeses, takes its name from the village of Roquefort sur Soulzon, where it matures in the local caves.

SERVES 4

100 g walnuts
185 g unsalted butter, plus extra for greasing
3 eschalots, finely chopped
170 g plain flour
500 ml milk
75 g Roquefort, crumbled
75 g parmesan, grated
2 tablespoons finely chopped chives
3 egg yolks
5 egg whites
80 ml pouring cream
micro herbs and baby cress (optional), to serve

1. Process the walnuts in a food processor until finely chopped. Grease four 250 ml capacity souffle dishes with extra butter and scatter over the finely chopped walnuts, shaking out any excess. Place the dishes on a baking tray and set aside.

2. Preheat the oven to 160°C.

3. Heat 15 g of the butter in a small frying pan over medium heat, then add the eschalot and cook for 5 minutes or until softened. Set aside to cool.

4. Melt the remaining butter in a large saucepan over low heat. When the butter starts to foam, add the flour and stir for 2–3 minutes or until the mixture becomes sand-coloured (this is called a roux). Slowly whisk in the milk, whisking continuously until the mixture boils and thickens. Reduce the heat to low and cook for 6–8 minutes or until thickened and smooth. Stir in the eschalot, Roquefort, 40 g of the parmesan, the chives and egg yolks and mix until well combined.

5. Using hand-held electric beaters, whisk the egg whites in a large bowl until soft peaks form. Stir one-third of the egg white into the cheese mixture to loosen it, then gently fold in the remaining egg white.

6. Divide the mixture among the souffle dishes, filling them right to the top. Bake for 20 minutes, then remove from the oven and set aside to cool a little. Meanwhile, increase the oven temperature to 180°C.

7. When the souffles are cool enough to handle, unmould them onto a baking tray, then pour some cream over each one and sprinkle with the remaining parmesan. Bake the souffles for 15–20 minutes or until warmed through and the cheese is bubbling.

8. Transfer the souffles and cream sauce to plates, then top with a little pile of micro herbs and baby cress (if using). Serve.

WINTER

MENU

ENTREES

Cou de canard farci aux pistaches
Stuffed duck neck with pistachios 63

Velouté de chou-fleur et Roquefort
Cauliflower soup with Roquefort 10

Soufflés au gruyère
Twice-baked cheese souffles 23

Cassolettes d'escargot à l'ail
Garlic snail pies 42

Tartelettes à l'oignon et au bacon
Onion & bacon tartlets 36

MAINS

Filet de 'kingfish' et brandade
Kingfish with brandade 87

Bourride
Seafood stew 81

Parmentier de lièvre
French-style hare pie 120

Confit de porc et purée de pommes
Confit pork belly with apple puree 130

Joues de bœuf braisés et purée de carotte
Braised beef cheeks with carrot puree 142

DESSERTS

Tarte au chocolat parfaite
Perfect chocolate tart 158

Soufflés à la framboise
Raspberry souffles 161

Riz au lait et son gâteau à la ricotta citronné
Rice puddings with lemon ricotta cake 178

Beignets à la confiture de framboise
Nat's raspberry jam donuts 168

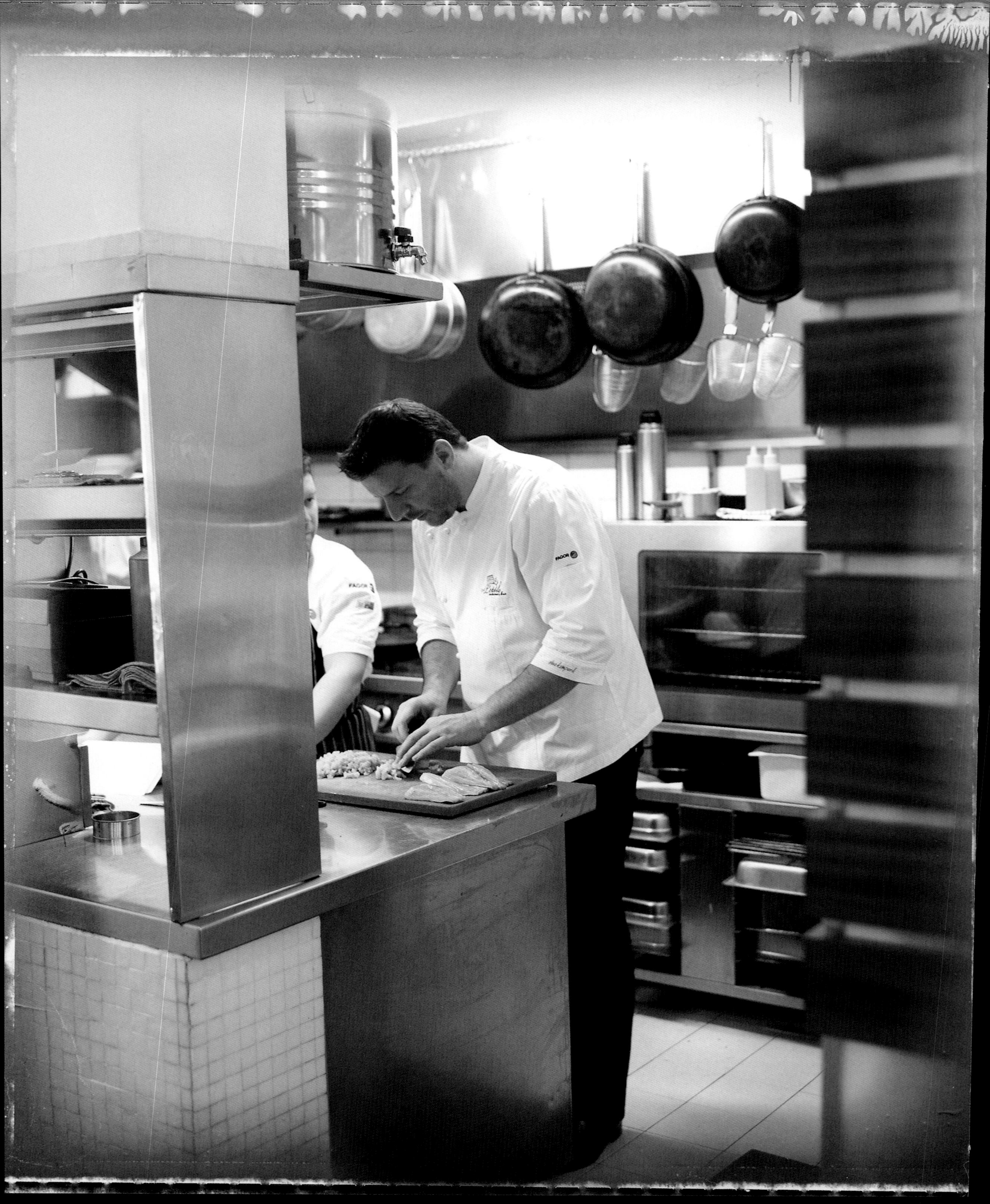
FAGOR

PÂTE SABLÉE   AÏOLI   BISQUE SAUCE
SWEET SHORTCRUST PASTRY

BASICS

FOND BLANC DE VOLAILLE

CONFITURE DE PRUNEAUX   DUCK JUS
WHITE CHICKEN STOCK   SMOKED BUTTER

FOND BRUN DE VOLAILLE
BOIS BOUDRAN DRESSING

MAYONNAISE

MAKES ABOUT 250 ml

1 egg yolk, at room temperature
1½ tablespoons French Dijon mustard (see page 208)
sea salt and freshly ground pepper
250 ml grapeseed oil
1 teaspoon lemon juice, or to taste
boiling water (optional)

1. Place the egg yolk, mustard and a pinch each of salt and pepper in a bowl and whisk to combine well. (Place the bowl on a tea towel to help stabilise it as you whisk.) Whisking continuously, add the oil, drop by drop at first, then in a slow, steady stream until the mixture is thick and emulsified. Whisk in the lemon juice and adjust the seasoning. If the mayonnaise is too thick, whisk in a little boiling water.

AÏOLI
AIOLI

MAKES ABOUT 375 ml

1 small brushed potato such as sebago (about 125 g), scrubbed
5 cloves garlic, peeled
sea salt
2 egg yolks, at room temperature
1 teaspoon lemon juice, or to taste
250 ml olive oil
pinch cayenne pepper

1. Preheat the oven to 200°C. Prick the potato with a fork, then bake it directly on an oven rack for 35–40 minutes or until tender. When cool enough to handle, scoop out the flesh and discard the skin.

2. Place the garlic and a large pinch of salt in a mortar and pound with a pestle until a paste forms. Transfer to a food processor. Add the egg yolks, lemon juice and 30 g of the potato and process until smooth. With the motor running, gradually add the oil, drop by drop at first, and then in a slow, steady stream until the mixture is thick and emulsified. Season to taste with salt, the cayenne pepper and a little more lemon juice if needed.

ROUILLE

MAKES ABOUT 430 ml

1 small brushed potato such as sebago (about 125 g), scrubbed
1 red capsicum (pepper)
5 cloves garlic, peeled
sea salt
2 egg yolks, at room temperature
1 teaspoon lemon juice, or to taste
pinch saffron threads
250 ml olive oil
pinch cayenne pepper

1. Preheat the oven to 200°C.

2. Prick the potato all over with a fork, then place it directly on an oven rack and bake for 35–40 minutes or until tender. When cool enough to handle, scoop out the flesh and discard the skin.

3. Meanwhile, roast the capsicum directly on a gas flame until the skin blackens and blisters. (Alternatively, place under a hot grill, turning until the skin blackens and blisters.) Transfer to a bowl, cover with plastic film and leave for 10 minutes or until cool enough to handle. Peel the capsicum, then discard the seeds and chop the flesh.

4. Place the garlic and a large pinch of salt in a mortar and pound with a pestle until a paste forms. Transfer the garlic paste to a food processor, then add the egg yolks, capsicum, lemon juice, saffron threads and 30 g of the potato and process until smooth. With the motor running, gradually add the oil, drop by drop at first, and then in a slow, steady stream until the mixture is thick and emulsified. Season to taste with salt, the cayenne pepper and a little more lemon juice if needed.

BISQUE
BISQUE SAUCE

MAKES ABOUT 1 LITRE

1 kg raw blue swimmer crabs (about 4)
50 ml olive oil
1 small onion, chopped
1 bulb baby fennel, trimmed and chopped
2 stalks celery, chopped
4 eschalots, chopped
8 cloves garlic, chopped
5 cm knob ginger, chopped
5 roma (plum) tomatoes, chopped
50 ml brandy
250 ml dry white wine
1 tablespoon tomato paste
2 star anise
5 black peppercorns
1/4 teaspoon coriander seeds
1/4 teaspoon fennel seeds
3 sprigs thyme
1 bay leaf
2 litres cold water
250 ml pouring cream
50 g cold unsalted butter, chopped
sea salt and freshly ground black pepper

1. Working with one crab at a time, hold a crab upside down, then lift the tail flaps ('apron') and insert a small knife under the top shell. Twist the knife to loosen and pull off the top shell, then remove and discard the grey gills ('dead man's fingers'). Leave the coral ('mustard') as it holds a lot of flavour. Using a kitchen cleaver or large sharp knife, cut each crab body into 8 pieces and tap the large claws firmly to break open the shell. Set aside.

2. Heat the olive oil in a large heavy-based saucepan or stockpot over high heat. Place the crab pieces in the pan and cook, stirring often, for 6–8 minutes or until the shells change colour. Add the onion, fennel, celery, eschalot, garlic and ginger and stir for 8–10 minutes or until lightly coloured. Add the tomato and brandy and simmer until reduced by half. Pour in the wine and simmer for 5–6 minutes or until reduced by half again, then add the tomato paste, star anise, peppercorns, coriander seeds, fennel seeds, thyme, bay leaf and water and bring to the boil. Reduce the heat to low and simmer, without skimming, for 40 minutes.

3. Strain the mixture through a colander placed over a large bowl, then return the solids to the pan and reserve the stock. Using a heavy-duty blender (or the end of a rolling pin), crush the shells as much as possible – the more you crush them, the more flavour will be released. Return the stock to the pan, combine well, then strain the mixture through a fine-mesh sieve into a large bowl, pressing with the bottom of a ladle to remove as much liquid and flavour as possible. Discard the solids.

4. Transfer 1 litre of the stock to a clean saucepan. Add the cream and simmer over low heat for 15–20 minutes or until the bisque has reduced enough to coat the back of a wooden spoon. Whisk the butter into the hot bisque sauce, then season with salt and pepper.

SAUCE BOIS BOUDRAN
BOIS BOUDRAN DRESSING

MAKES ABOUT 125 ML

70 ml walnut oil
2 tablespoons tomato sauce
few drops Tabasco
1 tablespoon champagne vinegar
1 teaspoon Worcestershire sauce
1 eschalot, finely chopped
1 tablespoon finely chopped French tarragon (see page 208)
1 tablespoon finely chopped chervil
1 teaspoon finely chopped chives
sea salt and freshly ground black pepper

1. Place the oil, tomato sauce, Tabasco, vinegar and Worcestershire sauce in a bowl and whisk to combine. Add the eschalot, tarragon, chervil and chives and combine well. Season to taste with salt and pepper.

FOND BLANC DE VOLAILLE
WHITE CHICKEN STOCK

MAKES ABOUT 2 LITRES

1 kg chicken bones, rinsed well
3 litres water
1 carrot, diced
1 onion, diced
1 small leek, white part only, well washed, diced
1 stick celery, diced
1 clove garlic, peeled
1 bouquet garni (see page 208)

1. Place the chicken bones and water in a large saucepan or stockpot. Bring to the boil over medium heat, skimming any impurities from the surface. Add the carrot, onion, leek, celery, garlic and bouquet garni and return to the boil. Reduce the heat to low and simmer for 3 hours, skimming regularly.

2. Strain the stock through a fine-mesh sieve placed over a large bowl and discard the solids. (To keep the stock as clear as possible, do not press on the vegetables when straining.) Cool to room temperature, then refrigerate until cold. (The fat will solidify on top of the stock, making it easy to remove and discard.) Refrigerate for up to 7 days or freeze for up to 3 months. (Freeze the stock in ice-cube trays so you can take out only as much as you need.)

FOND BRUN DE VOLAILLE
BROWN CHICKEN STOCK

MAKES ABOUT 1.7 LITRES

1 kg chicken bones, rinsed well
1 carrot, diced
1 onion, diced
1 stick celery, diced
100 g button mushrooms, quartered
500 ml dry white wine
2.5 litres water
1 clove garlic, peeled
1 bouquet garni (see page 208)
2 tomatoes, halved widthways

1. Preheat the oven to 200°C. Place the bones in a large roasting pan and roast for 30 minutes, stirring occasionally. Add the carrot, onion, celery and mushrooms, stir to combine well, then roast for another 30 minutes or until the vegetables are golden. Transfer the bones and vegetables to a large saucepan or stockpot and reserve the roasting pan.

2. Place the roasting pan over medium heat. Add the wine and scrape with a wooden spoon to remove any cooked-on bits. Pour the wine mixture over the bones, then add the water. Bring to the boil over high heat, then skim any impurities from the surface. Add the garlic, bouquet garni and tomato to the pan, reduce the heat to low and simmer for 4 hours, skimming the surface regularly.

3. Strain the stock through a fine-mesh sieve placed over a large bowl. Discard the solids. (To keep the stock as clear as possible, do not press on the vegetables when straining.) Cool to room temperature, then refrigerate until cold. (The fat will solidify on top of the stock, making it easy to remove and discard.) Refrigerate for up to 7 days or freeze for up to 3 months. (Freeze the stock in ice-cube trays so you can take out only as much as you need.)

FOND BRUN DE VEAU
BROWN VEAL STOCK

MAKES ABOUT 1.7 LITRES

1 kg veal bones
1 carrot, diced
1 onion, diced
1 stick celery, diced
100 g button mushrooms, quartered
500 ml dry red wine
2.5 litres water
1 clove garlic, peeled
1 bouquet garni (see page 208)
2 tomatoes, halved widthways

1. Preheat the oven to 200°C. Place the bones in a large roasting pan and roast for 30 minutes or until well browned, stirring from time to time. Add the carrot, onion, celery and mushrooms and stir, then roast for another 30 minutes or until the vegetables are well browned. Transfer the vegetables and bones to a large saucepan or stockpot and reserve the roasting pan.

2. Place the roasting pan over medium heat. Add the wine and scrape with a wooden spoon to remove any cooked-on bits. Pour the wine mixture over the bones, then add the water. Bring to the boil over high heat and skim any impurities from the surface. Add the garlic, bouquet garni and tomato, then reduce the heat to low and simmer for 4 hours, skimming the surface regularly.

3. Strain the stock through a fine-mesh sieve placed over a large bowl. Discard the solids. (To keep the stock as clear as possible, do not press on the vegetables when straining.) Cool to room temperature, then refrigerate until cold. (The fat will solidify on top of the stock, making it easy to remove and discard.) Refrigerate for up to 7 days or freeze for up to 3 months. (Freeze the stock in ice-cube trays so you can take out only as much as you need.)

FUMET DE POISSON
FISH STOCK

MAKES ABOUT 2.75 LITRES

1 kg white fish heads and bones, cleaned and washed
100 ml dry white wine
3 litres water
1 onion, diced
1 small leek, white part only, well washed, diced
1 small bulb fennel, diced
1 clove garlic, peeled
1 bouquet garni (see page 208)

1. Place the heads, bones and wine in a large saucepan or stockpot and bring to the boil over high heat. Add the water and return to the boil. Reduce the heat to low, then add the onion, leek, fennel, garlic and bouquet garni and simmer, skimming the surface regularly, for 20 minutes, then remove from the heat. Strain the stock through a fine-mesh sieve placed over a large bowl and discard the solids. (To keep the stock as clear as possible, do not press on the vegetables when straining.) Cool to room temperature, then refrigerate for up to 7 days or freeze for up to 3 months. (Freeze the stock in ice-cube trays so you can take out only as much as you need.)

NAGE DE LÉGUMES
VEGETABLE STOCK

MAKES ABOUT 1.25 LITRES

2 sticks celery, diced
2 leeks, white part only, well washed, diced
2 carrots, diced
1 onion, diced
2 cloves garlic, peeled
2 litres water
500 ml dry white wine
1 bouquet garni (see page 208)

1. Bring all the ingredients to the boil in a stockpot and skim any impurities from the surface. Reduce the heat to low and simmer for 2 hours, skimming regularly. Strain the stock through a fine-mesh sieve placed over a bowl. Discard the solids. (To keep the stock as clear as possible, do not press on the vegetables when straining.) Cool to room temperature, then refrigerate for up to 7 days or freeze for up to 3 months. (Freeze the stock in ice-cube trays so you can take out only as much as you need.)

BASICS

JUS DE CANARD
DUCK JUS

MAKES ABOUT 1 LITRE

50 ml olive oil
1 kg duck bones
1 onion, finely chopped
2 carrots, finely chopped
2 sticks celery, finely chopped
5 cloves garlic, bruised
5 sprigs thyme
325 ml dry white wine
1 teaspoon black peppercorns
3 litres water
50 g unsalted butter, chopped
sea salt and freshly ground black pepper

1. Heat the olive oil in a large stockpot over high heat. Add the bones and cook, stirring, for 8–10 minutes or until browned. Add the onion, carrot, celery and garlic and cook for a further 5–6 minutes or until the vegetables are golden. Add the thyme and cook for another 5 minutes. Deglaze the pan with the wine, scraping to remove any cooked-on bits from the base of the pan, then simmer for 20 minutes or until reduced by half. Add the black peppercorns and water. Bring to the boil, then reduce the heat to low and simmer for 1 hour, skimming the surface now and then to remove impurities. Strain through a fine-mesh sieve into a clean large heavy-based saucepan.

2. Return the stock to the stove, then bring back to the boil. Simmer over medium heat for 30–35 minutes or until reduced to a thick sauce consistency. Reduce the heat to low and whisk in the butter, one piece at a time; this makes the jus glossy. Season to taste with salt and pepper, then refrigerate until needed.

JUS DE VOLAILLE À L'ESTRAGON
CHICKEN & TARRAGON JUS

To make chicken jus, simply omit the tarragon.

MAKES ABOUT 375 ML

60 ml vegetable oil
450 g chicken wings
1 carrot, cut in half lengthways
1 leek, white part only, cut in half lengthways, well washed
1 stick celery, coarsely chopped
4 eschalots, peeled
4 cloves garlic, crushed
125 g unsalted butter, chopped
6 sprigs thyme
1 bunch French tarragon (see page 208)
250 ml white wine
1.5 litres White Chicken Stock (see page 204) or water
1 bay leaf
sea salt and freshly ground black pepper

1. Heat the oil in a large heavy-based saucepan over high heat. Add the wings, then cook for 8 minutes, turning until they are golden brown on both sides. Set aside on paper towel to drain. Add the carrot, leek and celery to the pan, then cook for 5–6 minutes, turning until golden brown. Add the eschalots and cook for 5 minutes. Return the wings to the pan, then add the garlic and butter and stir to coat the wings and vegetables. Add the thyme and half of the tarragon, then cook for 2–3 minutes. Add the wine, scraping the base of the pan to remove any cooked-on bits. Add the stock or water and bay leaf. Bring to the boil, then reduce the heat to low and simmer for 3 hours, skimming the surface now and then to remove impurities.

2. Strain through a fine-mesh sieve into a clean saucepan, discarding the solids. Add the remaining tarragon, then bring to the boil. Simmer over medium heat for 30 minutes or until reduced by one-third; it should have reached a sauce consistency. Season to taste with salt and pepper, then refrigerate until needed.

BASICS

BEURRE FUMÉ
SMOKED BUTTER

I use this smoked butter to add an addictively smoky quality to the potato puree on page 152. I have included instructions here for using a wok to smoke the butter. However, at the restaurant, we place the soaked hickory chips in a heavy-based roasting pan on the stovetop, then carefully set the chips on fire with a gas torch (we have a fire extinguisher and a fire blanket handy). After leaving the hickory chips to smoulder, we sit the butter in a roasting pan over the pan of smouldering chips, then leave the butter to smoke for 2–3 hours. Hickory smoking chips are available from specialty food and barbecue stores and need to be soaked in cold water overnight before use.

500 g hickory smoking chips, soaked overnight, drained
100 g unsalted butter

1. Line a wok with foil, then place over high heat and add the hickory chips. Place the butter in a heatproof bowl on a wire rack sitting over the hickory chips in the wok and smoke over medium heat for 20 minutes; the butter will melt (but will harden in the fridge later). Transfer to an airtight container and refrigerate for up to 2 days.

PÂTE BRISÉE
SHORTCRUST PASTRY

MAKES ENOUGH TO LINE A 30 CM TART TIN

250 g plain flour, plus extra for dusting
large pinch fine sea salt
1 egg yolk
125 g unsalted butter, chopped and softened
50 ml cold water

1. Sift the flour and salt into a large bowl and make a well in the centre. Add the egg yolk, butter and water and use your fingertips to work the wet ingredients into the dry ingredients until a dough forms; it doesn't have to be perfect.

2. Turn the dough out onto a lightly floured work surface and knead gently and quickly, using the palm of your hand, until just combined. (It is better for the dough to be a little rough rather than to overwork it, and you must work quickly to prevent the butter from melting.) Shape the dough into a disc, wrap in plastic film and refrigerate for 1 hour before using.

PÂTE SABLÉE
SWEET SHORTCRUST PASTRY

MAKES ENOUGH TO LINE A 30 CM TART TIN

125 g unsalted butter, chopped and softened
1 egg
90 g icing sugar, sifted
30 g ground almonds
250 g plain flour, sifted, plus extra for dusting

1. Place the butter, egg, icing sugar and ground almonds in the bowl of an electric mixer with a paddle attachment and beat until smooth and well combined.

2. Add the flour a little at a time and, as soon as all the flour is just incorporated, stop mixing. Transfer the dough to a lightly floured work surface and shape into a disc, then wrap in plastic film and refrigerate overnight. Remove from the refrigerator 30 minutes before using.

CONFITURE DE PRUNEAUX
PRUNE JAM

MAKES A 500 ML CAPACITY JAR

2 tablespoons green tea leaves
150 ml boiling water
150 g pitted prunes, finely chopped
280 g caster sugar
125 ml water
2 tablespoons Armagnac or brandy

1. Place the green tea in a small heatproof jug and pour the boiling water over, then leave to cool for 10 minutes. Place the prunes in a heatproof bowl and strain the tea-infused water over the prunes, discarding the tea leaves. Set aside for 1½ hours, then drain and discard the liquid.

2. Place the sugar and water in a large heavy-based saucepan over medium heat and stir until the sugar has dissolved. Add the prunes, then reduce the heat to low and cook, stirring, for 35–40 minutes or until the liquid has thickened. Remove from the heat, then stir in the Armagnac or brandy and set aside to cool. Transfer to a sterilised 500 ml capacity jar and store in the fridge for up to 1 week.

BASICS

GLOSSARY

BATONS
Vegetable sticks cut to a uniform size.

BOUQUET GARNI
A bundle of herbs (usually parsley, thyme and a bay leaf and sometimes including lemon or orange zest) tied together with kitchen twine and used in soups, braises or stocks to add flavour. My standard bouquet garni consists of two thyme sprigs and a fresh bay leaf, wrapped in a piece of the green part of a leek, then tied with kitchen twine.

CARTOUCHE
A round of baking paper placed directly over a braise, casserole, stew or custard to prevent the liquid from evaporating and stop a skin forming on the surface.

CORNICHONS
Small pickled cucumbers. Available from delicatessens and specialty food stores.

COUVERTURE CHOCOLATE
Top-quality chocolate containing a high level of cocoa butter. Couverture chocolate must contain a minimum of thirty-two per cent cocoa butter and fifty-four per cent combined total of cocoa solids and cocoa butter. Available from specialty food stores. I like to use chocolate with at least seventy per cent cocoa solids in my cooking for a deeper, richer flavour.

FRENCH DIJON MUSTARD
Made with brown or black mustard seeds, with various herbs, according to traditional methods. Wholegrain Dijon mustard is made by mixing whole mustard seeds with white wine and spices. I use the French brand, Maille, available from most supermarkets.

FRENCH TARRAGON
An essential herb in French cookery, and generally considered to be superior in flavour to the more widely available Russian tarragon. Worth seeking out from specialty greengrocers.

GELATINE
A gelling agent derived from collagen used to set jellies, mousses and sweets. It comes in powder or sheet form. The sheets come in different grades (titanium, gold and silver), according to how easily they set. Titanium-strength sheets are the strongest and silver are the weakest, with gold somewhere in the middle. Gelatine sheets must be soaked in cold water prior to use. Available from specialty food stores and delicatessens.

JULIENNE
A technique for cutting vegetables into matchstick-size strips of uniform length.

KITCHEN BLOWTORCH
Gives a blast of heat to brown or caramelise foods. Most commonly used to give creme brulee its hard, crunchy topping.

LARDONS
Small pieces of pork fat, bacon, speck or pancetta that are sauteed. Used as a salad garnish or inserted into large pieces of meat to keep them moist during cooking.

LEMONS (HOW TO SEGMENT)
To segment a lemon, remove the skin and pith, then cut the flesh into segments, discarding the frame.

LIQUID GLUCOSE
A 'single' sugar in syrup form. Used in commercial kitchens instead of sugar to make ice cream, sorbet and confectionery. It often replaces a proportion of white sugar in recipes. Available from health food stores.

NUTS (ROASTING)
Roast on a baking tray in the oven at 180°C for 3–4 minutes or until golden.

PORK BACK FAT
A fatty cut of pork from the pig's back. It can be wrapped around other meats and also used in terrines and pates. You will need to order this in advance from a good-quality butcher.

QUATRE EPICES
A combination of four spices, usually pepper, ginger, nutmeg and cloves, used to flavour casseroles, sausages and terrines. You can make it yourself or buy it from specialty food stores.

QUENELLE
Traditionally a kind of dumpling made from minced fish or meat, bound with seasoning and egg, then formed into an oval shape and poached in stock or water. Today the term describes the process of shaping soft foods, such as ice cream, vegetable puree or chocolate mousse, between two spoons to form a three-sided egg-like shape.

SHERRY VINEGAR
A type of vinegar made in Spain from sherry and aged in oak for at least six months. Used in salad dressings and for deglazing. Available from specialty food stores.

SNAILS
The most widely used snails in cooking are the petit gris, the common or garden snail, and the larger vineyard or burgundy snail. Tinned snails are ready to eat and are available from specialty food stores.

SPECK
This spiced, salt-cured, smoked pork product is used to flavour soups and casseroles, or can be cut into lardons and used to garnish salads.

SUGAR/DEEP-FRY THERMOMETER
Used when making jams and sugar syrup-based sweets to measure the different stages of sugar syrup leading to caramel. Also measures oil temperature for deep-frying.

TOMATOES (PEELING)
Make a cross at one end of the tomato and remove the core at the other end. Immerse the tomatoes in boiling water for 30 seconds, then immediately transfer to a bowl of iced water. Drain, then peel off the skins and squeeze out the seeds.

WILD MUSHROOMS (CEP AND MOREL)
Cep is the French name for porcini mushrooms. Morels are hollow with a honeycomb-like surface that traps dirt. Available from specialty food stores.

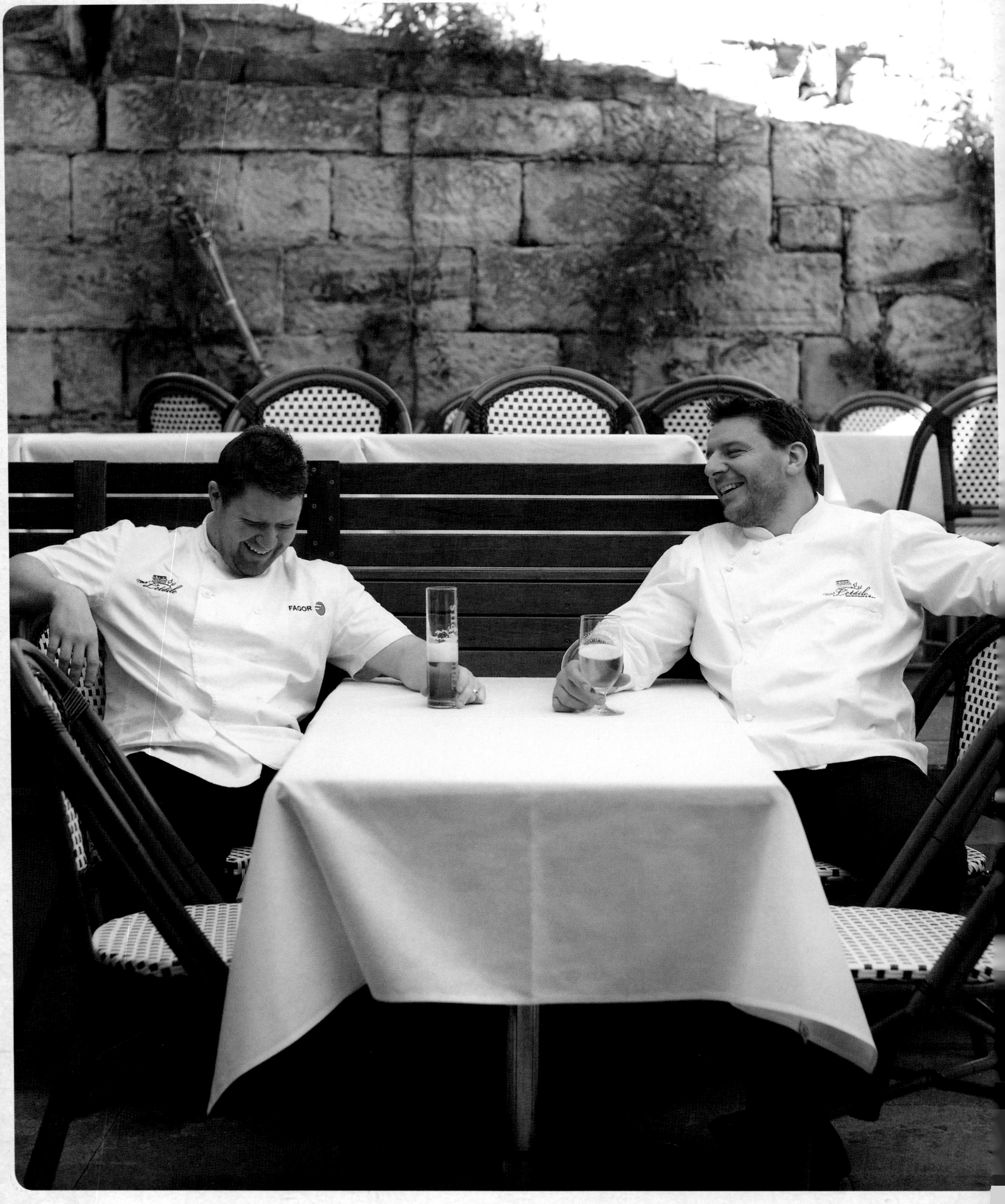
FAGOR

MERCI

This book is all about the last few years of my professional life. It includes the restaurant recipes I want to share with the many home cooks who are willing to be adventurous and try something new, and hopefully learn a little more about French cooking along the way. As this is not something I could have done by myself, I have a few people to thank.

Firstly, huge thanks to the team at Penguin: Julie Gibbs, my publisher, thank you for letting me continue my writing journey and share more of my recipes; Ingrid Ohlsson, who is such a wonderful help and support; Kathleen Gandy, for her endless hours of editing, and Virginia Birch and Alison Cowan for eleventh-hour assistance; Kirby Armstrong, who came up with the original design concept, and Emily O'Neill, for designing the final book. Thanks also to Elena Cementon, Clio Kempster, Nicole Abadee and Leanne Kitchen for their invaluable contributions, and to Peta Dent, for translating my restaurant-speak for the home cook.

To the wonderful photographer Chris Chen and her assistant Natalie Hunfalvay, thanks so much for making all the recipes look great on the page. Big thanks also to Geraldine Muñoz for her brilliant food styling, and to her assistant, Bhavani Konings.

To Troy Spencer, thanks for all your help and for sharing some of your recipes, as well as for running L'étoile restaurant the way I would if I could be in the kitchen. You're not only a great member of staff and a terrific chef, but now a great friend too — thank you so much!

Enormous thanks to Natalie Street, who continues to tell me where to be, what to do and when to do it. It's because of you, and all you do, that I don't think I'll be able to live the rest of my life without an assistant!

Also, thanks to my agent, Justine May, for your continued support.

Thanks to Yannick, Michele, Miguel and Don, my four business partners, for being patient and giving me the time to do everything else but run a restaurant!

To all my friends, who are patient, understanding and always there for me, even though I so rarely get to see any of you — thanks!

Thanks also to all the chefs and colleagues I've worked with over the years who have taught me, shared their knowledge and shaped me into the chef I am today.

And finally, enormous thanks to my family, especially my son Jonti. Jonti, you are my inspiration; you make me so proud and give me the passion to follow my dreams. Always follow your dreams — I love you! x

INDEX

A

Aioli 202
almonds
    Almond Blancmange with Berry Salad 172
    Almond Gazpacho with Crab & Almond Salad 17
    Almond Praline 183
    Almond Shortcrust Pastry 180
    Apple & Almond Frangipane Tarts 175
    Preserved Lemon & Almond Dressing 92
apples
    Apple & Almond Frangipane Tarts 175
    Apple Puree 130
    Black Pudding with Caramelised Apple 126
    Celeriac & Apple Remoulade 74
    Pork Stuffed with Apple & Sage 128
asparagus
    Egg-yolk Ravioli with Green Asparagus & Shaved Parmesan 67
    Spanner Crab & Tarragon Salad with Grilled Asparagus 70
    White Asparagus Barigoule 30
Asperges blanches 'en barigoule' 30
autumn menu 155
Avocado Cream 54

B

Baba au rhum 189
Ballottine d'aubergines sauce bois boudran 34
beans
    Cassoulet 146
    Spiced Flageolet Beans 153
    Warm White Bean Salad 100
Bearnaise Sauce 134
beef
    Braised Beef Cheeks with Carrot Puree 142
    Rib-eye of Beef with Bearnaise Sauce 134
    Rib-eye of Beef with Bone Marrow & Bordelaise Sauce 132
    Scotch Fillet Beef with Rich Red Wine Sauce 138
    Sirloin Steak with Eschalot Sauce 135
beetroot
    Salad of Goat's Curd & Baby Beetroot 38
Beignets à la confiture de framboise 168
Berry Compote 174
Berry Salad 172
Bisque Sauce *(Bisque)* 203
'Black flathead', salade tiède de haricots blanc vinaigrette 100
Black Flathead with Warm White Bean Salad 100
Black Olive Oil 14
Black Pudding with Caramelised Apple 126

C

blancmange
    Almond Blancmange with Berry Salad 172
Blanc-manger aux amandes et salade de fruit rouge 172
blueberries
    Sugar-coated Blueberries 189
Bois Boudran Dressing 203
Bombe Alaska 171
Bordelaise Sauce 132
Boudin blanc de volaille aux morilles 59
Boudin noir 126
Bourride 81
Braised Beef Cheeks with Carrot Puree 142
Braised Lamb Shoulder with Potato Puree 152
Braised Lentils 112
Braised Lettuce 124
Brandade 87
Brown Chicken Stock 204
Brown Veal Stock 205
butters
    Hazelnut Butter 49
    Smoked Butter 206

C

Cailles farcies aux raisins et au thym, lentils braisées 112
cakes
    Lemon Ricotta Cake 178
    Warm Chestnut & Olive Cake with Tomato Chutney 22
Calmar farci à la paella 97
Calmar farci aux moules, merguez et épinards 103
Canard rôti au miel et aux épices 106
Cannelloni de thon et de crabe et crème d'avocat 54
caramel
    Caramel Sauce 189
    Chewy Walnut & Caramel Tart 162
Carpaccio noix de Saint-Jacques 27
Carpaccio of Scallop 27
Carré de pork rôti 124
carrots
    Carrot Puree 142
    Glazed Carrots & Parsnip 106
Cassolettes d'escargot à l'ail 42
Cassoulet 146
Cauliflower Puree 88
Cauliflower Soup with Roquefort 10
Celeriac & Apple Remoulade 74
Cep Cream 28
Ceviche de 'kingfish', vinaigrette à la coriandre et aux pignons 66
Champagne Dressing 70
cheese
    Cauliflower Soup with Roquefort 10

Fromage Blanc Mousse with Berry Compote 174
    Goat's Cheese Salad 33
    Herbed Goat's Curd 38
    Lemon Ricotta Cake 178
    Mornay Sauce 50
    Oven-baked White Mould Cheese 194
    Pont-L'Evêque Cheese Gratin 20
    Roquefort Cheese Souffles 197
    Salad of Goat's Curd & Baby Beetroot 38
    Twice-baked Cheese Souffles 23
chestnuts
    Chestnut Puree 117
    Quail & Chestnut Pies 114
    Warm Chestnut & Olive Cake with Tomato Chutney 22
Chewy Walnut & Caramel Tart 162
chicken
    Brown Chicken Stock 204
    Duck Jus 206
    Chicken Leg Confit 105
    Chicken Liver Parfait 56
    Chicken & Morel Mushroom Sausages 59
    Chicken & Tarragon Jus 206
    Coq au Vin 108
    Pan-roasted Chicken Breasts with Baby Turnips 111
    Salad of Chicken Leg Confit 44
    White Chicken Stock 204
Chickpea Crepes Filled with Wild Mushrooms 41
Chickpea Panisse 150
Chilled Nougat Souffles 183
Chilled Pea Soup with Crab Salad & Black Olive Oil 14
Chilled Tomato Consomme with Prawn Salad 18
chocolate
    Chocolate Crème Brulee 164
    Chocolate & Hazelnut Mousse 190
    Chocolate Souffles 165
    Perfect Chocolate Tart 158
    White Chocolate Mousse with Dark Chocolate Tuiles 186
'Chowder' de Saint-Pierre 8
chutney
    Tomato Chutney 22
clams
    John Dory Chowder 8
    Razor Clams Mariniere 98
Confit de porc et purée de pommes 130
confit
    Chicken Leg Confit 105
    Confit Pork Belly with Apple Puree 130
Confiture de pruneaux 207
Consommé de tomates et salade de crevettes 18
Coq au Vin 108
Coquilles Saint-Jacques au beurre de noisette 49
Coquilles Saint-Jacques au fondue de poireaux 51

Coriander & Pine-nut Dressing 66
Côte de boeuf et moelle, sauce bordelaise 132
Côte de boeuf sauce béarnaise 134
Cou de canard farci aux pistaches 63
Couteaux de mer marinières 98
crab
    Bisque Sauce 203
    Crab & Almond Salad 17
    Crab Salad with Preserved Lemon Vinaigrette 14
    Crab-stuffed Zucchini Flowers 90
    Spanner Crab & Tarragon Salad with Grilled Asparagus 70
    Tuna & Crab 'Cannelloni' with Avocado Cream 54
creams
    Avocado Cream 54
    Cep Cream 28
    Hazelnut Cream 190
    Horseradish Cream 68
    Oyster Chantilly 16
Crème brûlée au chocolat 164
creme brulee
    Chocolate Creme Brulee 164
Crémeux au chocolat et à la noisette 190
Crêpe suzette citronnée en millefeuille 184
Crêpes a la farine de pois chiche fourrées aux champignons sauvages 41
crepes
    Chickpea Crepes Filled with Wild Mushrooms 41
    Lemon-curd Crepes Suzette Millefeuille 184
Croquettes d'escargots au beurre d'ail 45
Cuisse de poulet confite 105

D

Dill Oil 88
donuts
    Nat's Raspberry Jam Donuts 168
dressings
    Bois Boudran Dressing 203
    Champagne Dressing 70
    Coriander & Pine-nut Dressing 66
    French Dressing 100
    Preserved Lemon & Almond Dressing 92
    Walnut Dressing 33
    see also creams; vinaigrettes
duck
    Duck Jus 206
    Duck Terrine with Prune Jam 60
    Roast Duck with Spiced Honey Glaze 106
    Stuffed Duck Neck with Pistachios 63

E

Eggplant Rolls with Bois Boudran Dressing 34
Eggplant Tarts with Cep Cream 28
Egg-yolk Ravioli with Green Asparagus & Shaved Parmesan 67
Épaule d'agneau braisée, purée de pommes de terre 152
escabeche
    Red Mullet Escabeche with Celeriac & Apple Remoulade 74
    Sardines Escabeche 46
Eschalot Sauce 135

F

Faux filet de boeuf sauce marchand de vin 138
Filet de 'kingfish' et brandade 87
Filet de 'kingfish', purée de panais, petits oignons au vinaigre et bacon 82
Filet de Saint-Pierre, chou-fleur et noisette 88
Filet mignon de porc aux pommes et sauge 128
Fillet of Venison with Pepper Sauce 144
fish
    Black Flathead with Warm White Bean Salad 100
    Bourride 81
    Brandade 87
    Fish Stock 205
    Matelote of Skate Wing with Preserved Lemon & Almond Dressing 92
    Ocean Trout with Crab-stuffed Zucchini Flowers & Onion Soubise 90
    Papillote of Snapper & Foie Gras 94
    Red Mullet Escabeche with Celeriac & Apple Remoulade 74
    Sardines Escabeche 46
    see also John Dory; kingfish; tuna
Fond blanc de volaille 204
Fond brun de veau 205
Fond brun de volaille 204
fondue
    Leek Fondue 51
    Tomato Fondue 45
French Dressing 100
French-style Hare Pie 120
French Toast with Yoghurt Sorbet 192
Fromage au four 194
Fromage Blanc Mousse with Berry Compote 174
Fumet de poisson 205

G

garlic
    Aioli 202
    Garlic Snail Pies 42
    Garlic Soup 12
    Rouille 202
Gaspacho aux amandes et sa salade de crabe 17
Gâteau tiède aux marrons et à l'huile d'olive et son 'chutney' de tomates 22
Glazed Carrots & Parsnip 106
Gnocchi à la Parisienne 50
Gnocchi Parisian-style 50
Goat's Cheese Salad 33
Grape & Thyme-stuffed Quail with Braised Lentils 112
Gribiche Sauce 73

H

ham
    Smoked Ham Hock Terrine with Gribiche Sauce 73
hare
    French-style Hare Pie 120
hazelnuts
    Chocolate & Hazelnut Mousse 190
    Hazelnut Butter 49
    Hazelnut Cream 190
    Hazelnut Vinaigrette 44
    Pan-fried John Dory with Cauliflower & Hazelnuts 88
herbs
    Bois Boudran Dressing 203
    Bourride 81
    Coriander & Pine-nut Dressing 66
    Grape & Thyme-stuffed Quail with Braised Lentils 112
    Gribiche Sauce 73
    Herbed Goat's Curd 36
    Spanner Crab & Tarragon Salad with Grilled Asparagus 70
    Chicken & Tarragon Jus 206
honey
    Glazed Carrots & Parsnip 106
    Honey Madeleines 166
    Honey-roasted Pears with Warm Honey Madeleines 166
    Roast Duck with Spiced Honey Glaze 106
Horseradish Cream 68

J

jam
    Nat's Raspberry Jam Donuts 168
    Prune Jam 207
Jerusalem artichokes
    Jerusalem Artichoke Soup 13
John Dory
    John Dory Chowder 8
    Pan-fried John Dory with Cauliflower & Hazelnuts 88
    Pochouse of John Dory with Mussels 104
Joues de boeuf braises et purée de carotte 142

K

kingfish
    Kingfish Ceviche with Coriander & Pine-nut Dressing 66
    Kingfish with Brandade 87
    Kingfish with Parsnip Puree, Pickled Onions & Bacon 82

L

lamb
    Braised Lamb Shoulder with Potato Puree 152
    Lamb Rump with Spiced Flageolet Beans 153
    Lamb Saddle with Chickpea Panisse 150
    Roast Lamb Shoulder in Salt Crust 149
Lapin aux pruneaux 123
Leek Fondue 51
lemon
    Lemon Curd 180
    Lemon-curd Crepes Suzette Millefeuille 184
    Lemon Ricotta Cake 178
    Verrine of Lemon 'Tart' 180
lentils
    Braised Lentils 112
lettuce
    Braised Lettuce 124

M

madeleines
    Honey Madeleines 166
Matelote of Skate Wing with Preserved Lemon & Almond Dressing 92
Mayonnaise 202
    Celeriac & Apple Remoulade 74
    Rouille 202
Mornay Sauce 50
Moules à la bourguignonne 91
Mousse au chocolat blanc et tuile de chocolat amer 186
Mousse de foie de volaille 56
Mousse de fromage blanc et compote de fruites rouge 174
mousse
    Chocolate & Hazelnut Mousse 190
    Fromage Blanc Mousse with Berry Compote 174
    White Chocolate Mousse with Dark Chocolate Tuiles 186
mushrooms
    Cep Cream 28
    Chicken & Morel Mushroom Sausages 59
    Chickpea Crepes Filled with Wild Mushrooms 41
    Mushroom Duxelles 139
    Pearl Barley Risotto with Wild Mushrooms 118
mussels
    Mussels Bourguignon 91
    Pochouse of John Dory with Mussels 104
    Squid Stuffed with Merguez, Mussels & Spinach 103
Mustard Sauce 141

N

Nage de légumes 205
Nat's Raspberry Jam Donuts 168
nuts
    Stuffed Duck Neck with Pistachios 63
    see also almonds; hazelnuts; walnuts

O

Ocean Trout with Crab-stuffed Zucchini Flowers & Onion Soubise 90
olives
    Black Olive Oil 14
    Warm Chestnut & Olive Cake with Tomato Chutney 22
Omelette Norvègienne 171
Onion & Bacon Tartlets 36
Onion Soubise 90
Oven-baked White Mould Cheese 194
Oyster Chantilly 16

P

paella
    Squid Stuffed with Paella 97
Pain perdu et sorbet au yaourt 192
Pan-fried John Dory with Cauliflower & Hazelnuts 88
Pan-roasted Chicken Breasts with Baby Turnips 111
Papillote of Snapper & Foie Gras 94
parfait
    Chicken Liver Parfait 56
Parmentier de lièvre 120
parsnip
    Glazed Carrots & Parsnip 106
    Parsnip Puree 82
partridge
    Partridge Jus 117
    Roast Partridge 'En Salmis' 117
pastry
    Almond Shortcrust Pastry 180
    Shortcrust Pastry 207
    Sweet Shortcrust Pastry 207
Pâté brisée 207
Pâté de tête au sauce gribiche 73
Pâté sablée 207
Pavé de truite de mer et fleurs de courgette farcies au crabe, sauce soubise 90
Pearl Barley Risotto with Wild Mushrooms 118
pears
    Honey-roasted Pears with Warm Honey Madeleines 166
peas, fresh
    Chilled Pea Soup with Crab Salad & Black Olive Oil 14
Pepper Sauce 144
Perdrix rôtie en salmis 117
Perfect Chocolate Tart 158
Pickled Vegetables 68
pies
    French-style Hare Pie 120
    Garlic Snail Pies 42
    Quail & Chestnut Pies 114
    Veal Sweetbread Pie 139
Pithivier de ris de veau 139
Pithiviers de cailles et marrons 114
Pochouse de Saint-Pierre 104
Pochouse of John Dory with Mussels 104
Poires rôties au miel, madeleines tièdes 166
Pont-L'Evêque Cheese Gratin 20
pork
    Confit Pork Belly with Apple Puree 130
    Pork Stuffed with Apple & Sage 128
    Roasted Pork Rack 124
potatoes
    Brandade 87
    Pont-L'Evêque Cheese Gratin 20
    Potato Puree 152
Prawn Salad 18
Preserved Lemon & Almond Dressing 92
Preserved Lemon Vinaigrette 14
prunes
    Prune Jam 207
    Rabbit Stew with Prunes 123
pudding
    Rice Pudding with Lemon Ricotta Cake 178
Pumpkin Puree 144

Q

quail
    Grape & Thyme-stuffed Quail with Braised Lentils 112
    Quail & Chestnut Pies 114

R

Rabbit Rillettes 64
Rabbit Stew with Prunes 123
Raie 'en matelote', citron confit et d'amande vinaigrette 92
raspberries
    Nat's Raspberry Jam Donuts 168
    Raspberry Souffles 161
Ravioli au jaune d'oeuf, asperges verte et parmesan 67
Razor Clams Mariniere 98
Red Mullet Escabeche with Celeriac & Apple Remoulade 74
Rib-eye of Beef with Bearnaise Sauce 134
Rib-eye of Beef with Bone Marrow & Bordelaise Sauce 132
Rice Pudding with Lemon Ricotta Cake 178
Rich Red Wine Sauce 138
Rillettes de lapin 64
rillettes
    Rabbit Rillettes 64
Risotto d'orge perlé aux champignons sauvages 118
risotto
    Pearl Barley Risotto with Wild Mushrooms 118
Riz au lait et son gâteau à la ricotta citronné 178
Roast Duck with Spiced Honey Glaze 106
Roast Lamb Shoulder in Salt Crust 149
Roast Partridge 'En Salmis' 117
Roasted Pork Rack 124
Rognons de veau à la moutarde 141
Romsteck d'agneau aux flageolets 153
Roquefort Cheese Souffles 197
Rôti d'agneau en croûte de sel 149
Rouget à l'escabeche et céleri rémoulade 74
Rouille 202
Rum Baba 189
Rum Syrup 189

S

salads
    Crab & Almond Salad 17
    Crab Salad with Preserved Lemon Vinaigrette 14
    Goat's Cheese Salad 33
    Prawn Salad 18
    Salad of Chicken Leg Confit 44
    Salad of Goat's Curd & Baby Beetroot 38
    Spanner Crab & Tarragon Salad with Grilled Asparagus 70
    Warm White Bean Salad 100
Salade de chèvre chaud 33
Salade de crabe et d'estragon, asperges grillées et pommes de terre nouvelles 70
Salade de cuisse de poulet confite 44
Salade de fromage de chèvre frais et de petites betteraves 38

salt cod
    Brandade 87
Salt Crust 149
Sardines Escabeche 46
Sardines à l'escabèche 46
Sauce bois boudran 203
sauces
    Bearnaise Sauce 134
    Bisque Sauce 203
    Bordelaise Sauce 132
    Caramel Sauce 189
    Eschalot Sauce 135
    Gribiche Sauce 73
    Matelote Sauce 92
    Mornay Sauce 50
    Mustard Sauce 141
    Onion Soubise 90
    Pepper Sauce 144
    Rich Red Wine Sauce 138
sausages
    Chicken & Morel Mushroom Sausages 59
    Squid Stuffed with Merguez, Mussels & Spinach 103
    Stuffed Duck Neck with Pistachios 63
scallops
    Carpaccio of Scallop 27
    Scallops with Hazelnut Butter 49
    Scallops with Leek Fondue 51
Scotch Fillet Beef with Rich Red Wine Sauce 138
seafood
    Bourride 81
    Prawn Salad 18
    Seafood Stew 81
    Vichyssoise with Oyster Chantilly 16
    see also clams; crab; mussels; scallops
Selle d'agneau rôtie et panisse 150
Shortcrust Pastry 207
Sirloin Steak with Eschalot Sauce 135
skate
    Matelote of Skate Wing with Preserved Lemon & Almond Dressing 92
Smoked Butter 206
Smoked Ham Hock Terrine with Gribiche Sauce 73
snails
    Garlic Snail Pies 42
    Snail Croquettes 45
Snapper et foie gras 'en papillote' 94
snapper
    Papillote of Snapper & Foie Gras 94
Sofrito 97
sorbet
    Yoghurt Sorbet 192
Soufflés à la framboise 161
Soufflés au chocolat 165
Soufflés au gruyère 23
Soufflés au nougat glacés 183
Soufflés au roquefort 197
souffles
    Chilled Nougat Souffles 183
    Chocolate Souffles 165
    Raspberry Souffles 161
    Roquefort Cheese Souffles 197
    Twice-baked Cheese Souffles 23
Soupe à l'ail 12
Soupe de petit-pois froide et sa salade de crabe, d'huile d'olive noir 14
Soupe vichyssoise et chantilly à l'huîtres 16

soups
    Almond Gazpacho with Crab & Almond Salad 17
    Bourride 81
    Cauliflower Soup with Roquefort 10
    Chilled Pea Soup with Crab Salad & Black Olive Oil 14
    Chilled Tomato Consomme with Prawn Salad 18
    Garlic Soup 12
    Jerusalem Artichoke Soup 13
    John Dory Chowder 8
    Vichyssoise with Oyster Chantilly 16
Spanner Crab & Tarragon Salad with Grilled Asparagus 70
Spiced Flageolet Beans 153
spinach
    Squid Stuffed with Merguez, Mussels & Spinach 103
Spring menu 5
Squid Stuffed with Merguez, Mussels & Spinach 103
Squid Stuffed with Paella 97
Steak à l'échalote 135
stews
    Bourride 81
    Rabbit Stew with Prunes 123
    Seafood Stew 81
stock and jus
    Brown Chicken Stock 204
    Brown Veal Stock 205
    Chicken & Tarragon Jus 206
    Duck Jus 206
    Fish Stock 205
    Vegetable Stock 205
    White Chicken Stock 204
Stuffed Duck Neck with Pistachios 63
Sugar-coated Blueberries 189
Summer menu 77
Supreme de volaille, petits navets glacés et parfumé à l'estragon 111
Sweet Shortcrust Pastry 207

T

Tartare de Chevreuil 24
Tarte au chocolat parfaite 158
Tarte au citron en verrine 180
Tarte aux noix et au caramel mou 162
Tarte fine aux pommes 175
Tartelettes à l'oignon et au bacon 36
Tartes d'aubergine et d'échalote, crème de cèpes 28
Tartiflette 20
tarts
    Apple & Almond Frangipane Tarts 175
    Chewy Walnut & Caramel Tart 162
    Eggplant Tarts with Cep Cream 28
    Onion & Bacon Tartlets 36
    Perfect Chocolate Tart 158
    Verrine of Lemon 'Tart' 180
Terrine de canard et confiture de pruneaux 60
terrine
    Duck Terrine with Prune Jam 60
    Smoked Ham Hock Terrine with Gribiche Sauce 73
    Stuffed Duck Neck with Pistachios 63
Thon façon Rossini 84

Thon mariné à la vodka et au citron vert, petits légumes au vinaigre et crème au raifort 68
tomatoes
    Chilled Tomato Consomme with Prawn Salad 18
    Tomato Chutney 22
    Tomato Fondue 45
Tournedos de chevreuil sauce au poivre 144
tuna
    Tuna & Crab 'Cannelloni' with Avocado Cream 54
    Tuna Rossini 84
    Vodka & Lime-cured Tuna with Pickled Vegetables & Horseradish Cream 68
turnips
    Pan-roasted Chicken Breasts with Baby Turnips 111
Twice-baked Cheese Souffles 23

V

veal
    Brown Veal Stock 205
    Veal Kidneys with Mustard Sauce 141
    Veal Sweetbread Pie 139
vegetables
    Pickled Vegetables 68
    Vegetable Stock 205
    see also specific vegetables
Velouté de chou-fleur et Roquefort 10
Velouté de topinambour 13
venison
    Fillet of Venison with Pepper Sauce 144
    Venison Tartare 24
Verrine of Lemon 'Tart' 180
Vichyssoise with Oyster Chantilly 16
vinaigrettes
    Hazelnut Vinaigrette 44
    Preserved Lemon Vinaigrette 14
Vodka & Lime-cured Tuna with Pickled Vegetables & Horseradish Cream 68

W

walnuts 10
    Chewy Walnut & Caramel Tart 162
    Walnut Dressing 33
Warm Chestnut & Olive Cake with Tomato Chutney 22
Warm White Bean Salad 100
White Asparagus Barigoule 30
White Chicken Stock 204
White Chocolate Mousse with Dark Chocolate Tuiles 186
winter menu 199

Y

Yoghurt Sorbet 192

Z

zucchini flowers
    Crab-stuffed Zucchini Flowers 90

LANTERN

Published by the Penguin Group
Penguin Group (Australia)
250 Camberwell Road, Camberwell, Victoria 3124, Australia
(a division of Pearson Australia Group Pty Ltd)
Penguin Group (USA) Inc.
375 Hudson Street, New York, New York 10014, USA
Penguin Group (Canada)
90 Eglinton Avenue East, Suite 700, Toronto, Canada ON M4P 2Y3
(a division of Pearson Penguin Canada Inc.)
Penguin Books Ltd
80 Strand, London WC2R 0RL, England
Penguin Ireland
25 St Stephen's Green, Dublin 2, Ireland
(a division of Penguin Books Ltd)
Penguin Books India Pvt Ltd
11 Community Centre, Panchsheel Park, New Delhi – 110 017, India
Penguin Group (NZ)
67 Apollo Drive, Rosedale, North Shore 0632, New Zealand
(a division of Pearson New Zealand Ltd)
Penguin Books (South Africa) (Pty) Ltd
24 Sturdee Avenue, Rosebank, Johannesburg 2196, South Africa

Penguin Books Ltd, Registered Offices:
80 Strand, London, WC2R 0RL, England

First published by Penguin Group (Australia),
a division of Pearson Australia Group Pty Ltd, 2012

10 9 8 7 6 5 4 3 2 1

Copyright © Manu Feildel 2012
Photography © Chris Chen 2012

The moral right of the author has been asserted

All rights reserved. Without limiting the rights under copyright reserved above, no part of this publication may be reproduced, stored in or introduced into a retrieval system, or transmitted, in any form or by any means (electronic, mechanical, photocopying, recording or otherwise), without the prior written permission of both the copyright owner and the above publisher of this book.

Initial design concept by Kirby Armstrong © Penguin Group (Australia)
Design by Emily O'Neill © Penguin Group (Australia)
Styling for food and incidental photography by Geraldine Muñoz
Typeset in Adobe Garamond Pro by Post Pre-Press Group,
Brisbane, Queensland
Colour separation by Splitting Image, Clayton, Victoria
Printed and bound in China by 1010 Printing International Ltd

National Library of Australia
Cataloguing-in-Publication data:

> Feildel, Manu.
> Manu's French bistro / Manu Feildel; photographer, Chris Chen.
> 9781921382697 (hbk.)
> Includes index.
> Cooking, French.
> Other Authors/Contributors: Chen, Chris.
>
> 641.5944

penguin.com.au/lantern

Thank you to the following people and businesses for generously supplying props for the photographs: All Hand Made Gallery; Aeria Country Floors; Attic; Sally Beresford; Ici et La; Paper 2; Riedel; Sandy Lockwood; Thonet; Mud; Newtown Furniture Haven; Coast Clothing; and Perfect Pieces.